# Assembly Language Programming
## on the IBM PC

**Chris Hawksley and Neil White**
University of Keele

ADDISON-WESLEY PUBLISHING COMPANY

Wokingham, England · Reading, Massachusetts · Menlo Park, California
Don Mills, Ontario · Amsterdam · Bonn · Sydney · Singapore
Tokyo · Madrid · Bogota · Santiago · San Juan

The programs in this book have been included for their instructional
value. They have been tested with care but are not guaranteed for
any particular purpose. The publisher does not offer any warranties
or representations, nor does it accept any liabilities with respect to
the programs.

Cover photography by Jay Myrdal.
Publishing services by Ponting-Green, Basingstoke and London.
Typeset by Parker Typesetting Service, Leicester.
Printed and bound in Great Britain at The Bath Press, Avon
First printed in 1987, Reprinted in 1987

**British Library Cataloguing in Publication Data**

Hawksley, Chris
    Assembly language programming on the IBM
    PC. — (IBM personal computer series)
    1. IBM Personal Computer — Programming
    2. Assembler language (Computer program
    language)
    I. Title   II. White, Neil   III. Series
    005.2'65      QA76.8.I2594

    ISBN 0–201–14569–3

**Library of Congress Cataloging in Publication Data**

Hawksley, Chris, 1949–
    Assembly language programming on the IBM PC.

    (IBM personal computer series)
    Includes index.
    1. IBM Personal Computer — Programming.   2. Assembler
    language (Computer program language)   I. White,
    Neil, 1954–   . II. Title.   III. Series.
    QA76.8.I2594H385   1987      005.265      86–7961
    ISBN 0–201–14569–3 (pbk.)

**This book is to be returned on or before
the last date stamped below.**

| | | |
|---|---|---|
| 09. JAN 88 | 1. ST WA | 13. JAN 89. |
| 05. FEB 88 | 26. AUG | 28. ... 89. |
| | 09. NOV | |
| 27. FEB 88 | 01. DEC 88 | |
| 19 MAR (WN) | 22· Dec· 88  F I | 18. APR 89 |
| −5. APR 1988 | | 4 May 8? |
| 26. APR 89 | 28. JAN 89. | |
| | 2I. FEB 89 | 30. MAY 89 |
| | | 14. JUN 89 |
| 1? MAY 1??? | | 20. JAN 93 |
| 25. 27. JUN 88 JUL 8? | | 1 0 FEB 1996 |

**WALLINGTON LIBRARY**
Shotfield
Wallington   SM6 0HY
01-647 4458/9

RENEWALS    *Please quote:* date of return, your ticket number
and computer label number for each item.

*To Ann and Ron,*
*Anna Jane and Simon John.*

# Preface

This book is an introductory text in assembly language programming on the IBM Personal Computer for use on its own or as a supporting textbook in a course. The material is divided into two parts: a general introduction to computer architecture and assembly language programming, followed by a specific introduction to programming the IBM PC.

Where appropriate, examples relate directly to programming an IBM PC (of any variety) running a version of the operating system DOS or CP/M-86. The text is equally suitable for programmers of IBM compatible computers. In practice, most of the text concerns programming the Intel 8086 (now renamed the iAPX 86/10) and its family of microprocessors on which the IBM PC is based; hence the book is also suitable as an introduction to this family of microprocessors in a wider sense.

The reader is not expected to have prior knowledge of the general architecture of computer systems nor of assembly language programming on any computer. This material is introduced in the first part of the book. Experience of digital logic design or a background in electronics is not assumed, nor is it directly relevent to the material covered. However, a knowledge of the fundamentals of programming a computer in a high-level language is desirable for anyone learning to program at assembly level, and previous exposure to the elementary principles of programming in a language such as Pascal, FORTRAN or BASIC is assumed at a few points in the text.

The entire instruction set of the 8086 microprocessor is covered. As well as introducing assembly language features at appropriate points in the book an attempt has also been made to present them in a format which allows the book to be used subsequently as a reference text.

The first three chapters provide background material for readers who are not familiar with the low-level organization of computer systems. Except in choice of examples the material in these chapters is relevant to any computer, not just the 8086. Chapter 1 introduces the basic structure and operation of a computer in terms of the logical components involved. The notion of a more convenient representation for programs than binary code is developed in Chapter 2 to give an illustration of the typical facilities to be found in assemblers. Chapter 3 is rather different. It provides an introduction to basic data structures, particularly number and character representations with which the reader may not be entirely familiar.

If preferred, Part 1 can be skipped over fairly quickly and retained as background reference material. Chapter 4 provides an overview of 8086 structure and operation, including a brief look at groups of all the instructions of this processor. These are revisited in later chapters but, first, Chapter 5 introduces the framework in which to develop programs: the essential details of assemblers in DOS and CP/M-86. This chapter also introduces a *skeleton* program – a complete starter-kit for the assembly language programmer using one of these operating systems. Even the simplest assembly language program needs supporting instructions and data definitions (for initializing registers, defining constants or establishing communication with the operating system, for example) and this is the purpose of the skeleton program which is then used as the basis of subsequent programs in the book.

Chapters 6 to 9 develop the essential programming techniques required in an assembly language programmer's armoury. The first of these emphasises the importance of the subroutine as a fundamental program unit and illustrates its use with examples. Control structures are described in Chapter 7 by matching the familiar constructions in high level languages, such as conditional and loop statements, to the mechanisms used to implement these in assembler. Logical and arithmetic operations on data follow in Chapter 8, including a survey of the facilities offered by the numeric processor available in some 8086 systems. Again using high level language parallels, Chapter 9 extends the range of programming techniques to embrace compound data structures such as strings, arrays and records.

The discussion on programming methodology in Chapter 10 combines a selection of general topics on good program design features with a practical guide to locating an error in a program using the IBM PC debugging programs. This is followed by an explanation of the extensive operating system facilities for input and output using files. In addition to a general introduction to these features and a number of examples, Chapter 11 also includes a complete guide to all file function calls in the various versions of the operating systems for reference purposes. Both the 'File Control Block' oriented and tree-structured filing systems are covered. The final chapter presents a more advanced treatment of the 8086 segmentation scheme.

For easy reference, Appendix A documents all of the 8086 instruction set in a concise representation. The remaining three appendices provide listings of the skeleton programs and, in tabular format, the ASCII character set and file control block layouts used in DOS and CP/M-86.

Finally, we are pleased to record a debt of gratitude to a number of people who assisted us in producing this book. Hugh Proudman at IBM International Products Limited was most helpful in supplying several versions of operating systems and associated documentation. Our thanks are due also to Dr Dennis Andrews, Managing Director of a Keele University Science Park company for providing the excuse and encouragement to develop a sizeable commercial assembly language product on the IBM PC which gave us vital insight into the particular problems which arise in such an undertaking. Last, but by no means least, Sarah Mallen, ably aided and abetted by Kathryn Kergozou, engaged in the subtle art of gentle persuasion to coax us back to the word processor from time to time.

Chris Hawksley
Neil White
*Keele, February 1986*

**Acknowledgements**

The authors would like to thank Intel Corporation (UK) Ltd for permission to reproduce Tables 8.1 and 8.2 which are taken from the Intel iAPX86/88/186/188 User's Manual, Programmer's Reference, May 1983.

**Trademark notices**

IBM and Personal Computer are tradenames of International Business Machines. DOS was written for the IBM PC by Microsoft Inc. CP/M, CP/M–86, ASM–86 and DDT–86 are registered trademarks of Digital Research. Intel is a registered trademark of Intel Corporation. Zilog is a registered trademark of Zilog Inc. UNIX is a trademark of AT & T Bell Laboratories.

# Contents

# Part 1 | ASSEMBLY LANGUAGE PROGRAMMING

# 1 | Microprocessor Structure and Operation

## 1.1  HISTORICAL CONTEXT

It does not take an expert in computer science to be aware of the enormous revolutions in technology which have taken place in the short history of the computer. Born out of the necessities of a war the pace of development seems to accelerate perpetually. The ponderous dinosaurs of the 1950s which, according to the predictions of that era, would saturate the market demand for computation when they numbered 200, gave way to a line of electronic integration which opened up new horizons and new aspirations. By the time the first microprocessors came out of the ovens in the early 1970s, several complete generations of electronic components had come and gone, and a new era was about to begin. Who would have believed in 1950 that the technology for Orwell's *Nineteen Eighty-Four* would have arrived just about on cue?

But, should the reader be misled into thinking that this is the start of a science fiction novel, there is a most pertinent point to make regarding this train of development. If one discards the trimmings surrounding each new computer, and cuts through each manufacturer's glossy specifications, one is left with a set of basic principles of operation which are common to almost all electronic digital computers: unchanged and unchanging as the technology surrounding them gallops ahead. These principles, ascribed by John Von Neumann in the 1940s, govern the primitive behaviour of the heart of a computer: its central processing unit (CPU). From this point of view it is irrelevant whether the various components making up a computer are located physically in a single package (a microprocessor 'chip') or spread over a whole room or building. Thus, though the following introduction is aimed specifically at microprocessor architecture, it should be borne in mind that these are general principles applicable to any general-purpose digital computer.

## 1.2  GENERAL STRUCTURE

The essential logical components of a computer are illustrated in Figure 1.1.

3

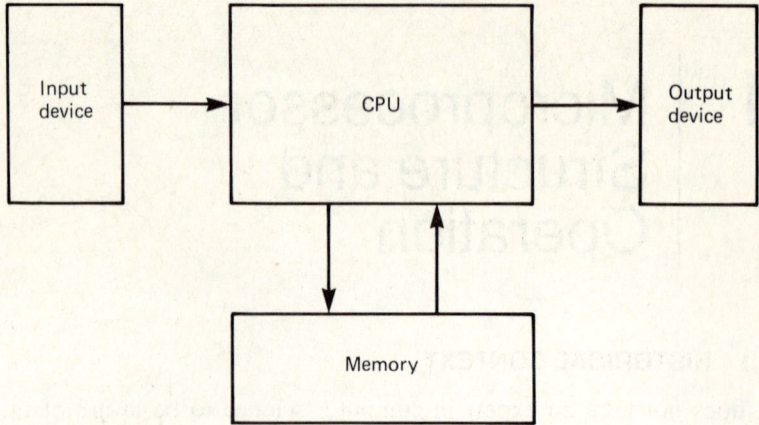

**Figure 1.1**  Basic components.

Lines and arrows reflect the flow of data passing through the computer. By 'data', current technology implies the use of electrical signals capable of representing two states, and a single item of data is called a **binary digit** or **bit**. This is not an absolute requirement and computers using more than two states have been constructed. However, such machines are unusual and there is a simplicity and elegance associated with a notation requiring only two symbols: 1 or 0, on or off, +5 volts or 0 volts, etc. By convention, the values of bits are written using '1' and '0', leaving the translation of these symbols into physical signals to be done by the particular computer equipment being used (the **hardware**). Thus, the paths marked in Figure 1.1 will carry trains of 0s and 1s representing information from the real world.

As an aside, there is a popular habit of using the terms 'information' and 'data' synonymously in the context of 'information processing' and 'data processing'. This is potentially misleading because the notion of **information** implies meaning, whereas **data** are merely the symbols used to represent a piece of information. Technically, human beings are the only ones capable of information processing: computers are blind processors of symbols – data processors. A pedantic distinction, perhaps, but it serves as a reminder that the digital computer is a deterministic device quite incapable of personal interpretation as we know it.

In this simple model, the input device represents any unit capable of providing binary signals from an external source and, similarly, an output device is any unit accepting binary signals for transmission to the external environment. Collectively, they are referred to as I/O devices or **peripherals** of the computer, though many different techniques are required to communicate with peripherals ranging from e.g. a single-bit 'on/off' input sensor to a complex graphical output display.

Turning attention to the memory, sometimes called the store of the computer, a storage unit of only one bit in size would be too restrictive and, hence, bits are grouped into larger units, commonly called **words** of storage. The memory of a computer is made up of a set of storage locations, each of the same size and each capable of holding one word of data. The number of bits per word, or **wordlength**, varies from computer to computer, and words are often split or combined with others to produce units of more convenient length. One such unit is the **byte**, a unit nowadays considered to be of exactly eight bits. It is important because the number of different binary patterns in eight bits is 256 ($2^8$), a particularly useful size in which to store the code for a single **character**. The **character set** of a computer is the set of printable and non-printable symbols communicated to peripherals and this set can vary, often only slightly, from computer to computer. Since a computer is primarily a symbol-processing machine, not a super calculator, much of its basic operation is concerned with moving around data in the form of characters.

In order to locate data in the memory, each of the memory locations has a unique identifier or **address**. In the simplest case, locations are numbered from zero upwards, to the maximum size of memory in the computer. A more subtle approach is to partition the memory into segments, with locations in each segment numbered from zero upwards. A memory location is then identified by both its segment number and the address within that segment. Such an address is often called an **offset** within the segment. This dodge avoids the necessity for very large addresses and provides a technique for separating areas of memory if this is desirable. Note that the term **addressing** is used to denote the action of identifying a given location in memory by its address.

The most common kind of memory is called **RAM**, short for **random access memory**. It is random access in the sense that the contents of any address in the memory can be retrieved in any order in the same length of time. Contrast this with the varying lengths of time it takes to locate tracks on a music cassette, for example, where the tape must be run from one end to the other before some tracks can be located. RAM is also referred to as read/write memory since data may be both read from, and written to, addresses in the memory. A simple analogy to RAM is a rack of pigeon-holes designed to hold mail. Each pigeon-hole is marked with a name (the 'address'), and letters (the 'data') may be placed into, and taken out of, that pigeon-hole at will. The name is fixed but the contents are variable. Any data written into a location in RAM will remain there until they are overwritten by a new value. Many RAMs, though not all, will lose data when the power to the computer is turned off – stores of this nature are said to be **volatile**.

A further kind of memory, called **ROM (read only memory)** has the property that, in normal use, data can only be read from the memory. In other respects, however, ROM is similar to RAM: data in either may be accessed randomly by the same addressing technique. Special ways of writing data into ROMs are used – sometimes data are established in the ROM once only, during manufacture – and the memory is non-volatile, i.e. it retains its contents even without power being applied. The uses of these two kinds of memory will be considered at the end of this chapter.

The **central processing unit (CPU)** is the centre of activity in the computer, containing elements responsible for initiating and controlling the processing of the data. Figure 1.2 shows its most important components from a computational (rather than, say, an electronic) point of view.

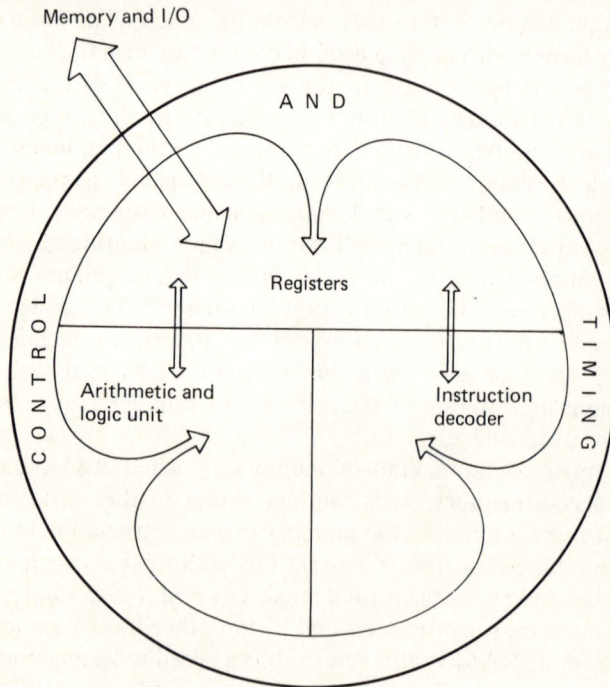

**Figure 1.2**   CPU logical structure.

A **register** is a single storage location similar to those found in the memory but having a unique name rather than a numerical address. There are usually far fewer registers than memory locations and they are used to hold items of data most relevant to that part of the program currently being obeyed. Some registers are linked with particular functions in the CPU; others are called **general-purpose**

**registers**. One, or perhaps more, of the registers is referred to usually as an **accumulator** and this tends to be the most used storage location in the computer. Other registers may hold addresses of memory locations which are about to be accessed. Although the precise names and numbers of registers vary from microprocessor to micro-processor, it is usually possible to place them into one of the categories listed in Table 1.1, which will be explained in more detail later.

**Table 1.1**   Register types.

| Register category | Description |
| --- | --- |
| Accumulator | General-purpose arithmetic and logical operations |
| Counters | Current values and limits of counts |
| Address registers | General-purpose addressing |
| Pointers | Special addressing, e.g. stacks, indexing |
| Flags | Bits set according to results of operations |
| Instruction register | Holds the current instruction |
| Instruction pointer | Address of current (or next) instruction |

The **arithmetic and logical unit** (ALU), known also as the 'mill' is the part of the CPU responsible for carrying out the arithmetic and logical operations which will be performed on data. In the ALUs of most microprocessors, values of data may be added or subtracted, or combined with logical operations such as AND, OR and NOT. In the more advanced microprocessors, integer multiplication and division functions are supported. Although hardware to perform floating-point ('real') arithmetic is now long established in larger computers, this facility is still relatively uncommon in microprocessors and the alternative of using software routines based on integer functions is normally preferred. As the technology improves it is almost certain to embrace a greater sophistication in arithmetic facilities for micro-processors though, in practice, the need for these features in the vast majority of microprocessor applications is not entirely established.

Involved in virtually all processes within the CPU is the timing and control unit. Without a rigidly controlled sequence of events the operation of any computer is reduced to chaos. Central to this timing function is the microprocessor clock which delivers a steady stream of pulses from which all transitions from event to event within the CPU are derived. The speed of operation of the microprocessor is governed by this clock, which is usually made to run as fast as possible within the limitations of the technology; too fast and there is a risk that one event will not be completed before the next is initiated. The essence of the control unit is to deliver the correct sequence of 'trigger' signals to relevant parts of both the CPU and its external partners, that is the memory and I/O devices, enabling the whole system to work in harmony. Directing the control unit to carry out a given sequence is the responsibility of the instruction decoder which in turn has its actions dictated by the instructions written by the programmer.

Note that the CPU of a microprocessor has become known as the **microprocessing unit** or **MPU** and this term will be preferred in later discussion on the architecture of microprocessors.

## 1.3   OBEYING STORED PROGRAMS

The key feature of a computer, distinguishing it from a simple electronic calculator, is the control of its operation by a **stored program**. The set of instructions which make up a program are placed in the memory of the computer before that program is obeyed instruction by instruction (the terms **executed** and **run** are also used for this process). Thus, unlike an artefact that requires constant manual direction to make it work, such as a garden spade or a motor car, the program guides the operation of a computer step by step. An **algorithm** is developed, possibly in total isolation from the computer, as a sequence of steps to solve a given problem and this is translated by the programmer, and perhaps by another program, into the language obeyed by the computer. (Note the deliberate avoidance of the notion of 'understanding' in this context. Anthropomorphisms in this discipline foster the shifting of blame for mistakes onto the so-called 'shoulders' of the computer itself – a clearly absurd, but often successful, scapegoat for the incompetent.) Only when the instructions are resident in the memory can the computer be put to work by executing the stored program.

The basic set of instructions used in a computer is called the **machine code** of that computer. A machine code program consists of instructions represented by binary codes which are stored in the computer memory prior to execution. This primitive code tends to be different for each new computer. Some degree of compatibility between machine codes may be achieved by including the instructions of one computer as a sub-set of the machine code of a new one, thus providing, in principle, an easy means of transporting programs from the older to the newer computer (an alternative is to provide compatibility at the assembly code level rather than at the machine code level). In general, however, a program written in machine code for one computer will not run on another computer which uses a different CPU.

The term 'machine code' aptly describes the fundamental language of computers since its instructions reflect the basic computer architecture outlined in the previous section. We shall see, for example, that there are instructions for transferring data from the input devices to the CPU; from registers to memory; from registers to the ALU and from the CPU to output devices. Another term for a language of this kind is **low-level**, contrasting with the **high-level** or problem-oriented languages which are designed to provide tools geared to the needs of programmers writing algorithms.

The basic structure of a machine code instruction is shown in Figure 1.3.

| Opcode field | Operand field |
| --- | --- |

**Figure 1.3**　The instruction.

The first part ('field') of the instruction is a binary code identifying the operation performed by that instruction: the operation code or **opcode**. In principle, if a microprocessor requires an instruction set of at most 256 instructions then the opcode field would need to be one byte wide ($2^8 = 256$) to provide a unique code for each instruction. In practice, it is usual to group instructions into types and to use specific bits of the opcode to indicate the type – with remaining bits used to differentiate between instructions of the same type. All instructions that transfer data between registers, for example, may have several bits in common. Furthermore, instructions transferring data to or from a particular register may use a consistent pattern of bits to represent the register in question. Thus, for uniformity, not all possible bit patterns in the opcode field are necessarily used to represent instructions.

The **operand field** of an instruction contains information about one or more **operands** (arguments) on which that instruction is to operate. In the simplest case, the operand field is empty and the opcode is itself sufficient to identify the sources and destinations of data and the actions to be performed. More commonly, perhaps, an instruction needs to refer to a location in memory in order to retrieve or to store an item of data. The operand field in this case will contain a pertinent means of identifying that location; sometimes this will be the memory address itself, but there are several alternatives discussed later in this chapter. The operand field may also contain information that is not to be used as an address. In particular, constant values may be included in some instructions to allow, for example, a constant integer to be placed in a register. The operand in this case is called a **literal** or **immediate** operand.

A program is obeyed by taking instructions from memory, one by one, in a process called the **fetch–execute cycle**: a process fundamentally unchanged since the advent of the first computers. The main components involved in this cycle are illustrated in Figure 1.4.

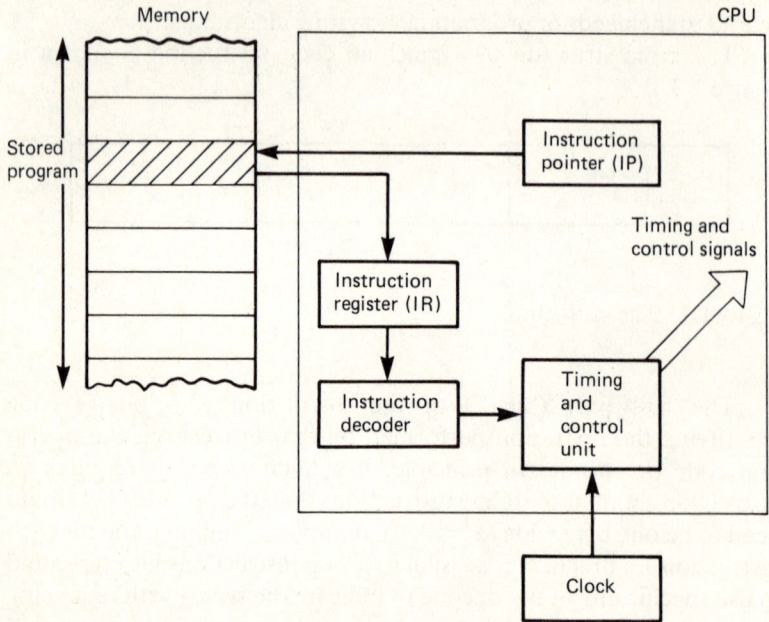

**Figure 1.4**    Fetch–execute cycle components.

Before execution can commence, the **instruction pointer** register (IP) must be set to (the term 'loaded with' is more often used) the address of the first instruction of the program stored in the memory. An alternative name for this register is the program counter (PC) but this abbreviation has come to be more commonly used for the term 'Personal Computer'. A register containing an address in this manner is said to 'point to' the location in memory identified by the address and this is shown in Figure 1.4 and in subsequent diagrams as a line and arrowhead 'pointing' at the location in question.

Each basic step of the fetch–execute cycle is triggered by a clock pulse from the microprocessor clock which is running, perhaps, at several million beats per second, and each period is referred to as a

**clock cycle**. Completing one instruction will take several clock cycles, perhaps several tens of cycles, depending on the microprocessor and on the complexity of the instruction. An instruction to perform arithmetic division, for example, will take many times as long to complete as a simple transfer of data between two registers. In all cases, it is the timing and control unit which is responsible for supplying the signals to force the required actions in a given cycle to take place.

In the fetch–execute cycle, the first task is to retrieve the next instruction to be obeyed from its location in memory and to place it in the **instruction register** inside the CPU. This instruction fetch may take one or more clock cycles, depending on the particular architecture and, in particular, on how many memory locations are occupied by the instruction. Microprocessors with a small wordlength, e.g. eight bits, may require two, three, or even more locations in which to store a single instruction. The instruction is then analysed by the **instruction decoder** to determine the set of control and timing signals appropriate for that instruction.

The 'execute' part of the cycle which follows is conditioned by the type of instruction being obeyed. In an internal transfer of data from one CPU register to another, for instance, the timing and control unit will open up a route between the two registers and force the transfer to take place in a short time, often a single clock cycle. If the instruction requires an operand which is to be obtained from memory, however, more work must be done by the timing and control unit and a further 'fetch' is initiated, this time to retrieve the data from memory. Some instructions will require the services of the ALU, and the operations performed in this unit may take numerous clock cycles to complete. Data may also be sent out of the CPU to a location in memory or, perhaps, to an output device. The behaviour of various types of instruction is considered in the next section.

The timing and control unit has one other important task to perform. The instruction pointer (IP) has to be updated to contain the address of the next instruction to be fetched and executed. In many cases, the IP will be incremented by one to point to (i.e. hold the address of) the instruction held in the memory location next to the one just obeyed. Where an instruction occupies more than one memory location then the IP will be incremented by more than one. The timing and control unit is aware of the length of all instructions and will adjust the IP increment accordingly. Most importantly, some instructions will modify the flow of control, i.e. they will cause a jump to take place to another part of the program. These transfer of control instructions result in the IP being loaded with the start address of the new section of program.

With the IP set for a new instruction the fetch–execute cycle begins again and in this way the execution of a program continues until stopped by removal of the power, the issue of a 'halt' instruction or by a hardware interrupt (described later).

## 1.4  INSTRUCTIONS

In Part 2 we shall examine in detail the instruction set of the 8086 microprocessor. For the moment, consider the general categories of instruction:

- data management;
- arithmetic and logical;
- transfer of control;
- input and output.

These categories are not only appropriate for the 8086; they are relevant to most microprocessors. Whereas a particular instruction set may contain a very large number of instructions, the great majority will fall naturally into one or other of these categories and it is useful to have a general awareness of these different types.

**Data management** instructions are those which move items of data from one point in the computer to another without modification. They include the set generally referred to as **load** instructions, allowing data to be loaded from memory into MPU registers or vice versa, and allowing register-to-register transfers inside the MPU. A mark of a well-designed processor is the degree of flexibility permitted in the use of these loading instructions. Allowing transfer of data from virtually any memory location or register to another, using consistent formats, greatly simplifies the job of 'managing' data and reduces the number of special cases to be learned.

The second group of instructions, the **arithmetic and logical** set, contains instructions which use the functions of the ALU to perform basic arithmetic – addition, subtraction and, perhaps, multiplication and division – between items of data held in registers and memory. These machine code instructions are very basic, in contrast to the wealth of arithmetic facilities provided in most high-level languages. The programmer must have a very clear idea of the action of an 8- or 16-bit add instruction, for example, particularly in the boundary cases of positive and negative overflow. (Overflow occurs when the result of an operation is too large to fit into the specified number of bits.) The basic characteristics of arithmetic and logical operations are considered later, in Chapter 3 and in Chapter 8.

Most arithmetic and logical instructions affect the special status, or **flag** register in the MPU. Individual bits of this register are defined to represent the general status or result of an operation. For example, one of the bits will almost certainly be set if the result of an arithmetic operation is zero. Another may be used to show whether the result is positive or negative and yet another will provide information to detect the occurrence of overflow. The flag register carries forward a variety of information resulting from one instruction to be used, perhaps, by a subsequent instruction. Thus, a positive or negative result may be used to force a transfer of control to a different part of the program using a 'conditional jump' instruction.

It is the **transfer of control**, or **branch** instructions which provide much of the power of programming. Instructions in this category are able to cause a jump to another part of a program by modifying the value of the instruction pointer register in the MPU. In general, the address to which control is transferred is specified in some way in the operand field of the instruction, but control transfer instructions may be further divided into the types:

- unconditional jumps;
- conditional jumps;
- subroutine calls and returns;
- interrupt handling.

An **unconditional jump**, as the name suggests, forces a change to the IP resulting in a branch to a new part of the program. A **conditional jump** will behave in the same way if, and only if, the relevant condition prevails. The conditions are usually determined by settings of bits in the flag (status) register, such as 'jump if not zero' or 'jump if negative'. If a condition is false, as determined by the relevant bit or bits in the flag register, then control passes to the instruction following the jump.

Subroutine calls operate in a different way because control should return, eventually, to the instruction below the call (cf. procedure calling in a high-level language). Thus, provision must be made to store away the **return address** of this next instruction, usually on a stack (see later), before jumping to the new address. Special **return** instructions are used to leave the subroutine and return to the instruction whose address was saved by the previous subroutine call.

The handling of interrupts is very different to the other control transfer instructions. An **interrupt** is a signal to the MPU to stop executing the current program and to transfer control to an interrupt **service routine**.

A **hardware interrupt** may be generated by a peripheral such as a disk drive as a means of demanding the immediate attention of the MPU – to transfer some data, perhaps. The interrupt is not coded into the program as an instruction: it arrives on a special control line to the MPU. Thus, a program may be interrupted potentially anywhere and at any time. Control is transferred rapidly (by one of several techniques) to the start of a section of program which is written specifically to cope with that event. On completion of this interrupt service routine control will be returned to the interrupted program to allow it to continue as if no interrupt had ever taken place.

A **software interrupt** is a program instruction which forces a transfer of control to take place in a similar manner to the above. The use of software interrupts in communications with the microcomputer operating system is considered in later chapters.

**Input and output** instructions usually effect very primitive transfers of data values to or from input/output **ports**, the connections between a computer and its peripherals. A common unit of input and output is one byte containing, perhaps, a character code generated by, or transmitted to, a character-based peripheral such as a visual display unit (VDU). Some processors include instructions for block transfer of I/O data. I/O ports are distinguished by addresses, and there are two common approaches to identifying an I/O port. The first is called **memory-mapped** input/output in which an I/O port is addressed in the same way as a memory address. Thus, if data are 'stored' in the address corresponding to an output port, they pass instead through this port to the outside world. Using this scheme, normal memory addressing instructions may be used for I/O if desired. An alternative approach is for the microprocessor to use a separate set of addresses to identify I/O ports, and to have a special set of I/O instructions with which to address the ports.

In many ways, the operation of input/output instructions resembles that of the data management type of instruction, particularly in the case of memory-mapped I/O where the addressing is the same in both I/O and memory accessing. Treating them separately is advantageous, however, since in the case of I/O there is a need to consider the notion of **control** in addition to the data transfer. I/O control is concerned with the synchronization of data transfer between the computer and its peripheral devices. A simple case of this is the necessity to limit the rate of data transfer to a printer that is quite incapable of printing at the speed with which a processor could provide the data. The usual way of communicating this control information is to use further I/O addresses which contain status information concerning the peripheral data transfers.

## 1.5   ADDRESSING MODES

As mentioned earlier, the operand field of an instruction can be used to specify one or more operands in a variety of ways. A given instruction may exist in several forms, differing only in the way in which the operand field is interpreted. One form of a simple add instruction, for example, may take an operand as a literal value to be added to a register; a second may interpret the operand as an address in memory which contains the value to be added, and so on. The way in which an operand field is interpreted is determined by the **addressing mode** of that particular instruction. Some examples of addressing modes are:

- implied;
- immediate;
- direct;
- indirect;
- relative;
- stack;
- indexed.

It should be recognized that not all processors allow all of these addressing modes and that some processors combine two or three modes together. Precise details of the 8086 addressing modes are given in Chapter 4 and we shall confine comments here to a general overview of the primary modes of addressing.

Many instructions, particularly those in the data management and arithmetic/logical groups, require both source and destination operands. A load instruction, for example, takes a value from one place and deposits it in another. The source and destination operands may be named registers or memory locations, for example. An `add` instruction requires two source operands and one destination operand. Note that a **one-address** computer uses instructions employing just one memory address in the instruction format. All other operands are identified implicitly, or via named registers within the CPU. Most instructions of most computers contain a maximum of one address in this way. Let us consider in general how instruction operands may be specified.

In **implied** addressing, an operand is conspicuous by its absence from the operand field! The instruction will always refer to data in the same place and, hence, the operand is inherent in the instruction itself. Some logical instructions, of the style 'negate the accumulator' use implied addressing, where the operand (in this case the accumulator) is perfectly clear from the opcode alone.

An **immediate** operand is the actual value on which one is to operate. Thus, an immediate load instruction can place a constant into a register; the constant is the operand in immediate addressing mode and this is a useful technique for initializing a register or memory location to a particular value.

If the value to be operated on is stored in memory at the address given in the operand field of an instruction then the mode is called **direct** addressing. It is shown diagrammatically in Figure 1.5.

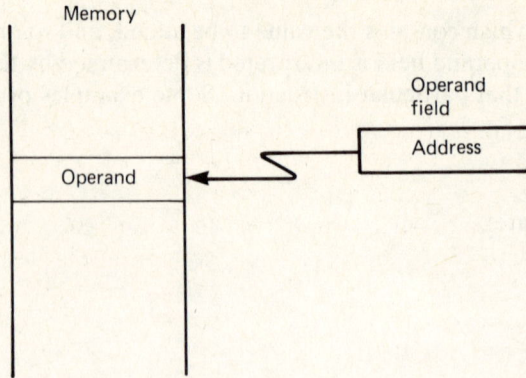

**Figure 1.5**   Direct addressing.

This is a simple and commonly used technique. Note that the range of addresses which can be located directly is limited by the number of bits allowed for the address in the instruction. Thus, a 1-byte address would allow direct addressing of only 256 locations but a 2-byte address would increase that to $2^{16} = 65\,536$ locations.

In **indirect** addressing, the address of the operand in memory is held in another memory location or in a register, and the instruction identifies this intermediate address. These two cases are represented in Figure 1.6. Accessing a memory operand via an addressing register (Figure 1.6(b)) is a particularly common technique, and the intermediate addressing register is said to 'point' to the operand in memory. It is particularly simple to access adjacent operands by incrementing (adding one to) or decrementing (subtracting one from) this register.

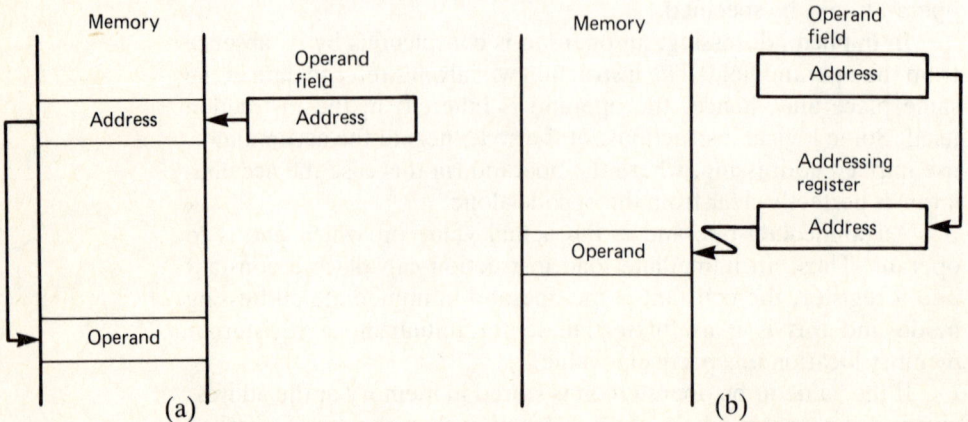

**Figure 1.6**   Indirect addressing: (a) memory indirect (b) register indirect.

**Relative** addressing is quite different to any of the above. A specific, or **absolute** address is not given in the operand field; rather an offset relative to some base address. Often, the base address is the address of the instruction itself, and relative addressing of this type is associated particularly with one variety of the control transfer or 'jump' instructions. Since many transfers of control in a program are quite 'local' in the sense that the jump is made forwards or backwards over only a few instructions, then the relative address specifying just the offset will require only a short operand field. Thus, an 8-bit operand field permits a relative addressing range of approximately plus or minus 128 locations of memory: quite sufficient, it is argued, for the majority of machine code program jumps. A direct address would require at least twice that number of bits in a realistic memory size. It is also evident that a relative address is 'self-relocatable', i.e. the program may be moved into a different part of the memory and the relative address will still be valid; this is not true of direct addressing. On the other hand, a drawback of relative addressing is that the offset is limited in size and, hence, that the 'range' of a relatively addressed jump is limited in size. This can be a handicap in automatic generation of machine code by a high-level language compiler, for example, where the range of a jump is not always easy to predict.

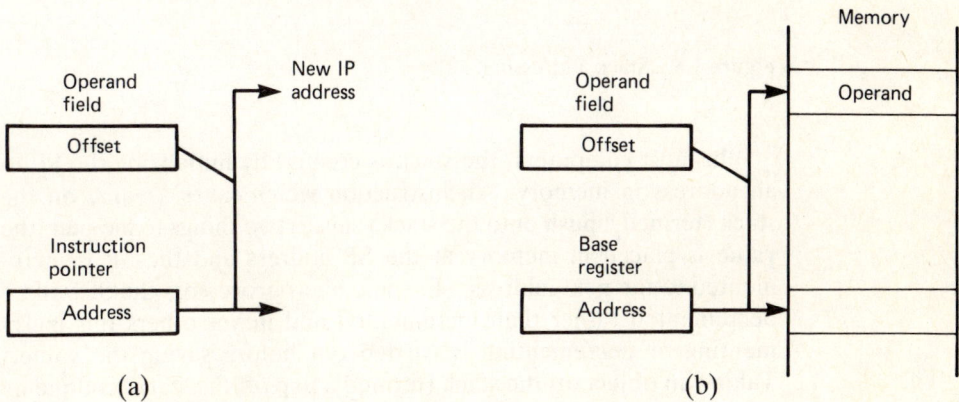

**Figure 1.7**   Relative addressing: (a) relative jumps (b) base relative.

Additionally, relative addressing is used as a means of accessing data in memory using a 'base' register to 'point at' (i.e. hold the address of) the start of a section of memory (Figure 1.7(b)). Base relative addressing can be used to partition the memory into sections, each accessed via a base register and each defined for a certain class of usage: instructions and data may be separated completely by this approach, for example. Multi-user computer systems may rely on each user being confined to a particular section of memory, restricted to addressing operands relative to the base of this section.

**Stack** addressing is a special case of register indirect addressing in which a register, called the **stack pointer** (SP) holds the address of a location in memory designated the 'top' of the stack, as shown in Figure 1.8. A **stack** is a list of stored data values with very limited rules of access: a value can be 'put onto' the top of the stack and a value can be 'taken off' the top of the stack. All operations take place on the top item and hence a stack is called a 'last-in, first-out' structure.

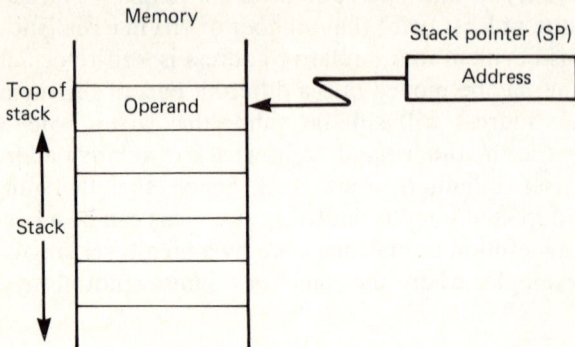

**Figure 1.8**    Stack addressing.

In most computers, the stack is created by initializing the SP to an address in memory. An instruction which saves a value on the stack (termed a **push** onto the stack) causes two things to happen: the value is placed in memory at the SP address and the SP is incremented to the next address. (In some microprocessors the SP will be decremented rather than incremented and in yet others this incrementing or decrementing is carried out before saving the value.) Taking an object off the stack (termed a **pop** off the stack) is done by performing the opposite of the above actions. Thus, a stack is a convenient, usually short term 'storage bin' for values, using only a pair of simple instructions (pop/push or their equivalents) and a strict adherence to the last-in, first-out rule. Most importantly, the stack is used 'behind the scenes' in other instructions, for example as a place to store the return address in a subroutine call.

**Indexed** addressing is introduced last of all because it is often available in conjunction with other addressing modes. Indexing implies calculating an address by adding a displacement, or offset, to a base address. An **index register** is used to hold one of these; the other is written in the instruction itself. In simple indexed addressing (Figure 1.9) the effective address (i.e. the memory address of the operand) is the sum of the base and displacement. However, combinations of indexed addressing with, for example, indirect addressing are frequently permitted, so that the effective address could be calculated in one of the ways shown in Figure 1.10. Not all variations are allowed in most microprocessors.

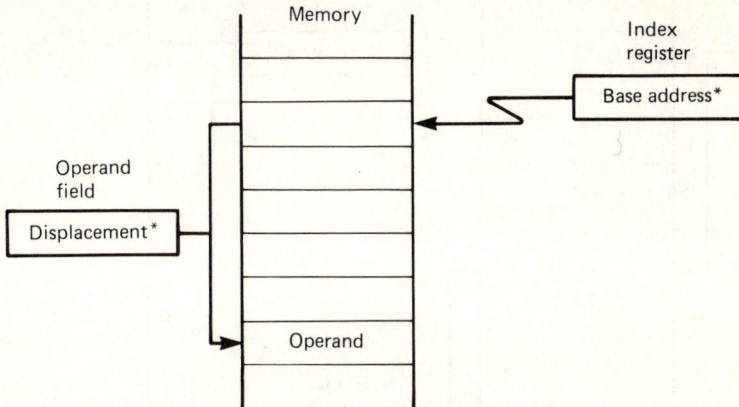

* In most microprocessors these two may be exchanged.

**Figure 1.9**    Simple indexed addressing.

## 1.6    CODE AND DATA

It is apparent from the previous discussion that program instructions (the 'code') and items of data occupy memory locations of precisely the same kind. In most processors, any area of memory can be used for either purpose and both instructions and data could be placed in adjacent locations, provided that suitable precautions are taken to prevent a program from obeying a data value instead of an instruction. Many current assembly language programs show a mixing of code and data in this way, with the variable data locations slotted in between subroutines or in gaps in the code created by forward jump instructions. The best advice in this matter is to avoid this intermixing of code and data at all costs. Code and data are logically distinct creatures and mixing the two is asking for trouble, usually as a result of one instruction modifying another by mistake.

There are two main aids to code/data separation; the first is to use the assembler facility to keep code and data in different regions of the memory and, secondly, some microprocessors provide registers whose function is to hold the base address of a code or a data region. Using base relative addressing in conjunction with these registers makes it difficult to confuse code with data.

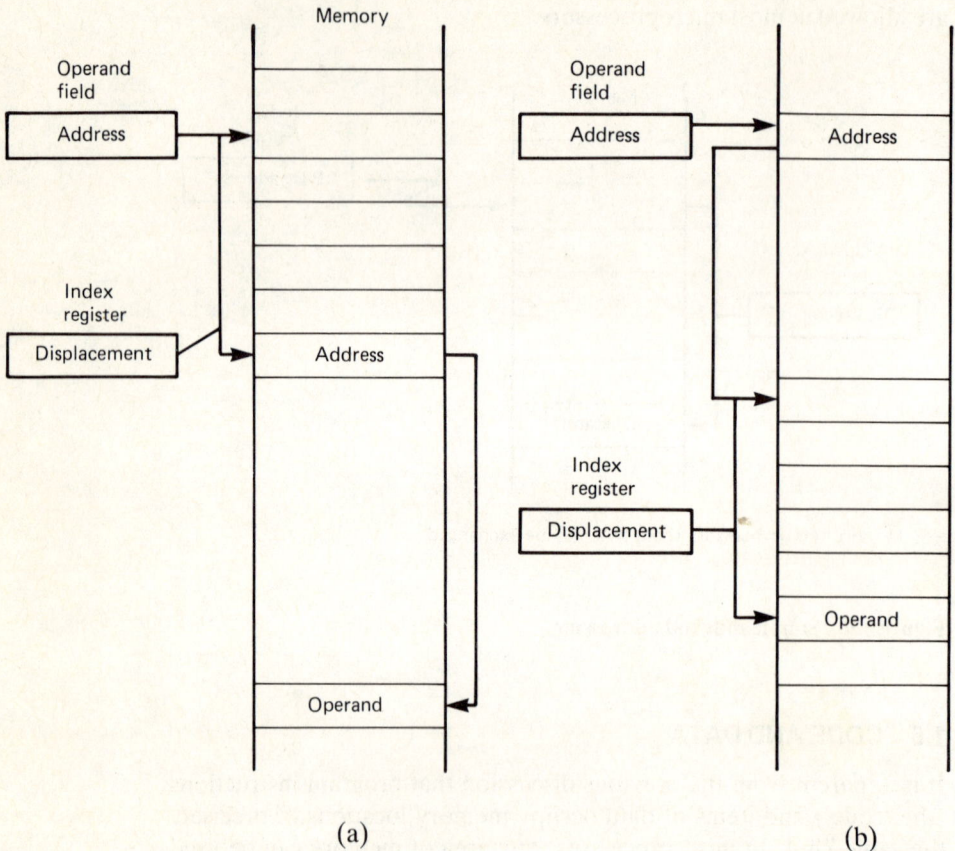

**Figure 1.10**  Indexing with other addressing modes: (a) indexed indirect addressing (b) indirect indexed addressing.

Separation of code and data is an important feature of micro-processor systems in which the program has to reside in non-volatile memory. A microprocessor-controlled instrument which must commence operation as soon as power is switched on would normally have its instructions stored in ROM, with hardware reset circuitry to force program execution to begin at a fixed address in the ROM on power-up. Constant data values for the program must also be stored in the ROM, but variable data locations require the 'write' access of RAM.

# 2 | Assembly Language Programming

## 2.1  ASSEMBLY LANGUAGE AND ASSEMBLERS

Some people enjoy the challenge of programming a microprocessor in machine code, entering instructions and data in binary or hexadecimal notation and calculating relative jump offsets by hand. Indeed, it is not a bad idea for every programmer to write at least one machine code program in his or her career to drive home just how demanding this task can be. In the longer term, however, there are convincing reasons for not programming directly in machine code, notably:

- the lack of an obvious correspondence between an instruction operation code and its meaning;
- the difficulty and inflexibility of writing all addresses as fixed numerical constants (called 'absolute addresses');
- the need to calculate manually all relative address offsets (which must be redone when the program is modified);
- the lack of program documentation and general readability.

**Assembly languages**, and their attendant assemblers, are devised to provide assistance in these areas. A characteristic of assembly language is its one-to-one relationship with machine code in nearly all situations. This means that although a few assembly languages possess instructions which cause several machine code instructions to be generated, in the vast majority of cases just one machine code instruction will be produced from one assembly language statement. This is in contrast to compiling a program in a high-level language such as Pascal, in which one high-level instruction (e.g. a loop statement) may compile into many basic machine code instructions. Both machine code and assembly language are referred to as **low-level** languages.

An **assembler** is a program that reads statements written in assembly language ·and generates as output the corresponding machine code instructions. As a side-effect, a listing file and syntax error report may be produced. An assembler running on the computer for which the assembly language is intended is called a **resident** assembler. When writing assembly programs for small microprocessor systems, especially those 'embedded' in other systems (e.g. instrumentation control) it is sometimes convenient to run the appropriate assembler on a larger computer, perhaps one based on a completely different processor. Although it is not possible to execute the resulting program directly on this 'host' computer, the machine code produced can be transmitted to the 'target' computer via a direct computer-to-computer link, or by using indirect storage on disk, magnetic tape or paper tape for subsequent reloading into the target system. An assembler of this nature is called a **cross-assembler**.

At one time, cross-assembly was recommended because of lack of speed or insufficient memory in small microprocessor systems. But the modern generations of microprocessors tend to have faster MPUs and larger stores, so this argument is much weaker now than only a few years ago. The main attractions of a cross-assembly system are linked more to the availability of reliable software (e.g. editors) and peripherals (e.g. printers, filestores) on a large computer, but perhaps not on the target computer.

It is important to recognize that, despite its rudimentary appearance, assembly code is made up of statements in a language and, hence, must adhere to the rules of grammar in that language. More particularly, in order to generate machine code, the assembly language instructions must be *syntactically* correct or an error message will be produced. Syntax constrains the form, or structure, of the assembler instructions. Correct syntax does not guarantee that the program will work, of course: this *semantic* correctness will be assessed by observation of how the program behaves when it is executed.

The syntax of an assembly language is usually very simple compared to that of a high-level language. An example is given in Figure 2.1, using a syntax diagram to define the syntax of an assembly language instruction in a hypothetical language. Note how an 'instruction' is defined by following arrowed lines through various boxes. An arrowed line can be read as 'followed by', and certain component items can be 'avoided' by following the by-pass links: i.e. they are optional components. In a full syntax definition, all the items in boxes must be defined themselves, in other syntax diagrams, to provide a complete and unambiguous specification of the legal forms of instructions in that language. Though common in high-level language texts, formal syntax definitions are rarely emphasized in the much simpler grammatical environment of assembly language and a more informal description of the components in Figure 2.1 follows in this chapter.

## 2.2  SYMBOLIC VALUES

A dictionary definition of a 'symbol' is 'a thing regarded as suggesting something' and this is an appropriate description of the use of symbols in assembly language.

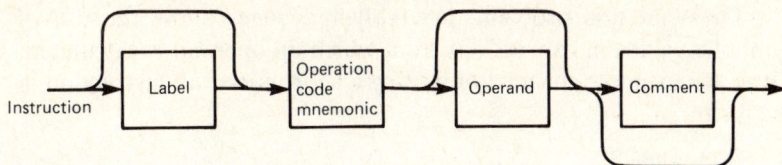

**Figure 2.1**   Instruction syntax.

## 2.2.1  Mnemonics

A pattern of bits corresponding to the operation code of an instruction means little to all but the most seasoned machine code addict. The practice of reading the bit pattern as a number does little to enhance its meaningfulness. A more sensible representation of an operation code is a short **mnemonic**, an 'aid to memory' made up of a few letters. Some examples of easily memorized mnemonics are ADD, IN, HALT, XOR (eXclusive OR) and MOV (MOVe data from place to place).

The use of mnemonics to represent instruction opcodes goes further than a one-to-one shorthand for a fixed bit pattern. From the discussion in the last chapter on addressing modes it is evident that there are many different opcodes that perform essentially equivalent operations; only the way in which the operands are identified varies. Thus, a single mnemonic (e.g. ADD) is used to represent the opcode of all variants, even though the bit pattern will be different in each case. It is left to the assembler to perform the necessary translation from the mnemonic into the correct bit pattern, taking into account the addressing mode of the operand.

A similar demand for mnemonics arises in the operand field of instructions as a means of representing particular registers by their names, for example AX (Accumulator), SP (Stack Pointer).

Note that, for emphasis, mnemonics of instructions, registers and other assembler reserved words will be written in an upper-case typeface in the text (e.g. BX, MOV), but will appear in lower-case in sections of programs. This distinction is made to improve readability: in practice, the assemblers considered here accept both upper- and lower-case letters interchangeably.

## 2.2.2  Symbolic addresses

Perhaps the most valuable aid provided by an assembler is that it permits symbolic addresses to be used in the operand field of an instruction. Where an instruction needs an address, the machine code programmer must give that address in *absolute* terms, that is, as a fixed numerical value. This is usually most inconvenient, forcing the programmer to commit the program to fixed locations in store and to perform distracting mental calculations.

To avoid this problem, assembly languages allow the use of symbolic values in expressions from which an operand is calculated. Thus, for example, instead of writing a subroutine call instruction in the form:

```
call 1000
```

which implies that the destination of the call (location 1000) has been calculated as an absolute address, it is sufficient to write:

```
call charout
```

where `charout` identifies a **symbolic address** whose value is defined elsewhere. The assembler builds up a table linking all symbolic names to their values, relieving the programmer of much tedious cross-referencing of numbers.

The value of a symbol is most commonly defined by the occurrence of a **label** attached to an instruction or data definition. Thus, the instruction at the destination of the above call could be labelled as:

```
charout:  <instruction>
```

The value of a label is the address of the location in which the `<instruction>` will be stored. As it passes through the source program, the assembler maintains a **current location counter**: a variable containing the address into which the next instruction will be assembled. When a label is encountered, both the symbolic name and its value (the current location counter value) are placed in the symbol table.

The syntax of a label is usually similar to that of a variable in a high-level language: a sequence of letters and digits starting with a letter, for example, (though it is often necessary to precede or follow this by a special character, such as a full stop or colon). Many assemblers place a limit on the length of labels, either on the actual number of written characters or on the number taken as significant in distinguishing labels. In this latter case, although:

```
mylabelno1:
mylabelno2:
```

may be acceptable in terms of length to a particular assembler, they would be considered to refer to the same label if that assembler considered only the first nine characters of symbols to be significant.

Consider the instruction:

```
mov     ax , firstvalue
```

Here, a symbol is used to represent the address of a data location in a direct addressing mode instruction. We may read this instruction as 'Move the contents of the location whose address is `firstvalue` into

the accumulator AX'. The way in which the data location addressed by
firstvalue is defined in this context is explained in Section 2.3. Note
that the programmer need never know the actual address corresponding to firstvalue; the assembler takes care of the address
allocation and substitutes the absolute address value into this instruction. Thus, any future alterations to the program which may result in
a change to the absolute address of this data value will be taken care
of automatically by the assembler.

The advantage of symbolic addressing can be seen even more
clearly in the following example which employs the relative addressing mode to specify a jump instruction.

```
        jmp     next
        ---
        ---        } intervening instructions
        ---
next:   ---
        ---
```

The operand field of this relative jump instruction will be assembled
to give the correct positive offset, i.e. the number of locations from
the present address (the current location counter value) to the
address of the location labelled next. We avoid the need to count the
number of intervening locations manually though we must ensure
that the calculated value lies within the range of the limited relative
addressing space (the assembler should warn of range overflow).

Program changes which involve inserting or deleting an intervening instruction in the above example will entail a change in the
relative address in the jump instruction. Allowing the assembler to
perform this adjustment avoids the inconvenience of recomputation
of the offset which is required in raw machine code programming and
the obscure errors which result from a failure to do so correctly.

### 2.2.3  Expressions
Most assemblers permit a limited use of arithmetic expressions in
operand fields. The location after firstvalue may be accessed using:

```
mov     ax , firstvalue + 1
```

for example. Addition, subtraction, logical and, perhaps, multiplication operators included between symbolic or constant integers are
evaluated by an assembler, but there are two important points to
note. Firstly, the evaluation of expressions is performed statically,
i.e. during assembly. Machine code is *not* produced to perform the
arithmetic when the program is obeyed. Secondly, only the more
comprehensive assemblers will provide the familiar rules of pre-
cedence from high-level languages; a strictly left-to-right evaluation
may be enforced so that the expression $4 + 6 \star 2$ evaluates to 20 rather
than the more usual result of 16.

It is sometimes useful to be able to include the value of the current location counter in an expression and many assemblers provide a special symbol (e.g. $) for this. Indeed, it may be necessary to write relative jumps using this symbol, as in

```
jmp     next-$
```

where the determination of the offset is represented as an explicit calculation.

Note also that there are some kinds of expressions which are rarely meaningful. Whereas the difference between two symbolic addresses, e.g. `tablestart - tableend` may be a sensible constant, the sum of two such addresses is most unlikely to make sense since it is not known, in general, what absolute values the assembler will give to such symbols.

Constants included in expressions are not usually limited to decimal numbers. A single character enclosed in quotes may be accepted, such that `'p'`, for example, is an acceptable alternative to the numerical internal code for this character. It is particularly useful to be able to write integer constants in number bases other than decimal – notably in hexadecimal (see Section 3.1) and, possibly, in binary.

## 2.3   DIRECTIVES AND COMMENTS

Assembler directives are commands written into an assembly language program to control some aspect of the assembly process. They are sometimes called **pseudo-ops** because of the syntactic similarity between a directive and an assembly language instruction. Directives can be divided into two classes: those which generate values in the machine code output from the assembler and those which do not. The former category includes directives for declaring and initializing data items. Directives which do not produce any code include those used to declare constants, to define start addresses for code and data segments, and to switch assembler options on and off. The ability to include comments in a program for the reader's benefit is also considered in this section, alongside assembler directives to aid the presentation of listings.

### 2.3.1   Space allocation

The label `firstvalue` used in expressions in Section 2.2 represents the address of a store location used to hold an item of data. There must be a way to define this location, in much the same way that a variable in a good high-level language has to be declared. In assembly language, however, it is not usual to fix the data type of a value placed in a labelled location, as is the case in a high-level language declaration. The representation and manipulation of data values is a matter for the assembly language programmer to establish. Thus, a bit pattern in a location may be interpreted, variously, as an integer, a character, or as any programmer-defined data type. The assembler requires guidance only in where to allocate the space in memory for a data value and in how much space to assign.

Space is usually allocated in units of bytes or words. Thus, in a microprocessor with a word length of 16 bits, we would expect to find directives for allocating space in units of 16-bit words and 8-bit bytes. Assuming firstvalue to be a single (16-bit) word value, an assembly language statement to define this label is:

```
firstvalue      dw 2000
```

The directive DW (define word) appears in the syntactic position of a normal assembly language mnemonic – hence the alternative term 'pseudo-op' – though many assemblers rather inconsistently forbid the terminating colon after the label, as shown in the above example. As in the case of an assembly language instruction, the label firstvalue will be defined as the value of the current location counter. Hence, the label value will be the address of the first byte of two allocated by the DW directive. The operand field contains the initial value placed in this data location (2000). A similar directive, such as DB – define byte – performs the equivalent definition of a single byte item; some assemblers will provide a range of directives for multiple-byte allocation and initialization.

In many cases, a data location will be initialized by the program and no initial value needs to be inserted by a defining directive. Furthermore, it is usual to provide a means of allocating a constant number of locations in a single directive, in which case the operand field will contain information regarding the number of bytes (or words) to be allocated and, perhaps, an initial value to be placed in each. This leads to the use of these directives for allocating space for vectors or tables: the arrays of assembly language. An example in one assembler is:

```
vec1            db 20 dup (0)
```

which results in the allocation of 20 consecutive bytes of store, initially all containing zero, with vec1 defined to be the address of the first of these bytes (DUP (0) is used here in the sense of 'duplicate the value zero' in all 20 bytes).

To establish a table of constant values, the DB or DW type of directive described above normally allows lists of values to be specified in the operand field, as in:

```
primes          db 1,2,3,5,7,11,13,17,19,23
```

which places the prime numbers in 10 successive bytes, labelling the first one primes.

### 2.3.2  Equating

Many high-level languages allow the declaration of constant identifiers which may then be used as more meaningful representations of
the constant value. A directive for equating a symbol and a value is
provided in most assemblers, e.g.:

```
noofprimes      equ 20
linefeed        equ 10
```

The second of these provides a symbol which is clearly more evoca-
tive of its meaning than the numerical character code on the right-
hand side.

No machine code is generated in assembling an equate directive.
The symbol and its value are placed in the table of symbols maintained by the assembler and this value is substituted for each use of
the symbol in the program.

### 2.3.3  Origin setting

The avoidance of absolute addressing inside an assembly language
program means that it is possible to arrange for the code to be placed
anywhere in store by informing the assembler of the desired starting
address. This is the initial value for the current location counter and,
hence, the directive to perform this initialization is usually placed at
the head of the program. For example:

```
org     1000
```

informs the assembler that the program should be assembled into
store from location 1000 onwards.

So far it has been assumed that there is only one current location
counter in use by the assembler. In practice, it is often convenient to
maintain two or even more such counters for the assembly of different component parts of a program, and assemblers may offer
separate counters for program instructions and for data, for example.
This is the device mentioned in Section 1.6 as a means of achieving
the desired separation of code and data in a program. Separate
location counters may be maintained by issuing different origin setting directives before the relevant sections of program.

### 2.3.4  Program documentation

Sections of programs written in assembly language are rarely self-
explanatory. Even the author of the code may have difficulty following the meaning of a sequence of assembly language instructions
written some short time previously. The purpose of program documentation is to improve the ease with which a source program can be
understood by a programmer and this is even more important in
assembly language programming than it is in high-level language
programming. Three reasons for documenting programs are:

- to assist in locating errors during program debugging;
- to help understand the program in subsequent program maintenance;
- to aid comprehension of the program by a new programmer.

The idea that a program requires 'maintenance' does not imply that it wears out with age, but that its specification continues to evolve even after testing and release into service. The task to be performed by the program is modified from time to time and modifications are implemented in a succession of releases of the software. It has been estimated that well over half of programming costs may be attributable to program maintenance. Add to this the high mobility of professional programmers and the importance of the third point above is emphasized.

We shall have much to say in the course of Part 2 regarding the importance of structured design specifications in all kinds of programming. At the coding stage, a useful facility provided by virtually all assemblers is the **comment**. Comments may be inserted in a program entirely for the benefit of the reader. They are ignored by the assembler except in the production of program listings.

The usual syntax of a comment is a special start comment character (often the semicolon ;) after which all characters on the current line are taken as part of the comment. This allows a comment to appear on a line of its own or as the tail end of an instruction.

```
;***************************
;      Input Subroutine
;***************************

inroute:  mov ax , instatus          ;Check the input
                                      ;status.
```

The style of commenting in a program is a matter of personal (or agreed) preference, as is the number of comments inserted in a program. As a very rough approximation it is not unusual to find about half of the source text (in number of characters) made up of comments: a considerably higher proportion than one would expect to find in a high-level language program.

For the longer comments that one may wish to include, at the head of a program or before an intricate subroutine, for example, a special comment directive may be available such as:

```
comment          %
Create-file Routine
-------------------
```

```
In the routine which follows:

register AX holds ....
...
... etc.
                        %
```

in which all text between the delimiting % symbols is taken to be a comment without the need for a comment delimiter on each line.

A number of assembler directives may be concerned with controlling the production of a program listing (an example of which is shown in Figure 10.1). The listing generated by the assembler contains more information than a simple copy of the source file – it includes the assembled machine code and address information which may be needed during program testing, for example. Furthermore, the layout of labels, instruction mnemonics and operands is usually cleaned up to present each component in a separate column, as shown.

Two additional features deserve mention. Either by default, or on request, an assembler will usually provide a listing of the symbol table created during the assembly process (as shown at the end of Figure 10.1). This gives cross-referencing information between a symbol and its value, organized in alphabetical order of symbols. Some assemblers provide this information at the head or tail of the listing file; others create a special cross-reference file. In a large program, a symbol table listing can be used to find a given label definition quickly by first obtaining its value and then scanning down the machine code address values in the listing. A more comprehensive cross-reference table may also include the numbers (or machine code addresses) of every line in the program on which that symbol appears. One potential application of this is in identifying symbols that are defined but never used – possibly due to alterations to a program.

The second feature is pagination and headings. A long listing may be split into pages, each numbered and headed with a title defined by the programmer. Details such as the title and number of lines per page are usually alterable by appropriate directives.

At the end of this section it is worth remarking on the relationship between program **documentation** and program **design**. The production of a neat listing complete with comments marks the completion of a design process which starts with the original specification of the problem to be solved. The most impressively commented assembly language program is no substitute for a higher-level algorithm explained in a more suitable language. We shall return to the principles of assembly language design in later sections.

### 2.3.5 Macros

An assembler such as the IBM Macro Assembler (MASM) provides directives to create and use macros. A **macro** is a sequence of instructions defined by the programmer and given a name. Whenever that name is used in the program the assembler will substitute in its place the predefined sequence of instructions. Thus, a macro name is a convenient shorthand term for a longer sequence of code presented in a **macro definition** and used in a **macro call**.

Note that this is not at all the same as the subroutine calling mechanism. A subroutine exists in one place only and the calling instructions transfer control to and from the subroutine at run-time. Each macro call results in the assembler expanding the name into the defined set of instructions and inserting them at that point in the program. After assembly there is no evidence of the macro's existence: it is entirely a text substitution facility within the assembly language.

Despite this apparent simplicity, macros can be extremely useful. A simple macro for saving the contents of a couple of registers (AX, BX) on the stack is:

```
save      macro
          push      ax
          push      bx
          endm
```

MACRO and ENDM are the pseudo-ops used in this macro definition. The name of the macro is SAVE and this can now be used in a program as if it were a new instruction mnemonic:

```
label1:
          mov       ax , avalue
          mov       bx , anovalue
          save
```

Here, the use of SAVE is exactly equivalent to writing PUSH AX followed by PUSH BX – the assembler will generate the same machine code. However, SAVE is shorter to write and, possibly, more meaningful than the two PUSH instructions.

Macros can have parameters to increase their usefulness. For example, a macro to save *any* two registers could be defined as:

```
pairsave          macro     r1 , r2
                  push      r1
                  push      r2
                  endm
```

and used to produce exactly the same code as before by calling with *actual* parameters (AX, BX) to replace the *dummy* parameters (R1, R2):

```
pairsave ax , bx
```

This brief introduction to macros has only covered the basic facilities available in a powerful macro assembler such as MASM. It is worthwhile investigating these in more detail as experience of assembly language programming is gained, particularly when larger programs are to be written.

### 2.3.6   More directives

The directives mentioned earlier in this chapter form a small subset common to many assemblers, though their actual names and syntax will vary from one to another. Some of the more advanced assemblers possess a large number of further directives and the IBM Macro Assembler is one of the more sophisticated assemblers in terms of the wealth of directives furnished for the convenience of the programmer. Over 20 pseudo-ops are provided for data allocation alone, for example.

## 2.4   THE ASSEMBLY PROCESS

The process of assembling a source code program into machine code is represented in Figure 2.2. Though the details will vary from assembler to assembler, it is usually possible to identify some or all of the separate processes in this diagram.

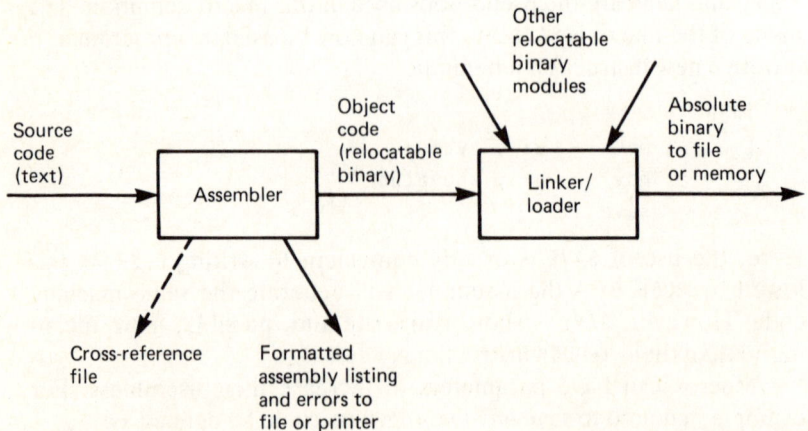

**Figure 2.2**   The assembly process.

### 2.4.1   File-oriented assembly

In most computer systems it is convenient to organize the assembly process as a series of operations on files stored, commonly, on magnetic disk. Thus, the assembler reads the contents of one file – the **source code** file – and generates a second file – the **object code** file – as its output. As an optional side-effect, a listing file and, perhaps, a cross-reference file may be created. A separate process is called after assembly in order to produce an absolute binary version of the program in a file or in memory.

Programmers who are used to the interpretive implementations of some high-level languages, especially BASIC, may find the separate translation phase of an assembler unfamiliar. In most BASIC systems, for example, a program is executed by taking the next BASIC statement to be obeyed, translating it into machine code and executing the code for that one statement before moving on to interpret the next BASIC statement. Thus, the program resides in store as high-level language instructions, not as machine code, and there is no separate translation phase as there would be in truly *compiled* implementations of high-level languages. A **compiler** is the high-level language equivalent of an assembler, generating an object program from source language statements as an activity quite distinct from the execution of that object program.

What may also be new to the BASIC programmer brought up in an interpretive environment is the use of a completely separate **editor** program to produce and maintain the source program file prior to submitting it for assembly. The detailed command structure of such editors is extremely variable and beyond the scope of this text, however, and the manufacturer's documentation on editing should be consulted. As a general word of advice, editors tend to be too complicated for mere mortals to master in every single feature. Hard-won experience suggests that apart from being competent at starting an edit, moving through the text and ending an edit, probably the only commands that are worth learning, particularly at first, are those to insert lines, delete lines, search for a string of text and substitute one string for another.

### 2.4.2  Assembler passes

One complete scan through the source program made by an assembler is called a **pass**. Some assemblers perform the entire assembly process in the course of a single pass, including syntax checking, symbol table construction, evaluation of expressions and code generation. Perhaps the majority of assemblers assign these tasks to one of two passes through the source program. Normally, pass 1 is concerned with syntax checking and symbol definitions, but no machine code is generated at this stage. Pass 2 makes use of the symbol table generated in pass 1 in order to evaluate expressions and generate machine code.

One-pass assemblers have to take particular care in translating references to symbols that have not yet been defined: for example forward jumps to labels. These must be marked in order to return later and fill in the missing symbol value. Arithmetic on forwardly defined symbols may be banned in one-pass assemblers because of the difficulty of deferring the expression evaluation.

The detection of many types of syntactic error will take place during pass 1 of a two-pass assembler; pass 2 is not usually attempted in the presence of pass 1 errors. A few assemblers make a third pass through the source file at the end of assembly, generating the listing file as a distinct activity.

### 2.4.3  Errors
Syntax errors detected by the assembler are reported in the listing file and, sometimes, messages are sent to the computer terminal stating the line number and nature of the error. A crude assembler will quote meaningless error numbers; a better one gives plain (more often cryptic) English phrases describing the nature of the error. As with all computer language translators, the reported error message may not point directly to the fault and some lateral thinking may be necessary. An `undefined label` error message, for example, may be due to a missing declaration or it may be caused by, among many other things, wrong spelling of the identifier in the operand field.

### 2.4.4  Linking, loading and relocation
A separate process of linking and loading is shown in Figure 2.2. In practice, some assemblers generate absolute machine code which requires trivial loading into store before execution. Indeed, the source program may be assembled directly into store for immediate execution after assembly, and this is a common choice on some of the smaller personal microcomputer systems.

For various reasons, it is often more convenient to have the assembler generate a **relocatable** object code file as shown in Figure 2.2. In relocatable object code, symbolic addresses in the source code are given values which are marked as being relative to a base address. Typically, this base address will be the origin of one of the current location counters. By tagging symbolic addresses in this way it is possible to delay the decision of where to place a program and its data in store. A **relocating loader** is a program which converts a relocatable object code file into machine code with absolute addresses. The user (or operating system) provides the loader with the base address value(s) to be added to relocatable addresses in order to create this absolute binary code.

Since a separate loading process adds to the complexity of assembly, it is reasonable to analyse why the distinction is advantageous. Firstly, a major task of an operating system is to manage resources. Here, resources are components of the system such as peripherals – printers, disks, etc. – or time allocated to different processes. The task of management entails deciding which programs running on the computer may use how much of which resource, and for how long. Even on single-user computers it is desirable to permit multi-tasking: the running of several programs concurrently. For example, one program may be printing out a file while the user edits another file. Storage allocation is an important resource to control in such an environment. Hence, it may be highly undesirable to commit a program to fixed addresses in store at assembly time, and flexible use of the memory resource is enhanced if the operating system (or user) can decide at the last possible moment where to locate a program.

Secondly, a program may be divided into several independently assembled modules. Splitting programs in this way offers benefits from a structured-programming viewpoint: a logical and physical segregation of ideas, that will be explored in more detail later. In practical terms, a set of subroutines performing common tasks, such as driving special peripheral devices, may be written once and saved in a library for use in future programs. Though such routines could be included in a program in source code form they increase the size of source code unnecessarily and slow down assembly. There is also the problem of ensuring non-duplication of identifiers used to represent symbolic quantities.

Modules, which are assembled independently into relocatable object code files, can be linked together in a separate process prior to loading. A **linker** makes the necessary cross-references of symbols between modules, inserting the correct addresses of subroutines called in one module but defined in another, for example. The programmer may have to assist the linker by stating, in each module, which symbols are defined externally and which are to be made available externally and pseudo-ops may be provided for these purposes.

# 3 | Basic Data Representations

For good or for bad, mankind is moving ever nearer to a unified system of number representation based on the decimal scale. In Britain, for example, school children no longer learn explicitly how to manipulate numbers in base 12 arithmetic: a prerequisite for pre-decimalized coinage and for counting in dozens or gross. Indeed, the convenience of a basic unit in human terms is sometimes sacrificed to the arithmetic simplicity of the decimal system. Not all units of measurement can be made to fit this system, however – even the decimalization lobby may have difficulty convincing us of the wisdom of converting to a decimal calendar.

At the basic architecture level, computers are not usually obliging in respect of decimals. Conventional technology favours a two-state representation of data at the hardware level: the binary system. Binary representation offers an elegance and economy in the number of different symbols required to represent values, but it suffers badly in human terms from the need to form long strings of digits to make up even the simplest data structures. Furthermore, since 10 is not an exact power of 2, it is not particularly straightforward to represent strings of binary signals by decimal digits and this has led to the recruitment of other number bases, particularly octal (base 8) and hexadecimal (base 16), as aids to low-level language programming. Users of high-level languages may not be familiar with the manipulation of numbers in bases other than 10, and this chapter introduces the basic principles of representing numbers of various types in various number bases. Also, the representation of characters in different character codes is considered at the end of the chapter.

Readers already familiar with the subject material of this chapter may prefer to skip on directly to Part 2 of the text. Bearing in mind that the computer is a general symbol manipulation machine and not a super-calculator, it is clear that some of the more involved numerical representations outlined in this chapter may be of only passing interest to many readers. At some point, therefore, readers may wish to skip forward to Section 3.5 (character codes).

## 3.1 NUMBER BASES

In the decimal system, numbers are represented using 10 distinct symbols – the decimal digits 0 to 9. The position of a digit in a number carries information relating to the 'weighting' of that digit: whether it is to be interpreted as a units, tens or hundreds digit, etc. More formally, the digits in a positive decimal integer are weighted by increasing powers of 10 as:

| weighting | $10^3$ | $10^2$ | $10^1$ | $10^0$ |
|---|---|---|---|---|
| digits | 1 | 2 | 3 | 4 |

decimal $1234 = 1 \times 10^3 + 2 \times 10^2 + 3 \times 10^1 + 4 \times 10^0$

(noting that anything to the power zero = 1)

Extending this convention to any number base, a positive, 4-digit integer in base $m$ is represented by:

| weighting | $m^3$ | $m^2$ | $m^1$ | $m^0$ |
|---|---|---|---|---|
| digits | $d_3$ | $d_2$ | $d_1$ | $d_0$ |

base$_m$ $d_3d_2d_1d_0 = d_3 \times m^3 + d_2 \times m^2 + d_1 \times m^1 + d_0 \times m^0$

Thus, the binary number 0101 is interpreted as:

| weighting | $2^3$ | $2^2$ | $2^1$ | $2^0$ |
|---|---|---|---|---|
| digits | 0 | 1 | 0 | 1 |

binary $0101 = 0 \times 2^3 + 1 \times 2^2 + 0 \times 2^1 + 1 \times 2^0$

Note that this expansion provides a simple technique for translating a binary number into decimal, since it is only necessary to evaluate each term in decimal and to sum the resulting values:

binary $0101 = 0 + 4 + 0 + 1 =$ decimal 5

Looked at another way, the digit weightings from right to left in a binary integer are 1, 2, 4, 8, 16 etc. (written in decimal) as opposed to 1, 10, 100, 1000 etc. in a decimal integer.

A more general technique for converting from one number base to another is repeatedly to divide the number by the new base, and this is illustrated in the conversion of decimal 35 into binary. Note how the remainder of the division at each stage becomes a digit in the new base, with the least significant digit generated first.

| | remainder | binary digit weight |
|---|---|---|
| 2 )35 | | |
| 2 )17 | 1 | $2^0$ |
| 2 )8 | 1 | $2^1$ |
| 2 )4 | 0 | $2^2$ |
| 2 )2 | 0 | $2^3$ |
| 2 )1 | 0 | $2^4$ |
| 0 | 1 | $2^5$ |

decimal 35 = binary 100011

Because of the number of digits in even quite small binary numbers it would be convenient to divide the number into small groups of digits and to replace them by digits of a higher number base. The decimal base is inconvenient for this purpose since 10 is not an exact power of two. If we group bits into threes, however, each group may be rewritten in base 8 or **octal** notation:

| decimal | 1337 | | | |
|---------|------|-----|-----|-----|
| binary | 010 | 100 | 111 | 001 |
| octal | 2 | 4 | 7 | 1 |

$$8^3 \qquad 8^2 \qquad 8^1 \qquad 8^0 \qquad \text{octal weightings}$$
$$2 \times 512 + 4 \times 64 \quad + 7 \times 8 \quad + 1 \qquad = 1337 \text{ decimal}$$

The most common groupings of bits in modern stores tend to be in units of eight (i.e. bytes) and multiples thereof. Thus, a byte could be represented by three octal digits, the most significant of which represents only two bits: an unfortunate mis-match.

| decimal | 101 | | |
|---------|-----|-----|-----|
| binary | 01 | 100 | 101 (one byte) |
| octal | 1 | 4 | 5 |

A more concise representation is achieved by grouping bits into fours and rewriting each group by the corresponding base 16 or **hexadecimal** digit. The 16 digits in this base (usually abbreviated to 'hex') are obtained by extending the decimal digits 0 to 9 by the first six letters of the alphabet, giving the correspondences in Table 3.1.

Table 3.1   Hexadecimal base.

| Decimal | Hexadecimal | Binary |
|---------|-------------|--------|
| 0 | 0 | 0000 |
| 1 | 1 | 0001 |
| 2 | 2 | 0010 |
| 3 | 3 | 0011 |
| 4 | 4 | 0100 |
| 5 | 5 | 0101 |
| 6 | 6 | 0110 |
| 7 | 7 | 0111 |
| 8 | 8 | 1000 |
| 9 | 9 | 1001 |
| 10 | A | 1010 |
| 11 | B | 1011 |
| 12 | C | 1100 |
| 13 | D | 1101 |
| 14 | E | 1110 |
| 15 | F | 1111 |

Hexadecimal representations of binary patterns are used extensively as a shorthand technique, improving the reliability with which binary numbers can be expressed. A 16-bit address, for example, can be written as a 4-digit hex address:

| binary | 1011 | 0000 | 0101 | 1010 |
|--------|------|------|------|------|
| hex | B | 0 | 5 | A |
| | $16^3$ | $16^2$ | $16^1$ | $16^0$ digit weightings |

$$11 \times 4096 + 0 \times 256 + 5 \times 16 + 10 = 45\,146 \text{ decimal}$$

Conversion from binary to hexadecimal and vice-versa can be seen to be far more straightforward than conversion to and from the decimal base.

Assemblers are usually designed to accept integer values in some, or all, of the bases mentioned above. The distinction is normally made by prefixing or postfixing a constant with a qualifier marking the base, or radix, of that constant. A value without a qualifier is assumed to be in the default base: a default which may be altered by pseudo-ops in many assemblers. Thus, the following constants may be equivalent:

| 145 | decimal (by default) |
|-----|---------------------|
| 10010001b | binary |
| 91h | hexadecimal |

Many assemblers insist that a hexadecimal constant start with a digit from 0 to 9, in order to distinguish the hex value A200h from a label of the same name, for instance. Writing this constant as 0A200h removes this ambiguity.

Note that 8-bit character codes such as ASCII (see the end of this chapter) are often presented as two hexadecimal digits. One half of a byte – a 4-bit value represented by one hexadecimal digit – is commonly referred to by the gastronomically influenced title of a **nibble**!

## 3.2 BINARY NUMBER REPRESENTATIONS

An 8-bit positive integer can be represented using the digit weightings described above:

| bit | 7 | 6 | 5 | 4 | 3 | 2 | 1 | 0 |
|-----|---|---|---|---|---|---|---|---|
| binary integer | 1 | 0 | 1 | 0 | 0 | 1 | 1 | 1 |
| weighting | $2^7$ | $2^6$ | $2^5$ | $2^4$ | $2^3$ | $2^2$ | $2^1$ | $2^0$ |
| decimal equivalent | 128 + | 0 + | 32 + | 0 + | 0 + | 4 + | 2 + | 1 = 167 |

The largest integer in this notation is $2^8 - 1 = 255$. The range of integers in $n$ bits is thus 0 to $2^n - 1$. There is no provision at this stage for the representation of negative numbers.

The notation can be extended to provide for negative integer representation in one of several ways. Perhaps the most obvious of these is called the 'sign plus modulus' technique in which one bit of the number is reserved for an indicator of sign. The modulus of the number, i.e. its magnitude ignoring sign, is expressed in the remaining bits in the same way as above. For example, $-51$ could be written in 8 bits as:

| bit | 7 (sign) | 6 | 5 | 4 | 3 | 2 | 1 | 0 |
|---|---|---|---|---|---|---|---|---|
| binary integer | 1 | | 0 | 1 | 1 | 0 | 0 | 1 | 1 |
| weighting | $-$ve | | $2^6$ | $2^5$ | $2^4$ | $2^3$ | $2^2$ | $2^1$ | $2^0$ |

The range of integers in $n$ bits by this approach is $-(2^{n-1}-1)$ to $2^{n-1}-1$.

Performing arithmetic on values in the sign plus modulus notation is feasible, with or without hardware designed to handle the manipulation of the sign bit, but it is not particularly straightforward. Note that the total number of integers that can be represented is $2^n-1$, one less than the all positive case. This is because there are two representations for zero – the sign bit may be 0 or 1 – and this is unfortunate since it means comparing values against two possibilities to detect a zero value. However, the most serious drawback of the sign plus modulus representation lies in the special organization which is needed to perform subtraction. Mentally, when we are confronted with a subtraction such as $31-53$ we may handle this in a different way to one such as $53-31$: by subtracting the smaller from the larger and adjusting the sign of the result. A system of representation of integers in which addition and subtraction are performed consistently is preferred in most computer systems.

This consistency is achieved if we consider what would happen if we actually did subtract 53 from 31:

$$\begin{array}{r} 0031 \\ 0053 \\ \hline \end{array}$$

(ignoring carry to left)  9978

The number 9978 is the *ten's complement* representation of $-22$ (the result of the subtraction in sign plus modulus terms). It is 'complementary' in the sense that the sum of the magnitudes of a pair of numbers either side of zero and equidistant from it is always zero (ignoring carry), as shown in Figure 3.1. For example:

| Ten's complement | Sign + modulus |
|---|---|
| 9997 | $-3$ |
| 0003 | $+3$ |
| 0000 | 0 |

Figure 3.1 is described by the following text and labels:

sign plus modulus

| −3 | −2 | −1 | 0 | + 1 | + 2 | + 3 |
|---|---|---|---|---|---|---|
| 9997 | 9998 | 9999 | | 0001 | 0002 | 0003 |

ten's complement          0000

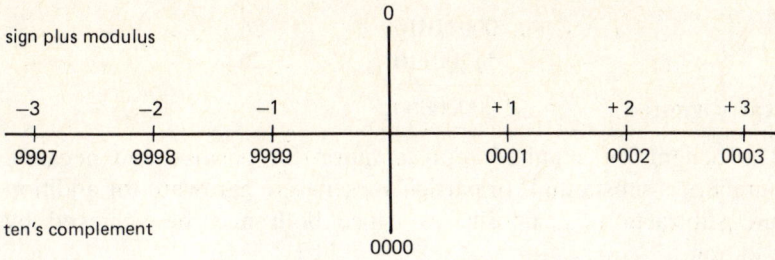

**Figure 3.1**  Ten's complement representation.

In the ten's complement case, arithmetic is always performed on integers with the same number of digits – four in the above example – and any carry from the left column of the sum is ignored. A negative number always starts with a 9 and the number of digits may be extended by adding further 9s to the left.

The corresponding notation in binary is two's complement (Figure 3.2), and this representation is expected by the signed arithmetic instructions in most computer architectures. The two's complement of a number is obtained by subtracting the modulus of the number from zero or, more usually, by the simple rule 'complement each bit of the binary integer and add 1, ignoring carry out of the left-hand column'.

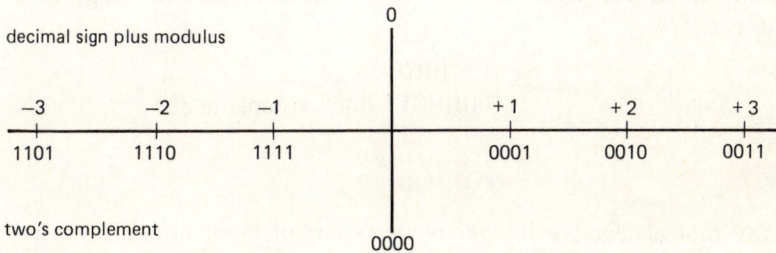

decimal sign plus modulus          0

| −3 | −2 | −1 | | + 1 | + 2 | + 3 |
|---|---|---|---|---|---|---|
| 1101 | 1110 | 1111 | | 0001 | 0010 | 0011 |

two's complement          0000

**Figure 3.2**  Two's complement representation.

*Example*   Find the two's complement of +26 in eight bits.

| 00011010 | Decimal 26 |
|---|---|
| 11100101 | Each bit complemented (the one's complement) |
| 1 | Add 1 |

11100110   −26 (two's complement)

This may be verified by adding +26 to −26 in two's complement form:

```
00011010          +26
11100110          −26
```
(carry ignored)      00000000

The benefits of a united representation for positive and negative numbers is substantial. In particular, separate hardware for addition and subtraction is superfluous, since both may be achieved by addition.

*Example*   Subtract +53 from +31 in eight bits.

The problem is first recast as the sum:

$$31$$
$$(-53) +$$

and the two's complement of 53 is calculated:

```
00110101   +53
11001010   one's complement
         1
11001011   two's complement (−53)
```

The subtraction is now performed by the addition:

```
00011111    +31
11001011    (−53) +
11101010    −22
```

This two's complement result can be checked by taking the two's complement again, thus returning to the complementary positive integer:

```
11101010   −22
00010101   one's complement
         1
00010110   +22
```

Note that a negative integer in two's complement notation always starts with a 1 and a positive integer with a 0 and, consequently, the most significant bit of a number is an indication of sign. For this reason, the most significant bit is called the **sign bit**. In terms of digit weightings, it is interesting to note that the two's complement notation can be interpreted by a simple change to the all positive representation described earlier. Consider, in eight bits:

| Bit | 7 | 6 | 5 | 4 | 3 | 2 | 1 | 0 |
|---|---|---|---|---|---|---|---|---|
| Two's complement binary integer | 1 | 1 | 1 | 0 | 1 | 0 | 1 | 0 |
| Weighting | $-2^7$ | $2^6$ | $2^5$ | $2^4$ | $2^3$ | $2^2$ | $2^1$ | $2^0$ |

Signed decimal equivalent   $-128 + 64 + 32 + 0 + 8 + 0 + 2 + 0 = -22$

Thus, in two's complement notation, the most significant bit (the sign bit) of an $n$ digit number is weighted negatively ($-2^{n-1}$). The largest positive and negative integers in 8 bits are:

binary 0 1 1 1 1 1 1 1 = 7F hexadecimal = +127 decimal

binary 1 0 0 0 0 0 0 0 = 80 hexadecimal = −128 decimal

The range in general is $-2^{n-1}$ to $2^{n-1}-1$ and, hence, the total number of integers that can be represented in $n$ bits is the full $2^n$ (there is only one representation for zero). The condition known as **integer overflow** occurs when an operation on integer operands produces a result which is outside this range. We can detect when this has happened by examining the sign bits of the operands and result, and the state of the carry after an operation. Overflow can only occur in two's complement addition when the signs of the operands are the same. Consider the following examples:

| Carry bit | Sign bit | | |
|---|---|---|---|
| | 0 1 1 1 1 1 1 1 | 127 |
| | 0 0 0 0 0 0 0 1 | 1 + |
| 0 | 1 0 0 0 0 0 0 0 | +ve overflow |

| Carry bit | Sign bit | | |
|---|---|---|---|
| | 1 0 0 0 0 0 0 0 | −128 |
| | 1 1 1 1 1 1 1 1 | (−1) + |
| 1 | 0 1 1 1 1 1 1 1 | −ve overflow |

The overflow has caused the sign of the result to be different to the sign of the operands. An alternative rule is that overflow occurs if the carry *into* the sign bit position of the sum is different to the carry *out of* that position.

Note finally that there is no obligation on the programmer to use two's complement notation; it is convenient to do so if signed arithmetic is required since the instructions and flag settings will behave in accordance with this convention. On the other hand, if operations are to be performed on positive integers only, with positive integer results, the programmer might choose to perform unsigned arithmetic using the full positive range from 0 to $2^n - 1$, perhaps, and interpret the settings of the flags accordingly.

## 3.3  RATIONAL NUMBERS

Integer numbers fall within the province of every computer user in virtually every task we undertake. They are used for counting things and for enumerating events. They are fixed, invariant objects, two of which may be compared with confidence of a predictable result. As soon as a decimal (or binary) point is introduced into numbers we create a data type with very different characteristics.

Any computer representation of fractional numbers carries with it a limited precision as well as an overall range. Thus, the number 3.14159 is written with a precision of six significant figures: it is an approximation stated to be accurate to this number of figures. Any manipulation of this fraction takes place in the context of that limited precision. For example, adding 0.000001 to the above number will not affect its value stored to this precision.

### 3.3.1  Fixed-point fractions

In terms of digit weightings, the decimal fraction 13.625 may be shown as:

| decimal | 1 | 3 | | 6 | 2 | 5 |
|---|---|---|---|---|---|---|
| weighting | $10^1$ | $10^0$ | | $10^{-1}$ | $10^{-2}$ | $10^{-3}$ |

decimal<br>point

$$10 + \quad 3 + \qquad\qquad 0.6 + \quad 0.02 + \quad 0.005 = 13.625$$

To the left of the decimal point, digit weightings are the same as in the integer case. Negative powers are used to the right of this point. Fractions of this kind are called **fixed-point fractions** because the position of the decimal point is fixed. The same fraction in binary is 01101.101 and one representation of this is:

| bit | 7 | 6 | 5 | 4 | 3 | | 2 | 1 | 0 |
|---|---|---|---|---|---|---|---|---|---|
| binary | 0 | 1 | 1 | 0 | 1 | | 1 | 0 | 1 |
| weighting | $-2^4$ | $2^3$ | $2^2$ | $2^1$ | $2^0$ | | $2^{-1}$ | $2^{-2}$ | $2^{-3}$ |

binary<br>point

signed
decimal           $0 + 8 + 4 + 0 + 1 + \quad \frac{1}{2} + \quad 0 + \quad \frac{1}{8} = 13.625$
equivalent                                                                    decimal

Compared to the integer case, the range of numbers which can be represented by this technique is reduced by the encroaching binary point. Thus, to achieve a usable range and precision of fixed-point fractions it is necessary to use considerably more bits than eight. Three bytes are sufficient to represent a fixed-point fraction with a precision of about six decimal places, for example.

The major drawback of using a fixed-point representation is that there is no stored record of the position of the binary point. The programmer must maintain its position independently of the representation and make suitable adjustments to this position when performing arithmetic. In some arithmetic operations it is easy to calculate the new position of the binary point. If two fixed-point fractions having $m$ and $n$ binary places respectively are multiplied together, for instance, then the result will have $m + n$ binary places, as shown in the next example.

```
  0101.101          3 binary places (5.625 decimal)
    01.01×          2 binary places (1.25 decimal)
  ─────────
  0101101
  010110100
  ─────────
  0111.00001        5 binary places (7 1/32 = 7.03125 dec.)
```

Addition or subtraction of fixed-point fractions is less straightforward, however. Before the operation can be performed, the binary point of the two numbers must be aligned, as in:

```
     binary               decimal
   0101.101                5.625
     01.01    +            1.25    +
   ─────────              ───────
   0110.111                6.875
```

An algorithm is required to shift the binary fraction (and its binary point) with the fewest binary places left by one place, to match the number of binary places of the other number. The result of the addition will then have the same precision as the operand with the largest number of binary places. There is an added complication, however. Shifting one number to the left may cause that number to go out of range, as would happen if the next 8-bit binary fraction were shifted one place left:

| | (sign) | | | | binary point | | | |
|---|---|---|---|---|---|---|---|---|
| bit | 7 | 6 | 5 | 4 | 3 | 2 | 1 | 0 |
| binary | 0 | 1 | 1 | 0 | 1 | 0 | 0 | 0 |
| weighting | $-2^3$ | $2^2$ | $2^1$ | $2^0$ | $2^{-1}$ | $2^{-2}$ | $2^{-3}$ | $2^{-4}$ |
| decimal | 0+ | 4+ | 2+ | 0+ | $\frac{1}{2} = 6.5$ | | | |

Any attempt to shift the above pattern left would move a one into the sign bit; an unnacceptable occurrence. The way out of this problem is to shift the other number to the right, i.e. to reduce its number of binary places. In doing so, information will be lost as the least significant bits of the fraction are shifted out of the right-hand end of the byte; this is an unfortunate but inevitable consequence of the need to align the binary point.

Quite separately from this preconditioning of the operands, the result of an arithmetic operation may go out of range. In practice, this can be detected in time to shift the result to the right, losing bits at the least significant end of the result but, in most cases, enabling a result of the given precision to be produced.

### 3.3.2    Floating-point fractions

In general, implementing arithmetic routines using fixed-point representation is not recommended in any but the simplest of cases. The juggling of binary point positions is particularly easy to get wrong, often in subtle ways. It is always better for a data structure to contain all the necessary information for its manipulation and in the case of fractions, this includes the position of the binary point as well as the magnitude of the number.

Floating-point representation of fractions is used almost universally in implementations of real arithmetic in high-level languages. Special-purpose hardware is often available on which to execute instructions to perform high speed operations on these data types.

There is a close analogy between floating-point binary representation and the scientific notation for fractions. In scientific notation, a decimal number may be expressed in two parts as:

$$a \times 10^b$$

for example:

$$1.6523 \times 10^3 \quad (= 1652.3)$$
$$6.345 \ \times 10^{-6} \quad (= 0.000006345)$$

Similarly, in binary floating-point representation, a number is expressed as:

$$a \times 2^b$$

where $a$ is called the **mantissa** and $b$ the **exponent** of the number.

In the decimal case, numbers are usually normalized so that the mantissa is either zero, or lies in the range 1 to 10 (or $-10$ to $-1$). For floating-point binary, the mantissa is often normalized to be either zero or lie in the range:

$$\tfrac{1}{2} \leqslant a < 1 \qquad \text{(positive numbers)}$$
$$-1 \leqslant a < -\tfrac{1}{2} \qquad \text{(negative numbers)}$$

for reasons which will be apparent shortly.

If the number of bits allocated to the mantissa is $m$ and that allocated to the exponent $e$, how should $m$ and $e$ be chosen? Note that the range of a floating-point number is dictated by $e$ whereas the precision (number of significant figures) is dictated by $m$. In integer representation it is often convenient to choose single or double word lengths of, for example, 16 bits as the basic integer size, but this is insufficient for sensible units in the floating-point case.

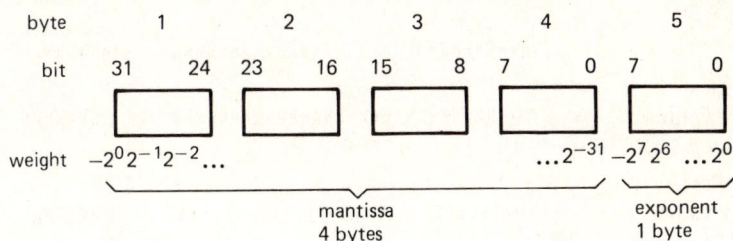

**Figure 3.3**   Floating-point representation.

A floating-point representation based on five bytes is shown in Figure 3.3. Respecting the common practice of addressing values in bytes, or multiples thereof, a choice of one byte for an exponent written in two's complement form gives a range of exponents from $2^{-128}$ to $2^{127}$. Given the above normalization, this implies that any number $n$ may be represented such that:

$$\tfrac{1}{2} \times 2^{-128} < |n| < 1 \times 2^{127} \qquad (\text{or } n = 0)$$
$$\text{i.e. } 2^{-129} < |n| < 2^{127}$$

where $|n|$ is the magnitude of $n$, ignoring the sign (the modulus of $n$). Thus, the range of numbers that can be stored is approximately plus or minus $2^{127}$, which is in the order of plus or minus $10^{38}$ – quite adequate for most applications (the world began less than $10^{17}$ seconds ago).

The 4-byte mantissa in Figure 3.3 is made up of a sign bit (bit 31) followed by the normalized fraction significant to 31 binary digits (about nine significant decimal digits). Again, this is a respectable precision in most, though certainly not all, cases.

Typically a floating-point number is normalized so that the most significant non-sign digit of the mantissa is a one for positive numbers or a zero for negative numbers. In this way, trains of leading zeros (positive numbers) or of leading ones (negative numbers) are avoided, thus maximizing the number of significant binary digits in the mantissa. Extreme values in this floating-point range and one other example are shown in Table 3.2.

**Table 3.2**   Floating-point examples.

| Value | Mantissa bits | Exponent bits |
|---|---|---|
| | 31... ... ... ... ... ... ... ... ... ... 0 | 76543210 |
| largest +ve value $(1 - 2^{-31}) \times 2^{127}$ | 01111111111111111111111111111111 | 01111111 |
| largest −ve value $-1 \times 2^{127}$ | 10000000000000000000000000000000 | 01111111 |
| zero | 00000000000000000000000000000000 | 00000000 |
| smallest +ve value $2^{-1} \times 2^{-128}$ | 01000000000000000000000000000000 | 10000000 |
| smallest −ve value $-2^{-1} - 2^{-31} \times 2^{-128}$ | 10111111111111111111111111111111 | 10000000 |
| $\pi$ 3.14159265 | 01100100100001111110110101010001 | 00000010 |

Two conditions which may occur during operations on floating-point numbers are worth mentioning at this point. Floating-point *overflow* occurs when the result of an operation is too large to fit the representation. Note that it is the exponent which overflows to cause this to happen. An overflow of the mantissa affects only the precision of the result and can be overcome by normalization. Floating-point *underflow*, on the other hand, occurs when the result is smaller than the smallest number which can be represented. Again, this is dictated by the exponent, the largest negative value of which represents the limiting case for small numbers. Whereas floating-point overflow is a condition from which there is no sensible recovery (other than by changing the size of the exponent), underflow can be handled reasonably by setting the result of the operation to zero.

There are many practical variations on this outline of floating-point representation. One of these is to add 128 to the exponent and store it as a positive integer between 0 and 256 rather than as a two's complement value between −128 and 127. This is referred to as an 'excess $N$' exponent, where $N = 128$ in this case. This may make arithmetic manipulation slightly easier in computers where the exponent does not fit into a convenient unit of storage for two's complement arithmetic or where operation on all positive integer exponents is preferred.

Some hardware facilities for manipulating floating-point fractions are introduced in Chapter 8.

## 3.4   BINARY CODED DECIMAL REPRESENTATION

Binary coded decimal (BCD) representation of numbers is an intuitively simple scheme in which four bits are used to represent one decimal digit. Of the 16 patterns available in four bits, only 10 are used, as shown in Table 3.3. Four-bit groups (half-byte 'nibbles') are placed side by side to represent multi-digit decimal numbers, as:

| BCD | 0101 | 0111 |
|---|---|---|
| Decimal | 5 | 7 |

Thus, one byte may hold BCD representations in the range 0–99; two bytes extend this to 0–9999.

**Table 3.3**   Binary coded decimal.

| BCD | Decimal | Unused |
|---|---|---|
| 0000 | 0 | 1010 |
| 0001 | 1 | 1011 |
| 0010 | 2 | 1100 |
| 0011 | 3 | 1101 |
| 0100 | 4 | 1110 |
| 0101 | 5 | |
| 0110 | 6 | |
| 0111 | 7 | |
| 1000 | 8 | |
| 1001 | 9 | |

The main attraction of BCD representation is the ease with which conversions to and from decimal may be made and, more particularly, the resulting simplicity of input and output of decimal digits. BCD is most useful in applications involving frequent decimal I/O, providing that relatively simple internal arithmetic is required. Many pocket calculators use BCD representation because of the need to display each stage of a calculation in decimal format.

Performing arithmetic in BCD on a computer designed primarily to handle two's complement binary numbers is not particularly difficult for fairly simple operations on short BCD integers. It is not recommended as a general technique for manipulations of fractions on the grounds of programming complexity and relatively poor performance from both speed and space viewpoints. The simple cases of addition and subtraction of positive BCD integers are considered next.

A pair of 2-digit BCD integers may be added together using a binary ADD instruction as:

```
decimal   BCD
  57      0101  0111
  21 +    0010  0001 +
  ──      ────────────
  78      0111  1000
         (7        8)
```

The result is only correct, however, because there is no carry from either of the two nibbles in the sum, and because both of these latter are valid BCD codes. Consider the sum of a second pair, in Example 1(a).

*Example 1(a)*

```
decimal   BCD
  57      0101  0111
  24 +    0010  0100 +
  ──      ────────────
  81      0111  1011
         (7        -)
```

This result is not the desired BCD sum and it contains an invalid digit code. The right-hand digit of the sum has moved into the group of six unused codes of Table 3.3. The pair in Example 1(b) also produce an incorrect sum though, in this case, the result contains two valid BCD codes.

*Example 1(b)*

```
decimal   BCD
  57      0101  0111
  29 +    0010  1001 +
  ──      ────────────
  86      1000  0000
         (8        0)
```

The problem here arises from the sum of two BCD digits (7 and 9) spanning completely the range of invalid codes.

There is a further problem in BCD arithmetic that arises when the result of an addition includes a 9 digit, and the digit to the right of this overflows the BCD range as in Example 1(c).

*Example 1(c)*

```
decimal    BCD
  147      0001  0100  0111
  253 +    0010  0101  0011 +
  ───      ──────────────────
  400      0011  1001  1010
          ( 3     9       -)
```

Here, not only has the least significant digit of the sum become one of the illegal BCD codes, but any subsequent carry from this position will produce a further anomaly when this carry is added to the BCD code 9 in the next column.

Fortunately, the remedy for these range problems is quite straightforward. In each incorrect case in these examples, the result may be corrected, after the binary addition has taken place, by adding a 'filler' of 6 to the offending result digit(s), as shown in Examples 2(a), 2(b) and 2(c).

*Example 2(a)*

| decimal | BCD | |
|---|---|---|
| 57 | 0101 | 0111 |
| 24 + | 0010 | 0100 + |
| 81 | 0111 | 1011 |
| | | 0110 + 'filler' 6 |
| | 1000 | 0001 = 81 |

*Example 2(b)*

| | | |
|---|---|---|
| 57 | 0101 | 0111 |
| 29 + | 0010 | 1001 + |
| 86 | 1000 | 0000 |
| | | 0110 + 'filler' 6 |
| | 1000 | 0110 = 86 |

*Example 2(c)*

| | | | |
|---|---|---|---|
| 147 | 0001 | 0100 | 0111 |
| 253 + | 0010 | 0101 | 0011 + |
| 400 | 0011 | 1001 | 1010 |
| | | 0110 | 0110 + two fillers |
| | 0100 | 0000 | 0000 = 400 |

Note the need to add in two fillers in the last example – one to correct the least significant sum digit and the other due to the presence of a 9 in the next column.

To summarize, we must correct a BCD result digit in any of the following cases:

- it lies outside the BCD range 0–9;
- a carry was generated by the binary addition;
- it is a 9 and the column to the right is to be corrected.

In order to be in a position to detect when any of these events has occurred, a pair of processor status flags may be used in conjunction with 2-digit (8-bit) BCD arithmetic. These flags are set by carries out of bits 3 and 7, respectively, of the 2-digit sum – i.e. they hold the BCD carries from the 2-digit sum. The carry from bit 7 is the normal 8-bit arithmetic carry of the processor; that from bit 3 needs to be a special carry flag (often called the auxiliary, or BCD half-carry flag).

If a processor provides the necessary flags, BCD addition is normally performed by a binary addition followed by a special 'decimal adjust' instruction. This instruction will consider the state of the two flags and the two 4-bit codes of the result, making the corrections by adding fillers according to the above rules. A similar instruction may be available for BCD subtraction, where the filler must be subtracted from the result rather than added to it.

Multi-digit BCD numbers may be added and subtracted by algorithms based on the 2-digit case with carry. Negative numbers can be represented in BCD by a sign plus modulus or ten's complement technique. Indeed, the keen programmer can inflict upon himself, or herself, the task of writing 20-digit BCD floating-point multiplication and division routines – and will get little further guidance from this book! In most cases of non-integer arithmetic, or even integer multiplication and division, it is better to perform the decimal-to-binary and binary-to-decimal conversions necessary to allow one to perform the arithmetic in binary.

## 3.5  CHARACTER CODES

Early computer codes representing characters were based on those used at that time for punched card machinery or for telegraphy. One of these, the **Baudot Code**, is a 5-bit character code which is context-dependent. It uses a pair of the 32 possible codes as special letter/figure 'shift' codes, thus extending the character set to 59 members (some symbols are duplicated in both shifts).

### 3.5.1  ASCII
A 5-bit code is, in general, unsuitable for the diversity of characters present on most modern computer terminals. Alphabetic characters in upper and lower case (52), plus digits (10), punctuation (approximately 10), arithmetic symbols (approximately 12) and other special symbols (%$&@ ...) take the number of required codes well into the 90s. In binary terms this suggests a 7-bit code able to offer 128 ($2^7$) patterns, and most of the popular codes are based on a 128-member character set. It is usual to store such a 7-bit code in a single byte, leaving the eighth bit unused or, perhaps, employed for **parity** checking.

In an *even* parity scheme the parity bit is set or unset in order to make the total number of 1s in the byte even (there is an odd number of bits set to 1 in an *odd* parity scheme). The purpose of including a parity bit is to detect single-bit errors in a byte caused, for example, by corruption in memory or during data transfer from a remote peripheral.

Standards are important to achieve in character coding because of the diversity of peripheral equipment made for computers by many different manufacturers. Also, character format is by far the most common vehicle for interchange of data between computer systems. It is extremely helpful if designers can agree about character coding within the large networks of computers currently in vogue. The most widely recognized character code is ASCII (American Standard Code for Information Interchange), presented in tabular form in Appendix B. There are a few minor international variations to this set, due mainly to the inclusion of different currency symbols.

To some extent, as long as one is consistent about the choice of code to represent a given character it would not seem to matter precisely which code is chosen. However, the ordering of the ASCII set is not chosen randomly and there are some useful groupings from a programmer's point of view. Perhaps the most obvious of these are the three groupings of alphabetic characters (upper and lower case) and digits shown in Figure 3.4.

| char | dec | hex | binary | | char | dec | hex | binary |
|------|-----|-----|--------|---|------|-----|-----|--------|
| A | 65 | 41 | 01000001 | | a | 97 | 61 | 01100001 |
| . | | | | | . | | | |
| . | | | | | . | | | |
| . | | | | | . | | | |
| Z | 90 | 5A | 01011010 | | z | 122 | 7A | 01111010 |

                  ↑                                 ↑

               bit 5                            bit 5

| char | dec | hex | binary |
|------|-----|-----|--------|
| 0 | 48 | 30 | 00110000 |
| . | | | |
| . | | | |
| . | | | |
| 9 | 57 | 39 | 00111001 |

**Figure 3.4**  Character code patterns.

Firstly, we note that the alphabetic characters and digits are consecutive within each of the three groupings, facilitating an easy method of identifying a member of a group by range checking. Better still, the code for an upper and lower case alphabetic character differs in only one bit – bit 5. Thus, a lower case character may be converted into its upper case equivalent by changing bit 5 to 0, for example – a logical AND with the constant pattern 11011111 is sufficient. Alternatively, the case of an alphabetic character can be reversed by 'flipping' bit 5 – with an operation which exclusively ORs the code with the constant pattern 00100000.

Note that the fact that all upper case characters come before all lower case ones explains why sorting algorithms will place 'Abu Dhabi' before 'aardvark' and 'York' before 'able' unless action is taken to normalize the case.

There is an obvious connection between a digit and its integer representation. The least significant nibble of a digit code contains the BCD code for that digit; a feature that may be used in conversions between binary (BCD) and character forms.

The first 32 codes in ASCII are called **control codes** and, for ease of reference, the $n$th control code is usually called CONTROL character $n + 40$hex (i.e. code 0 = CONTROL @, code 1 = CONTROL A, etc.). This also provides a means of generating control codes from a keyboard by using the CTRL key as a shift. Most of the control codes are non-printable characters in the sense that they have no visible effect when sent to a simple printing terminal. As their name suggests, many of them are used for control purposes: to signal the start or end of a message, for example. 'Smart' visual display units (they are never 'intelligent' as the sales leaflets claim) make use of control codes for effects such as positioning the cursor, flashing text on and off, clearing the screen, etc. One of the codes, CONTROL G (code 7), is defined as the signal for a terminal to sound off its bell or buzzer for a short burst. A small group of codes move the cursor on a VDU screen or the printing head/paper in a printer (see Table 3.4).

**Table 3.4**  Control characters.

| Code | CTRL | Effect | Comment |
|------|------|--------|---------|
| 8 | H | backspace | Move the cursor one place left |
| 9 | I | horizontal tab | depend on tab and top-of-form |
| 11 | K | vertical tab | settings in a terminal |
| 12 | L | form feed | |
| 13 | M | carriage return | often used together to |
| 10 | J | line feed | start a new line |

Note that the backspace character only has the effect of moving the cursor one place to the left. Actually to delete from the screen the character over which one has backspaced it might be necessary to type the 3-character sequence 'backspace', 'space', 'backspace' (though the controlling software may do this in response to receiving a single backspace or delete (code 127) character).

Unfortunately, beyond the above conventions there are few hard and fast rules about the interpretation of control characters and many VDUs use different sequences of codes to achieve the control functions referred to earlier. One must always be careful when defining control codes to have special significance in a program (as a terminator, for example) to ensure that the code will not inadvertently be sent to a peripheral that will interpret the code in a 'clever' way. It is worth noting that receipt of stray control codes is one of the most likely explanations for complete garbage on a VDU screen – e.g. blocks of flashing text – or for total cessation of operation of a VDU.

Note finally that the data conventions described in this chapter are only a very few of the many possible interpretations which may be placed on patterns of binary digits. A programmer is free to use whatever convention is most suitable in a given application: in many cases the choice of representation has a fundamental effect on the method of problem solution.

# Part 2 | PROGRAMMING THE 8086

# 4 | Introducing the 8086

## 4.1 INTRODUCTION TO THE 8086

One of the most popular microprocessors of its day was the Intel 8080 which was first made available in 1974. This processor is a 'second generation' microprocessor and many microcomputer systems exist which utilize it. A very similar but slightly more powerful micro-processor was produced by Zilog and called the Z80. These two microprocessors are probably the most widely used of the so-called 8-bit microprocessors and a vast range of programs is available for them. In particular, the very popular CP/M system was produced for the 8080.

With such wide use of the 8080 its limitations became increas-ingly apparent. It has a maximum memory size of 64 Kbytes (65 536 bytes) and most instructions apply to individual bytes only. While byte processing is ideally suited to text processing, it is inconvenient for arithmetic problems. The 8080 is also ill-equipped for arithmetic problems as it possesses no multiply or divide instructions. In order to perform most arithmetic operations on numbers larger than a single byte several 8080 instructions are required. This considerably reduces the effective speed of the processor.

In 1978 Intel produced the 8086 microprocessor – a 16-bit proces-sor. While this is very similar to the 8080 in architecture it is capable of very much more. It can access 1 Mbyte (1 048 576 bytes) of memory and is faster then the 8080. The 8086 has multiply and divide instruc-tions and can operate on larger units of memory – 16-bit objects – which are more suited to arithmetic problems than the 8-bit bytes. The 8086 also includes a whole range of string manipulation instruc-tions. Thus the 8086 is extremely powerful both for text processing and for arithmetic. Finally, in 1979 Intel produced the 8088 micro-processor. As far as the programmer is concerned the 8088 is equiva-lent to the 8086 – they have identical architecture and instructions. The only real difference between them is the way in which they communicate electrically. The 8086 always communicates 16-bit data objects. If the operation is supposed to be an 8-bit one then half of the 16 bits are ignored. The 8088 always communicates 8-bit data objects – like the 8080. These operations are completely invisible to the programmer but are of interest to the hardware designer who can more easily replace an 8080 microprocessor by an 8088 micro-processor.

For the rest of this book we shall refer to the 8086 microprocessor but this is taken to include the 8088.

This chapter describes the 8086 microprocessor in some detail. You may, at this early stage, plough through the chapter in depth. Alternatively you may browse through it and return to it for reference as and when necessary while reading the rest of this book. Some features of the 8086 are only mentioned in passing in this chapter. They are described in more detail in later chapters.

## 4.2   8086 COMPONENTS – REGISTERS

A processor within a computer system manipulates data objects and communicates with external devices. The 8086 has instructions to manipulate objects which are eight bits in length (bytes) and objects which are 16 bits long (words). In addition, the individual bits within these bytes and words can be accessed. Earlier microprocessors were largely restricted to 8-bit, or byte, operations. A byte is an object that is capable of having up to 256 (two to the power of eight) different values and can be conveniently used to represent a small number or character. A word is an object that is capable of having up to 65 536 (two to the power of 16) different values and is typically used to represent whole numbers when the small range of a byte is too restrictive.

While there are 8086 instructions which, for example, test the character in a particular byte or add together the two numbers held in two words, it is important to remember that these objects are simply groups of eight or 16 individual and independent binary digits whose meanings are in the mind of the programmer and entirely dependent upon the context in which they are used.

The 8086 operates on data objects which are within the MPU (registers) and on data objects within its memory. There are fourteen 16-bit registers and each is referred to by its own name. An 8086 system can have available to it a maximum of 1 048 576 bytes of memory (one Mbyte) and these objects are referred to by numbers counting from zero up to 1 048 575 (or 0 to FFFFF in hexadecimal). Any two consecutive bytes can be referred to as one 16-bit word, thus providing a very flexible arrangement.

The 14 registers are shown in Figure 4.1 grouped into four categories. Their names are shown on the left together with a more descriptive name on the right.

Before covering these four categories of register in more detail a brief explanation of their uses will be given.

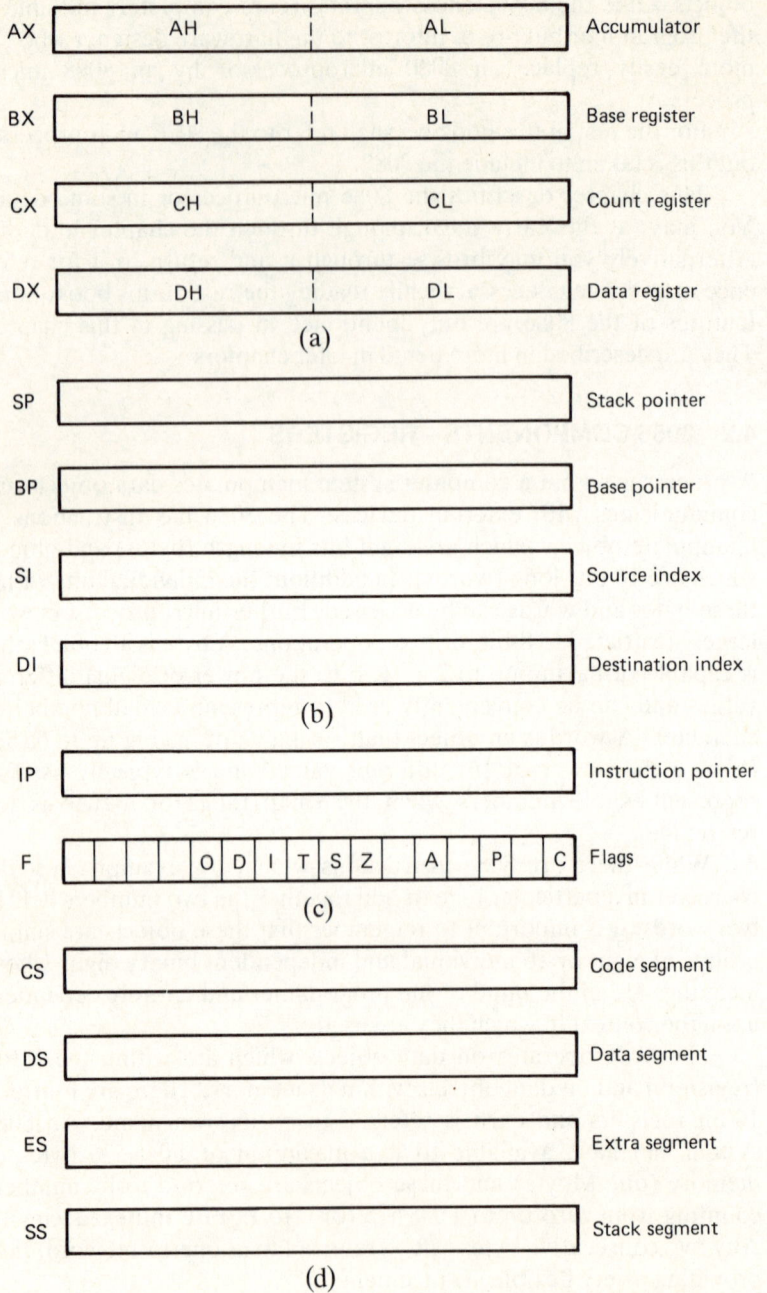

Figure 4.1    8086 registers: (a) general-purpose (b) addressing (c) status
(d) segment.

The general-purpose registers, as their name implies, can largely be used interchangeably. However, certain 8086 instructions interpret the contents of some of these registers in specific ways. The reason for this lies behind a successful attempt to compromise between the convenience of their general-purpose usage and the need, on efficiency grounds, to keep program instructions as short as possible and thus reduce the overall size of a program. For instance, the 8086 set of instructions range from fairly basic operations such as 'Add this value to that register' to reasonably powerful instructions such as 'Starting at byte number X, copy N bytes to byte number Y onwards'. The more complex instruction needs three values, namely the number of bytes to copy and the source and destination of this copy. We would not wish to be denied the facility to calculate these three values earlier in the program and so the instruction could include the names of three registers which contain these values. Instead, the 8086 demands that the three values be in three specific registers (the CX, SI and DI registers) and the instruction is short as no register names are given.

Generally speaking, the basic instructions allow the register(s) involved to be specified while the more complex instructions do not. As we shall see, this is rarely an inconvenience.

The addressing registers have some general capabilities but, because of their role in many of the more complex instructions, they tend to be used for fairly specific purposes by the programmer. As we shall see, any instruction which can operate on the (16-bit) general-purpose registers can also operate on the addressing registers.

The segment registers and the status registers have very particular functions.

### 4.2.1   General-purpose registers

There are four general-purpose registers AX, BX, CX, and DX. Each can be manipulated either as a whole 16-bit word or as two separate 8-bit bytes. To distinguish the two bytes in each register they are called the **high** and **low order** bytes. For example, the register AX is a 16-bit register. It can also be manipulated as two 8-bit registers called AH and AL (A High and A Low) which comprise the high and low order eight bits of AX. Eight-bit operations are restricted to the general-purpose registers.

When the 8-bit and 16-bit operations available within the 8086 are explained in more detail later, the benefits of such dual roles for the general-purpose registers will be appreciated. At this stage we will note that an operation may take place between two 16-bit registers or memory words, or between two 8-bit registers or memory bytes. We cannot directly add a byte to AX or add a word to BL.

The AX register or accumulator is the most general-purpose register of the four. Any operation that names a register may name AX (or AH, AL). This register is also used in input and output operations.

Each of the other three general-purpose registers has one or more implied extra functions – certain instructions apply to them alone without the need to name them. The BX register may be used as an addressing register and shares a lot in common with the BP register which is described below. Typically it contains the address of the start of a table of words or bytes in memory and there are instructions which operate on, for example, 'The Nth byte starting at the byte whose address is in BX'.

The CX register is commonly used by instructions which require a count. For instance, there exist instructions which perform an operation 'CX times'.

The DX register has two specialized functions. Firstly, input and output instructions may use the value in DX to select the device from/to which input/output is directed. Secondly, the multiplication and division instructions can operate upon 32-bit numbers, in which case the 32-bit number is stored in DX and AX which are temporarily regarded as one 32-bit register.

### 4.2.2   Addressing registers

The four addressing registers are SP, BP, SI and DI (as mentioned above, BX has additional honorary membership of this group). The words and bytes in memory are referred to by number. An operation which manipulates a memory byte would specify that byte's number which is more commonly called its address. An addition instruction may state:

```
Add byte 100 to AL
```

And the address/name of the two operands, byte 100 and AL, would appear within the instruction. Alternatively we may calculate the address and use a variant of the add instruction which may state:

```
Add the byte whose address is in SI to AL
```

We can then repeatedly obey this instruction while altering the value in SI. The four addressing registers contain addresses of data objects in memory. As is probably suspected by now, each of the addressing registers has its own unique implied extra function.

The SP register is called the stack pointer. It provides access to a section of memory which has been designated by the programmer as a stack. The operation of the 8086 stack is mentioned later both in this chapter and others.

The BP register is closely associated with the SP register, permitting access to other sections of the stack apart from the top. This register greatly assists the implementation of the high-level language facilities of nested procedures with their own local data objects. Because the BP register always accesses the stack it should not normally be used as a pointer.

The SI and DI registers are involved in the 8086's string manipulation facilities. A string is a sequence of bytes or words in memory. Operations include the facilities to compare strings, examine each byte/word in sequence and copy one string onto another. The addresses of the two strings involved in a copy or compare are held in the SI and DI registers. Where a string operation takes information from memory it uses the SI (source index) register. Where a string operation puts information into memory it uses the DI (destination index) register. A detailed description of the 8086's string operations appears later in this book.

### 4.2.3  Status registers

The two status registers are the instruction pointer (IP) and the flags register (F). The instruction pointer and the flags register are both 16 bits long. The IP contains the address of the next instruction to be obeyed and part of the processing of each instruction involves updating it accordingly. The range of addresses it can hold is 0 to 65 535. As we shall see later, very large programs can overcome this apparent restriction by manipulation of the code segment register.

The flags register is a collection of 16 individual flags – each either on or off – which are grouped to appear as one register for convenience. The flags represent the current state of the processor. Generally speaking, flags are set or cleared automatically by certain instructions depending upon the outcome. For example, flags will be altered if a subtraction instruction produces a negative or zero result. Some flags are set or cleared explicitly by an instruction in order to put the 8086 into a different mode of operation. Certain instructions have a different effect in different modes. Only nine of the 16 flags are defined. They are shown in Table 4.1.

**Table 4.1**  Status flags.

| Flag | Type | Bit Position | Use |
|------|------|--------------|-----|
| C | Status | 0 | Set on carry |
| A | Status | 4 | Set on half carry |
| S | Status | 7 | Set on negative result |
| Z | Status | 6 | Set on zero result |
| O | Status | 11 | Set on overflow |
| P | Status | 2 | Set on even parity |
| D | Mode | 10 | Direction |
| I | Mode | 9 | Interrupt enable |
| T | Mode | 8 | Trap |

The bit positions of the flags are largely irrelevant to the programmer since there are instructions to set or test individually named flags. A more detailed description of the flags now follows.

### Carry
This is set if the result of the last arithmetic instruction was too large to fit in the (8- or 16-bit) destination. This will happen if a carry occurs from bit 7 (byte) or bit 15 (word).

### Half carry
This is set if the result of the last arithmetic instruction involved a carry out of the least significant four bits. This is useful when using binary coded decimal (BCD) notation.

### Sign
This is set if the result of the last arithmetic instruction was negative using two's complement notation. This is therefore set to the value of bit 7 (byte) or bit 15 (word) of the result.

### Zero
This is set if the result of the last arithmetic instruction was zero. A very common use of this flag is to test for equality of two values. There are instructions which compare two values by subtracting one value from the other. The flags are set accordingly but neither value is affected. In particular the zero flag will be set if the two values are the same. For this reason the zero flag will often be referred to as the 'equal' flag. Indeed many instructions which refer to this flag have two alternative spellings such as JZ – jump if zero – and JE – jump if equal.

### Overflow
This is set if the result of the last arithmetic instruction was too large using two's complement notation as explained in Chapter 3.

### Parity
The parity flag is set if the result of the last arithmetic instruction had an even number of bits set to 1. For data transmission to other devices, where errors may occur, it is often the practice to send information as bytes. Each byte contains seven data bits and one parity bit. This parity bit is set such that the number of the eight bits which are 1 is even. If any one bit is altered during transmission then the received byte will no longer have even parity.

### Direction
Some string instructions operate on successive bytes or words in memory. The setting of this flag dictates whether these instructions will work forwards or backwards through memory.

### Interrupt
This flag enables or disables the 8086's ability to react to external stimuli known as interrupts. The use of interrupts is largely confined

to the operating system and need concern only the advanced programmer.

## *Trap*

When this flag is set, the 8086 pauses after the execution of each instruction to allow the program to be run one step at a time when testing.

The effects of each instruction on the flags are shown in Appendix A.

### 4.2.4   Segment registers

The 8086 has a segmented memory. There are four segments or areas of memory defined. Their starting positions are given by the addresses in the segment registers. For most purposes we can ignore the segment registers and it is sufficient to note that if they all contain zero then the 8086 behaves as a nonsegmented processor with 64 Kbytes of memory. More sophisticated (or larger) programs will manipulate these registers and such manipulation permits both access to a very large number of memory locations and the facility logically to split a program or several programs into independent sections.

These facilities are described later in the book. Until then, we will ignore the existence of segment registers.

## 4.3   INSTRUCTION CATEGORIES

In Chapter 1, the instructions of a processor were placed into four general classifications:

- data management;
- arithmetic and logical;
- transfer of control (jumps);
- input and output.

All the 8086 instructions are listed in Appendix A. Specific instructions are explained in detail, throughout the book, by example. This section aims to give a comprehensive overview of the 8086 instruction set in order that the potential of this processor can be appreciated. While most instructions can be placed into one of the above four categories easily, some instructions could be placed in more than one group. In particular there is some overlap between the first two categories.

### 4.3.1   Data management instructions

This category covers all instructions which move data within the 8086 system. This movement requires three operands: source, destination and the size of object (number of bytes) to be moved. The third operand will often be implied in the instruction to be a single byte or word (two bytes). In the general case, where any number of bytes are to be transferred, the 'string instructions' are used and the number of bytes to be moved is specified in a register rather than as part of the instruction. Note that in all moves of the form 'source → destination', a copy of the value of the source operand is put into the destination (overwriting whatever was there) and the source is left unaltered. None of the data management instructions affects the flags (except POPF).

### Move: MOV

The most general instruction is called the move (abbreviated to MOV) instruction. It appears in two forms: the first will move a byte; the second will move a word. The instruction is given a destination and a source operand. There are three types of operand – a register, a memory byte or word and a literal value. With these types, nine possible combinations of transfer exist, as shown in Table 4.2.

**Table 4.2**  Operands.

| Combination | Destination | Source |
|:---:|---|---|
| 1 | register | register |
| 2 | register | literal |
| 3 | register | memory |
| 4 | memory | register |
| 5 | memory | literal |
| 6 | memory | memory |
| 7 | literal | register |
| 8 | literal | literal |
| 9 | literal | memory |

The literal operand is either a byte or word value that is literally part of the instruction. It is a constant value and so combinations 7, 8 and 9 are meaningless. Whereas it makes sense to Move the number 10 into AX it does not make sense to Move the value in AX into the number 10! Finally, combination 6 – memory to memory – is not allowed in the 8086. A transfer from one memory location to another must be achieved by two MOV instructions: the first to move the memory source to, say, AX and the second to move the contents of AX to the memory destination. Note that instructions having destination and source operands are always written with the destination operand first.

### Exchange: XCHG

The exchange (XCHG) instruction performs a double move. The values of the two operands are interchanged. Both operands are therefore source and destination operands. For this reason, neither operand can be a literal.

### Stack operations: PUSH, POP

The two stack operations are PUSH which requires one source operand and POP which requires one destination operand. In both cases the operand must be a word operand and may be a (16-bit) register or memory word. Two special variants exist – PUSHF and POPF – which require no operand as they always refer to the flags register. These instructions allow fast and convenient methods of saving and restoring the state of the 8086.

### Translate: XLAT

The translate (XLAT) instruction is extremely special-purpose in its function. It is given no operands. It takes the (16-bit) address value in the BX register, adds to this the byte value in AL to produce a new address, and then moves the byte value at this address into AL. As its name suggests, it translates the byte in AL according to the ordered list of bytes running from the address currently held in BX. It could be used to encrypt and decode characters in English text by setting up suitable tables.

### String instructions: MOVSB(W), REP, LODSB(W), STOSB(W)

The two instructions MOVSB and MOVSW permit the move from memory to memory which MOV does not allow directly. MOVSB moves one byte and MOVSW moves one word. The value is moved from the byte (or word) whose address is in the SI (source index) register to the byte (or word) whose address is in the DI (destination register). After the move, MOVSB causes both SI and DI to be altered by one to index the next source and destination byte; MOVSW causes both SI and DI to be altered by two to index the next source and destination words respectively. These string instructions may be preceded by the special prefix REP. In this case the MOVSB or MOVSW is performed repeatedly. The number of moves is the value held in the CX register. The CX register is decremented by one (down to zero) by each move. This allows any number, between 0 and 65 535, of bytes or words to be moved from one area of memory to another.

The LODSB (and LODSW) instructions move one byte (or word) into AL (or AX) from memory addressed by SI. SI is then altered by one (LODSB) or two (LODSW).

The STOSB (and STOSW) instructions move the byte (or word) from AL (or AX) into memory addressed by DI. DI is then altered by one (STOSB) or two (STOSW).

These string instructions are explained in detail in Chapter 9.

### Others: LAHF, SAHF, LEA, LDS, LES

These instructions are only mentioned for completeness here. The first two are concerned with the specialized moves between AH and the flags. LEA, LDS and LES move an address into a given register. The last two move a value into either the DS or ES segment registers.

### 4.3.2    Arithmetic and logical instructions

This category of instructions includes the arithmetic operations of addition, subtraction, multiplication and division as well as the logical operations which manipulate the individual bits within bytes and words. While none of the data management group affects the flags, all of the arithmetic and logical instructions affect the flags (except the logical NOT instruction).

Most of these instructions require a source and a destination operand while the rest act upon a given single (destination) operand. Where an instruction requires two operands, the same combinations of register, memory and literal types which are permissible for the MOV instruction may be used, with the exception of the multiplication and division instructions. The instructions which act on a single operand may use a register or memory location.

#### Arithmetic instructions

The arithmetic instructions include addition, subtraction, multiplication and division of 8-bit and 16-bit whole numbers. There are, additionally, instructions to compare data objects, increment or decrement numbers by one and negate numbers using two's complement notation.

#### Addition and subtraction: ADD, SUB, ADC, SBB

The ADD and SUB instructions perform addition or subtraction between the source and destination operands. The value of the destination operand is overwritten by the result. ADC (add with carry) and SBB (subtract with borrow) include the carry flag. ADC will add the two specified operands and the carry flag together. SBB will subtract the source operand from the destination operand and subtract the carry flag. This facility permits very large numbers to be manipulated. We can represent such numbers by grouping two or more words (or bytes) together as shown in Figure 4.2.

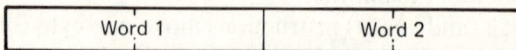

| Word 1 | Word 2 |
|--------|--------|

**Figure 4.2**    Two-word (4-byte) integer.

To perform an addition (or subtraction) of two such 2-word integers, we first use ADD (or SUB) between the least significant two words (word 2 above). Then we use ADC (or SBB) between the most significant two words. Any carry (or borrow) resulting from the first addition (or subtraction) is then included into the next word. For larger than 2-word integers we would continue with ADC (or SBB) until the most significant two words have been processed. This method is covered in greater detail in Chapter 8. Note that when an addition or subtraction or any other operation is carried out on half of a 16-bit register, the other half is not affected by any carry or borrow required.

### Multiplication and division: MUL, DIV, IMUL, IDIV

These four instructions always act upon the accumulator register AX and one given register or memory source operand.

If the source operand is a byte then these instructions perform an 8-bit multiplication or division. If the source operand is a word then a 16-bit operation is carried out. Multiplication of two objects produces a result requiring twice the space of either object. An 8-bit MUL always produces a 16-bit result which is stored in AX. A 16-bit MUL always produces a 32-bit result which is stored in DX and AX combined, with DX receiving the most significant 16 bits.

Whole number division (DIV) produces two answers – the division result and the remainder. A byte operand divides the full 16 bits of AX, placing the division result in AL and the remainder in AH. A word operand divides the 32 bits of DX and AX combined, placing the division result in AX and the remainder in DX. A summary of the effects of MUL and DIV is:

| Operation | Byte source | Word source |
|---|---|---|
| MUL | AL ★ source →AX | AX ★ source → DX:AX |
| DIV | AX/source →AL; | DX:AX/source → AX; |
|  | remainder → AH | remainder → DX |

Note that for a series of multiplications and divisions then, all other things being equal, a multiplication followed by a division on the result is the sensible order of events.

IMUL and IDIV act in the same way as MUL and DIV but assume signed two's complement operands and produce signed two's complement results.

### Compare: CMP

The compare instruction (CMP) acts in the same way as the SUB instruction, in that a subtraction is performed between the destination and source operands but the result is discarded, leaving both operands intact. However, as with all the SUB instructions, the flags O, C, Z and S are set according to the result. Thus after the CMP instruction we can test which is the larger of the two operands or whether they are equal by testing the relevant flags.

### Unary operations: INC, DEC, NEG

These instructions require one destination operand. INC and DEC increment and decrement the operand by one respectively. NEG negates the operand and is equivalent to subtracting the operand from zero.

## *Logical instructions*

The arithmetic instructions operate on integer values that the 8-bit and 16-bit registers and memory objects represent. The logical instructions treat the registers and memory objects simply as ordered groups of binary digits. They can be grouped conveniently into 'Boolean' instructions and 'shift' instructions.

## *Boolean instructions: AND, OR, XOR, TEST, NOT*

With the exception of NOT, the Boolean instructions operate between a source operand and a destination operand. These obey the same rules as operands in the move (MOV) instruction and for most of the arithmetic instructions. The source operand may be a register, memory object or literal value. The destination operand may be a register or a memory object. The Boolean operation is performed between each of the corresponding bits in the source and destination operands. The results of AND, OR and XOR between bits is:

| *Operand 1* | *Operand 2* | AND *result* | OR *result* | XOR *result* |
|:---:|:---:|:---:|:---:|:---:|
| 0 | 0 | 0 | 0 | 0 |
| 0 | 1 | 0 | 1 | 1 |
| 1 | 0 | 0 | 1 | 1 |
| 1 | 1 | 1 | 1 | 0 |

For example, if operand 1 is the bit pattern 01101110 and operand 2 is the bit pattern 11000111 then the results for AND, OR and XOR are:

```
01101110   AND   11000111      01000110
01101110   OR    11000111      11101111
01101110   XOR   11000111      10101001
```

The TEST instruction performs the same operation as the AND instruction but discards the result, leaving both operands intact. It does, however, set the flags according to the result – rather like the arithmetic CMP instruction. The NOT instruction flips all the bits of the destination operand, replacing 0s with 1s and 1s with 0s. The NOT instruction is exceptional within the arithmetic and logical group of instructions as it does not affect the flags register. This is a curious anomaly and, probably, a design fault.

Typical uses for these instructions involve using one operand as a 'mask' where the bits corresponding to the bits of interest in the destination operand are 1 and the other bits are 0. The results of AND, OR and XOR are then:

AND The bits of interest remain untouched – the others are zeroed (called masking bits out).

OR The bits of interest are set to 1 – the others remain untouched (called setting bits).

XOR The bits of interest are flipped from 1 to 0 and 0 to 1 – the others remain untouched (called flipping bits!)

A common use for masking (using AND) is to test whether any of the bits of interest are set to 1. After the AND instruction, the zero flag will be set if the result is all zeros. The TEST instruction is particularly useful here when we do not wish to alter the destination operand but merely to examine it. Masking is explained in detail in Chapter 8.

### Shift instructions: SHL, SHR, SAL, SAR, ROL, ROR, RCL, RCR

These instructions take one destination operand and a count. The count is specified either as one or as the value in the CX register. The operation is performed 'count times'. SHL (shift left) and SHR (shift right) move the bit pattern sideways one position. The incoming bit is 0 and the outgoing bit moves into the carry flag – which could then be tested. Shifting left or right is equivalent to multiplying and dividing by two and it is considerably faster then the multiply or divide instruction.

When using two's complement notation, negative numbers are represented by the most significant bit being 1. SHR would not give the required division by two on such a negative number as a 0 would appear in this position. The SAR (shift arithmetic right) instruction is provided for this case and acts like SHR except that there is no new incoming bit – the most significant bit remains unaltered (it is copied one place to the right) and this is often called 'propagating the sign bit'. SAL is the partner to SAR but is, in fact, exactly equivalent to SHL.

The remaining four instructions – ROL, ROR, RCL, RCR – also shift the bit pattern but in a cyclic manner: what goes out at one end reappears at the other end and overwrites the carry flag. Using ROR (rotate right) the bit pattern is shifted to the right with the least significant bit reappearing as the most significant bit. The ROL (rotate left) instruction moves the pattern to the left with the most significant bit reappearing as the least significant bit. RCR (rotate through carry right) and RCL (rotate through carry left) act in the same manner as ROR and ROL except that the carry bit appears within the cycle. The bit that is moved out of the bit pattern goes into the carry flag and the bit that was in the carry flag goes into the bit pattern. An example of the action of one shift or rotate on two bit patterns is shown in Figure 4.3.

### 4.3.3    Transfer of control instructions

Instructions are normally obeyed in order: once an instruction has been executed, the next instruction in memory is obeyed. There are some instructions which can break this sequential order of execution. One group of instructions can be obeyed repeatedly or, depending upon a variety of conditions, different groups of instructions can be obeyed.

Pattern 1: 01101011 and carry flag 1

Result after:

| | | | |
|---|---|---|---|
| SHR | 00110101 | CF | 1 |
| SHL | 11010110 | CF | 0 |
| SAR | 00110101 | CF | 1 |
| SAL | 11010110 | CF | 0 |
| ROR | 10110101 | CF | 1 |
| ROL | 11010110 | CF | 0 |
| RCR | 10110101 | CF | 1 |
| RCL | 11010111 | CF | 0 |

Pattern 2: 11001010 and carry flag 1

Result after:

| | | | |
|---|---|---|---|
| SHR | 01100101 | CF | 0 |
| SHL | 10010100 | CF | 1 |
| SAR | 11100101 | CF | 0 |
| SAL | 10010100 | CF | 1 |
| ROR | 01100101 | CF | 0 |
| ROL | 10010101 | CF | 1 |
| RCR | 11100101 | CF | 0 |
| RCL | 10010101 | CF | 1 |

**Figure 4.3**   The action of one shift or rotate on two bit patterns.

The transfer of control, or jump, instructions fall into four categories:

- unconditional jumps;
- conditional jumps;
- subroutine calls;
- interrupts/special events.

These four categories will now be described briefly. The ability to perform such jumps gives the computer its power and is the main difference between it and a simple calculator. These instructions will, as a result, reappear throughout this book and some form the basis for chapters in their own right.

### Unconditional jumps: JMP

There is an unconditional jump instruction: JMP. It takes one operand which produces a memory address as the destination of the jump. In its simplest form, this operand is a literal but the operand may be any 16-bit register or any 16-bit memory address.

Most jumps are to locations which are relatively close to the current instruction. When the operand to a JMP instruction is a literal, then this literal gives not the destination address itself but the distance in bytes between the JMP instruction and the destination. The literal is treated as a signed two's complement number. If it is negative then a jump backwards is performed. There is also a variant of the JMP instruction which takes a single-byte literal operand for use when the jump is known to be to a very close destination – this conserves space and time.

When the operand is a register then the contents of that register give the new address in the program. Similarly when the operand is a memory location the contents of that memory location become the new address for program execution.

The literal operand form is made simple to use by most assemblers. The assembler will allow the programmer to prefix any instruction with a label – a name chosen by the programmer. This label can then be used in a JMP instruction and the literal relative distance of the jump is calculated by the assembler.

## Conditional jumps

The conditional jumps all take only a literal 8-bit signed two's complement operand which specifies the distance to jump if that condition is true. This restricts the distance to 128 bytes backwards and 127 bytes forwards. For larger conditional jumps, a combination of a conditional jump and an unconditional jump (which can jump to any location in memory) must be used.

The conditional jumps test either the values of the flags or the CX register. Most of the assemblers for the 8086 allow some of the conditional jump instructions to be specified by two or more different names. For example, there exists an instruction which jumps if the carry flag is set. After a subtract (SUB) or compare (CMP) instruction, the carry flag will be set if the destination operand was smaller than the source operand. The two typical assembler names for the 'jump if carry set' are:

JC    Jump if carry
JB    Jump if below – i.e. smaller

This assembler facility makes the program slightly more obvious in its intent.

## Flag testing jumps

There are 16 conditional jump instructions which test the flags. Of these, there are five which test whether each of the O, C, S, Z and P flags is set and another five which test whether each of those same flags is clear. The remaining six test on combinations of settings of the O, C, Z and S flags so that, following a CMP or SUB instruction, jumps such as 'Jump if less than or equal to' may be performed. These six instructions consist of three such combinations – three jump if the combination is true and the other three jump if the combination is false. Thus for each of these 16 conditional jump instructions there is, within the same 16, a jump on the opposite condition. The 16 instructions are listed in Table 4.3, along with their equivalent assembler mnemonics.

**Table 4.3**   Flag testing jumps.

| Name(s) | Meaning | Flag conditions | Inverse |
|---------|---------|-----------------|---------|
| JO | Jump if overflow | Ov = 1 | JNO |
| JC   JB   JNAE | Jump if carry | C = 1 | JNC |
| JS | Jump if sign | S = 1 | JNS |
| JZ   JE | Jump if zero | Z = 1 | JNZ |
| JP   JPE | Jump if parity | P = 1 | JNP |
| JNO | Jump if not overflow | Ov = 0 | JO |
| JNC   JAE   JNB | Jump if not carry | C = 0 | JC |
| JNS | Jump if not sign | S = 0 | JS |
| JNZ   JNE | Jump if not zero | Z = 0 | JZ |
| JNP   JPO | Jump if not parity | P = 0 | JP |
| JA   JNBE | Jump if above | C = 0 and Z = 0 | JBE |
| JBE   JNA | Jump if below or equal | C = 1 or Z = 1 | JA |
| JG   JNLE | Jump if greater | Z = 0 and S = Ov | JLE |
| JLE   JNG | Jump if less or equal | Z = 1 or S < > Ov | JG |
| JGE   JNL | Jump if greater or equal | S = Ov | JL |
| JL   JNGE | Jump if less | S < > Ov | JGE |

Notes:

A = above       (unsigned comparison)
B = below       (unsigned comparison)
G = greater     (signed two's complement comparison)
L = less        (signed two's complement comparison)
E = equal
N = not
PE = parity even
PO = parity odd
Ov = overflow flag    (to avoid confusion with 0 (zero))

### CX testing jumps: JCXZ, LOOP, LOOPZ, LOOPNZ

The four jumps conditional on the CX (count) register are designed to facilitate constructs which obey a set of instructions a certain number of times. CX is typically used to hold a count. These instructions are:

- JCXZ   Jump if CX is zero.
- LOOP   Decrement CX and then jump if CX is still not zero.
- LOOPZ or LOOPE   As LOOP but do not jump if the Z flag is zero. Read as 'LOOP while zero' or 'LOOP while equal'.

- LOOPNZ or LOOPNE  As LOOP but do not jump if the Z flag is 1. Read as 'LOOP while not zero' or 'LOOP while not equal'.

These instructions are particularly powerful. For example, a section of program to find the first byte (if there is one) which has the value, say, 10 in a list of 20 bytes could take the form:

```
        mov     cx , 20             ;LOOP a maximum of 20 times.
        mov     si , startaddress - 1  ;Put the address of the first
                                    ;byte (less one) into SI.

looplabel:
        inc     si                  ;Increment SI to point at the
                                    ;next byte.

        cmp     byte ptr [si] , 10  ;Compare the byte pointed
                                    ;at by SI with 10.

        loopne  looplabel           ;Decrement CX and jump to
                                    ;looplabel if CX > 0 and
                                    ;the CMP was not equal.

        jne     notfound            ;Jump to the label 'notfound'
                                    ;if the zero flag is still
                                    ;unset. All 20 must have been
                                    ;tried unsuccessfully.
              .
              .                     ;SI points to the byte after
              .                     ;the first '10' byte.
              .
              .
              .
```

Note that, for emphasis in the text, instruction mnemonics and register names are written in upper case. In sections of programs a more appealing lower-case convention is adopted. Most assemblers will accept both upper-case and lower-case versions of instruction mnemonics and register names interchangeably. Note also that all text following a semicolon on the line is not part of the program but a comment for human consumption and understanding only. The instruction:

```
cmp     byte ptr [si],10
```

may appear strange at first sight. The first (destination) operand is a memory operand – that byte whose address is in the SI register. The different kinds of memory operand are the subject of the next section (4.4) of this chapter.

### Subroutine calls: CALL, RET

The two instructions CALL and RET (return) permit the use of subroutines. The CALL instruction acts in a similar way to the unconditional jump instruction JMP – it is given a destination of the same form. Additionally, the CALL instruction saves the instruction pointer (after it has been incremented to the address of the instruction after the call) by pushing its value onto the stack. The CALL instruction is equivalent to a combination of PUSH and JMP.

The RET instruction removes a word from the stack and places its value in the instruction pointer. The RET instruction is equivalent to a POP instruction with the instruction pointer being the destination. The effect is to jump back to the instruction following the original CALL instruction. The advantage of using the stack to save the instruction pointer (remember where the CALL originated) is that further CALL instructions can occur before the first RET instruction without any loss of information. Because the stack operates as a 'last in, first out' memory, the RET instruction will always cause a jump back to the instruction following the most recent CALL instruction. In this way, subroutines can be written to perform simple but frequently required tasks. Further subroutines can then be written which use these simple subroutines in order to provide more powerful facilities.

### Interrupts / special events: INT

The 8086 processor may be interrupted by a signal from an external device or it can be interrupted internally by executing the interrupt instruction INT. In either case the effect is that of an elaborate CALL instruction being performed immediately after the 8086 has finished executing its current instruction.

A discussion on interrupts is beyond the scope of this chapter but the INT instruction will be used in later programs as a convenient means of initiating input and output. A set of programs which perform input and output is part of an operating system. The two most popular operating systems available are called DOS and CP/M-86. It is one of the functions of an operating system to handle all interrupts or special events without the ordinary user or programmer being inconvenienced.

### 4.3.4  Input and output instructions: IN, OUT

Without the ability to communicate or interact with other devices, the processor is powerless. Unless at least the result of a calculation or other operation can be 'seen' by some other object then the processor may as well not be there. Input and output may take place, for example, by the 8086 communicating with devices controlling the thermostats and relays in a washing machine. Alternatively the 8086 in a microcomputer system will communicate with the keyboard and display screen and optional extras such as printers and disks.

Input and output is performed on the 8086 by the two instructions IN and OUT. These respectively receive and send information from and to the accumulator register. The use of these two instructions within a program which communicates with an external device is tedious to say the least and is also very specific to the device in question. For this reason there exist, within the operating systems of microcomputers, programs to perform this communication.

For our purposes we will assume the existence of such programs and call them by using the INT interrupt instruction.

The two most popular operating systems for the 8086, as mentioned in the previous section, are called DOS and CP/M-86. They appear very similar in the area of input and output. We can, for example, with one INT instruction read a character typed on the keyboard. The input and output facilities of these two systems are considered in Chapter 5, with disk input and output introduced in Chapter 11.

## 4.4   MEMORY ADDRESSING MODES

In Chapter 1, several different addressing modes were described. In earlier sections of this chapter it has been convenient to think of the operand(s) of an instruction as either:

- implied;
- literal (immediate);
- register;
- memory.

The **implied** operand exists where an instruction works on particular registers without the freedom to specify which registers. For example, the XLAT (translate) instruction will use the values in BX and AL to address memory.

The **literal** operand is a simple constant number and can be only a source operand – we cannot place a result into a number.

The **register** operand is one of the 16- or 8-bit registers.

The **memory** operand type allows the programmer to specify a memory object in a variety of ways. This type covers the addressing modes referred to in Chapter 1 as 'direct', 'indirect' and 'indexed'. The remaining modes given in Chapter 1 are 'relative' and 'stack'. The only relative addressing in the 8086 has been covered in the descriptions of the conditional jump instructions where the jump is relative to the current instruction. Stack addressing has been covered in the descriptions of the instructions PUSH, POP, CALL and RET.

The 8086 allows a memory operand to be specified in a way which can span the modes: direct, indirect and indexed. The memory operand is given by naming one, two or three values. These three values are:

1. An address (direct address).
2. A base register (either BX or BP).
3. An index register (either SI or DI).

All three values are optional with the proviso that at least one of them is given. From these three values the memory operand's address is calculated by the 8086 as follows:

Address + (address in BX or BP) + (address in SI or DI)

If any of the three values is omitted then its place in the above equation is also omitted.

Most 8086 assemblers have the same convention for writing such memory operands. The address is given as a number (or mnemonic name) followed by the register name(s) in square brackets. If both register names are given then they are separated by the plus sign ( + ). The examples in Table 4.4 illustrate some of the possibilities available.

**Table 4.4**   Example memory operands.

| Operand | Address used |
| --- | --- |
| 100 | 100 |
| [BP] | The value in BP |
| [SI] | The value in SI |
| 60 [BX] | 60 + the value in BX |
| [BP+DI] | The value in BP + the value in DI |
| 1000 [BX+SI] | 1000 + the value in BX + the value in SI |

As can be seen, the standard addressing modes of direct, indirect and indexed are obtained by varying combinations of address, base register and index register. It is worth repeating here that the BP register has a specialized function and is not normally used to refer to a program's data objects.

**Direct addressing** is performed by giving an address only.

**Indirect addressing** is performed by giving a base (or index) register only, the address having first been placed into this register.

**Indexed addressing** is performed by giving an address and a register.

The elaborate `address + base + index` mode provides a combination of indexed and indirect addressing.

For example, assume that a program is written to access a table of memory bytes and that the assembler has been given the name `table` to mean the address in memory of the start of the table. The instruction:

```
mov    al , table
```

would move the first byte of the `table` into `AL`. If we wished to access the *n*th byte, where *n* is any number, then we must first place the value of *n* into `SI` (or `DI`). Then, the instruction:

```
mov    al , table [si]
```

would move into `AL` the required byte. We could regard the table as a list of several sub-tables. For instance we could arrange for groups of bytes to represent information about people giving their names, addresses and ages. If we needed 40 bytes for each person and the last byte contained the person's age, then we could access the *n*th person's age as follows:

1. Multiply *n* by 40 (length of each sub-table).
2. Put the answer in `BX` (`table + BX` is the start of this person's sub-table).
3. Put the index of the age (39) into `SI` (or `DI`).
4. Obey:
   ```
   mov    al,table [bx + si]
   ```
   to put person *n*'s age into `AL`.

This flexible approach to memory addressing allows the programmer a large degree of freedom when accessing structured information.

Finally, you might have wondered how the assembler is told whether the memory operand is supposed to be a byte or a word. In the above examples, it was assumed that when `table` was introduced to the assembler two items of information were provided: firstly the address as a simple memory address and secondly the type – byte or word.

Each memory operand has these two attributes – address (position) and type (size). Sometimes the operand given to the assembler contains no information in order to deduce the type. Alternatively we may wish to access a word from `table` instead of a byte. In these cases, the assembler requires that the memory operand be given in full. The address is given as before and preceded by the word `PTR`. The word `PTR` is preceded by either the word `BYTE` or the word `WORD`. This provides the full specification of a memory operand. On the right-hand side of the word PTR is an address and on the left-hand side of the word PTR is a size. Then, the instruction:

```
mov     ax , word ptr table
```

would move the two bytes (one word) starting at table into AX.

A final word of warning is appropriate at this juncture. All addresses are given as the address of the first byte of the required object. Assuming that BX held the value 2, then:

```
mov     al , byte ptr table [bx]
```

would move the third byte of table into AL (BX = 0 gives the first byte).

```
mov     ax , word ptr table [bx]
```

would *not* move the third word of table into AX. The address is the same – table + 2. This instruction would move the third and fourth bytes of table into AX – the second word. This can be seen more clearly in diagrammatic form as:

```
table
byte 0  ⎫
        ⎬ word 0
byte 1  ⎭

byte 2  ⎫
        ⎬ word 1
byte 3  ⎭
   .
   .
   .
```

## 4.5  SUMMARY

The main architecture and instructions of the 8086 have been introduced in this chapter. The other instructions and facets of the 8086 which have been only briefly mentioned will appear in later chapters. At this juncture it is thought desirable to start programming the 8086 in earnest. The next chapter introduces some programs for the 8086 and describes the ways in which particular 8086 systems operate in order to run programs.

# 5 | 8086 Assembly Language Programs

## 5.1 INTRODUCTION

In the last chapter, all the basic 8086 instructions were introduced. That chapter showed the tools that are available but did not illustrate the ways in which these tools may be combined to produce programs. That chapter can be useful as a reference guide. This chapter introduces programming on an 8086 computer system by showing those stages involved in writing a complete program. It is assumed that an IBM PC is available using either the DOS or CP/M-86 operating systems. In fact, there are slight differences between the assemblers on these two systems and these are noted in the text. See the manufacturers' documentation for more details.

Section 5.2 serves as an introduction to the DOS and CP/M-86 assemblers. It shows how the data of a program are declared and how instructions are presented. Section 5.3 describes a 'skeleton program'. This program is provided in order to allow other programs to be constructed without the need, at this stage, to be aware of all the conventions of the interface between an 8086 program and the system. It includes all the expected assembly preamble, leaving the user the task of inserting data and instructions as required for each program. Section 5.4 takes the reader through the fairly straightforward procedure of assembling and running an assembly program. This procedure is different for the DOS and CP/M-86 systems and each is described separately. Finally, Section 5.5 describes the construction of an assembly program to detect palindromes. The program illustrates many of the features described in the earlier sections of this chapter and builds the assembly program up in several small stages.

## 5.2 8086 ASSEMBLY PROGRAMS

Chapter 2 described the common features of assemblers and assembly language programming. This section covers the specific assemblers available with the DOS and CP/M-86 operating systems.

Fortunately the two assemblers' dialects differ only slightly. The DOS assembler has many extra features which will not be covered.

### 5.2.1 Segments

It has been mentioned earlier that the 8086 processor operates a segmented memory. In fact, at any time, there exist four areas of memory called **segments**. They appear as individual areas of memory. The 8086 can have attached to it up to 1 Mbyte of memory. A segment is a part of this megabyte and can be as large as 64 Kbytes long: one-sixteenth of the total memory size.

The four segments each begin at an address derived from the value in the corresponding segment register. The segments are called:

- code;
- data;
- stack;
- extra.

Most 8086 instructions which refer to memory are capable of producing an address with a span of 64 Kbytes. The address applies to the byte or word with that address within one of these four segments.

In general, instructions which apply to data will refer to the data segment or, occasionally, to the extra segment. Instructions which produce an address to jump to refer to that address within the code segment. Instructions which apply to the stack will refer to an address within the stack segment. Consider the layout of memory as shown in Figure 5.1.

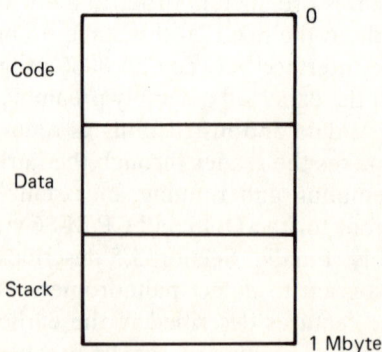

**Figure 5.1**  Example memory layout.

Three segments are shown. Instructions would appear in the code segment. Data objects are in the data segment and the stack is in the stack segment. A jump to instruction 10, say, actually jumps to instruction 10 within the code segment. An instruction which moves word 10 into the AX register will fetch word 10 within the data segment. A PUSH or POP stack instruction will refer to the word whose address is given by the stack pointer SP. This address will be relative to the stack segment. The extra segment, as its name implies, is an additional segment which can be used for extra data units or for a variety of temporary purposes. We shall not need the extra segment to be present in its own right – it will be equivalent in all respects to the data segment.

The benefits of this segmented arrangement are largely that, although the architecture of the 8086 addressing is limited to a range of 64 Kbytes, by separating logically distinct categories of memory use – code, data and stack – we can access up to 64 Kbytes of code and, separately, 64 Kbytes of data and use a stack of up to 64 Kbytes in length.

Further benefits of segmented memory are described in chapter 12 but they include the ability to access all the available 1 Mbyte of memory and the ability to include several independent programs in memory at the same time.

If this description of segments has been confusing then be consoled by the fact that, unless and until you need to write very large programs, all that you are required to envisage is that there appear to be three separate memories in the 8086, each 64 Kbytes in length. One always holds instructions, one holds data and the other is the stack. They are each addressed as bytes 0, 1, 2, ... up to 65 535. The system, in the form of the assembler and linker/loader, looks after the segments' registers for you and the 'skeleton program', given later in this chapter, ensures that the segments are presented to the assembler in a sensible manner.

The reason why this description of segments has been given is because the assembler expects a program to be presented in (usually) three sections – code, data and stack. When the program is run, these sections will be loaded into the appropriate three segments. In presenting the stack section, all that is necessary is to specify its maximum size. This is done for you by the skeleton program. This leaves you with the tasks of presenting your program's data declarations as one unit and then providing your program's instructions as a second unit.

### 5.2.2  Assembler code and data declarations

In this section the syntax of the assemblers for the 8086 is introduced. For data declarations we are concerned with presenting each separate data item used by the program. This presentation requires three pieces of information. Firstly the **name** of the data item is given. The program's instructions can then refer to this name rather than its actual address. Secondly the **type** of the data item is given – byte or word. Thirdly, finally and optionally the initial **value** of the data item is provided. This is the value that the data item will possess at the start of the program.

For instructions the mnemonic is provided followed by any operands. Each instruction may be preceded by a **label** or several labels. A label is a name immediately followed by a colon. The label can then be used as the operand or target of a jump instruction.

Within the assembler, data names and label names are equated with the address of either the data item or of the labelled instruction. These addresses are the offsets within the data and code segments respectively. As all memory items are given an address relative to the start of a segment this value will from now on be referred to as its **offset**.

Throughout an assembly program blank lines and spaces may be used to increase clarity. Comments may be introduced at the end of any line in the assembly program. A comment is introduced by the semicolon character ; . The semicolon and all other characters following it on that line are ignored by the assembler. They appear in the assembly listing but have no other significance. Comments should be used liberally. Assembly programs in particular are often very difficult to read or understand without comments explaining the use of each item of data and the function of each group of instructions. Even the original author of a program will find a comment-less program extremely difficult to understand just a few days after writing it.

### 5.2.3   Syntax terminology

In order to avoid ambiguity the following notations will be used:

*Name*

A name consists of any number of the characters:

```
A to Z, a to z, 0 to 9 and _
```

The first character of a name must be alphabetic. The underline is used for readability. For example the name:

```
No_of_characters
```

is more readable than the name:

```
Noofcharacters
```

While any number of characters may be used for a name, the assembler will only remember and distinguish a certain number of them. The 8086 assemblers will distinguish at least the first 30 characters. All names may be typed using either lower or upper case alphabetics without altering their meaning.

*Keyword*

A keyword is one of a set of names which have a special significance to the assembler. They represent instruction mnemonics, register names and assembler directives. They should not be used as the names of labels or data items.

## Variable

A variable is a name which refers to a data byte or word.

## Label

A label is a name which refers to the offset of an instruction.

## Constant name

A constant name is a name equated with a constant.

## Offset

The offset of a variable or label is its offset as related to the position of its declaration. The variable or label is replaced by this offset when the assembler produces the 8086 machine code instructions.

## Constant

A constant is a value which is fixed. It can be a number expressed in decimal or hexadecimal, a character surrounded by quotes, the offset of a variable or label or it can be a constant name. Any number of constants may be combined with arithmetic operators to produce another constant. The assembler will calculate the value of any such expression and substitute its value.

### 5.2.4   Data declarations

The keywords used to declare data (constant names and variables) are:

```
equ
db
dw
```

and additionally in the CP/M-86 assembler only:

```
rb
rw
```

DB and DW stand for 'define byte' and 'define word' respectively. They introduce variables which are bytes or words. EQU stands for 'equate' and serves to introduce constant names. RB and RW stand for 'reserve bytes' and 'reserve words' respectively. They are used in the CP/M-86 assembler to define several bytes or words.

## Defining constant names

A name can be associated with a constant value. This is accomplished by using the EQU keyword. The keyword EQU is placed between a name and a constant. For example:

```
No_of_items  equ  10
```

This allocates no data space but allows the name No_of_items to be used as any other constant. This facility can make a program more readable and, if used consistently, the program can be altered quite painlessly when the 'number of items' is altered at a later date. As a

constant name is just another example of a constant it may be used in
the definition of another constant name:

```
No_of_items          equ   10
Size_of_an_item      equ   6
Total_items_size     equ   No_of_items * Size_of_an_item
```

The above three definitions introduce three constant names. If either
the number or size of an item is to be changed then only the sole
corresponding definition need be altered. A constant, as used on the
right hand side of EQU, can be a number, character, constant name, an
offset or an expression involving any of these.

A number constant is expressed by default in decimal:

```
10
999
```

A number may be expressed in hexadecimal by using the characters
0–9 and A–F (upper or lower case). This number is then terminated
by the letter H:

```
10h          (Hexadecimal 10 = decimal 16)
1AFh         (Hexadecimal 1AF = decimal 431)
```

There is one ambiguity possible with a hexadecimal constant. Consider the following:

```
AOFh
```

This could be interpreted by the assembler as the hexadecimal value
AOF – 2575 in decimal – or as the name AOFh. The assembler will
always place the latter interpretation on it – an object starting with an
alphabetic character is a name. The ambiguity is resolved in these
situations by preceding the hexadecimal constant with the digit 0:

```
0AOFh
```

Character constants are introduced by enclosing a character in
quotes:

```
'A'
```

Such a constant has as its value the ASCII numeric code – 65 in this
case. Using character constants instead of their numeric codes makes
a program more readable and less error-prone. It is also of more
convenience to the programmer.

Offsets are produced by the keyword OFFSET. It is followed by
either a variable or label and produces the offset of that variable or
label:

```
offset count
```

Note that just using a variable name without the keyword OFFSET
would reference the contents of the variable instead of its location.

## Defining variables

A variable is defined by using the keywords DB and DW. A name is placed on the left hand side of the keyword and an initial value (a constant) on the right hand side. For example:

```
result  db      0
```

introduces a byte variable called result with an initial value of zero.

```
count   dw      1000
```

introduces a word variable called count with an initial value of one thousand. The name may be omitted, for example:

```
        db      'a'
```

will allocate a byte in the data segment with an initial value of 'a'. As it has no name it cannot directly be accessed by the program's instructions but the apparently limited worth of such a declaration will become clearer later.

Several data items, separated by commas, may be introduced with one DB or DW. The items are allocated successive offsets and the first item is associated with the name given. The declaration:

```
table   db      0,9,18,198,36
```

allocates five bytes with initial values as shown. The name table refers to the first byte. In this way an array or vector of data items may be built up. An item within this array can be selected by adding a value to the offset of table. The result is the offset of the required object. Alternatively an indexed address mode using table can select the required byte. Indexes of 0, 1, 2, 3, 4 will select the values 0, 9, 18, 198, 36 respectively.

A particular instance when a list of items is required is to produce a string of characters for printing. There exists a system function – described later in this section – which prints out a sequence of characters on the screen. It is provided with the offset of the first character and prints successive characters until a terminating character – a dollar – is encountered. Such a message could be defined as:

```
message db      'H','e','l','l','o','!','$'
```

Such a sequence of characters is so common that a shorthand representation is permitted. A list of characters surrounded by quotes is equivalent to each individual character appearing in succession. The above message declaration can be written as:

```
message db      'Hello!$'
```

## Reserving space

Sometimes a large table of data is required and no initial values are necessary. For instance the system function which reads data from a disk must be provided with an area of memory of typically 128 bytes length. Such data transfers from disk are more efficient if performed in bulk rather than one character at a time. In this case all that is required is a name associated with the start of 128 bytes of data with no special initial value. One way of achieving this space would be a declaration of the form:

```
disc_space        db        0,0,0,0,0, .....,0,0
```

Both the DOS and CP/M-86 assemblers allow a form of declaration which specifies how many bytes or words to allocate.

The CP/M-86 assembler achieves this with the extra keywords RB and RW (reserve bytes and reserve words). The declaration:

```
disc_space        rb        128
```

allocates 128 bytes of storage and disc_space is synonymous with the first byte. None of the bytes has a meaningful initial value. The declaration:

```
disc_space        rw        64
```

will achieve a similar effect in the CP/M-86 assembler but with an important difference. In this case disc_space refers to the first word (the first two bytes) of the allocated area.

The DOS assembler provides a different and more powerful approach. The DB and DW keywords are used as before. The assembler accepts in the place of any constant on the right hand side of either DB or DW a definition of the form:

```
<constant> dup (<constant-list>)
```

where <constant> is any constant and <constant-list> is any number of constants separated by commas. This represents <constant> occurrences of <constant-list>. The disc_space declaration can now be written in the DOS assembler as:

```
disc_space        db        128 dup (0)
```

This defines and allocates 128 occurrences of the constant byte zero. The DOS assembler also permits in a list of constants a question mark ? as a value meaning *don't care*. The disc_space area can then be declared with no specified initial values by:

```
disc_space        db        128 dup (?)
```

This has exactly the same effect as the above CP/M-86 alternative:

```
disc_space        rb        128
```

Further occurrences of DUP may appear within the brackets following DUP. In this way some interesting, if rarely used, initial data patterns may be created by an enthusiastic programmer.

### 5.2.5   Code instructions

The code section of a program consists of a sequence of instructions each on a separate line. Blank lines are ignored. Any instruction may be preceded by one or more labels. The occurrence of such a label serves to define it. Labels may be used – in a jump instruction for example – before they occur in the program, thereby permitting forward jumps.

Each instruction starts with a mnemonic for the operation. This mnemonic is called the **opcode**. Following this, and on the same line, are any operands that this opcode requires. A label may appear before the opcode on the same line and a comment may appear at the end of the line.

Some instructions require no operands – their effect is implicit. Such instructions include those to adjust the AX register to binary coded decimal format and the instructions to set or clear particular status flags.

Some instructions have a single operand and this follows the opcode with at least one space or tab intervening. Examples of such instructions are the jump instructions and the stack PUSH and POP instructions. Depending upon the nature of the instruction this operand is called either a **source** or a **destination** operand.

The remaining instructions require two operands. These follow the opcode on the same line with at least one space or tab intervening. The two operands are separated from each other by a comma and, optionally, more spaces or tabs. The first operand is called the destination operand and the result, if any, is placed in it. The second operand is called the source operand.

In the preceding chapter the different forms of an operand were listed. These are:

- implied;
- literal;
- register;
- memory.

The implied form relates to the first kind of instruction where no operand is given – it is implicit in the instruction.

The literal form is a constant and is only permitted as a source operand. Any of the forms of constant described for constant name declarations may be used here.

The register form is represented by one of the register names:

```
ax bx cx dx   ah al   bh bl   ch cl   dh dl
si di
bp sp
cs ds ss es
```

Note however that not all instructions permit all of the above registers as an operand. The availability of instructions which allow these registers as operands decreases as the list above is descended.

The memory form of operand consists of one, two, three or four sections:

1. Variable.
2. Index register SI or DI.
3. Base register BX or BP.
4. Constant modifier.

Examples of memory operands are:

| | |
|---|---|
| fred | the word or byte declared as fred; |
| [si] | the word or byte whose offset is the value currently in the SI register; |
| [bx] | the word or byte whose offset is the value currently in the BX register; |
| fred [si] | the word or byte whose offset is the offset of fred plus the value which is currently in the SI register; |
| fred [bx] | the word or byte whose offset is the offset of fred plus the value which is currently in the BX register; |
| fred [bx+di] | the word or byte whose offset is the offset of fred plus the value which is currently in the BX register plus the value which is currently in the DI register. |

The constant modifier may be written in square brackets at the end of the operand. This constant modifier is added onto the offset. For example:

```
mov     ah , fred [si] [2]
```

would move into the AH register the byte whose offset is the offset of fred plus two plus the value currently in the SI register. The assemblers also permit alternative forms:

```
mov     ah , fred [si+2]
mov     ah , fred [si] + 2
```

which will produce the same instruction. The constant may be negative and:

```
mov     ah , fred - 3
```

will move into the AH register the byte three bytes behind fred.

While the vast majority of operands used in practice are a single variable or a single register, the more complex variations permitted by the 8086 processor are worth remembering and using wherever appropriate.

The assembler requires that the two operands be compatible – they both refer to bytes or they both refer to words. Each 2-operand instruction has both a byte and a word variant but not a mixture of the two. Often the assembler can deduce the type. The instruction:

```
mov     ax , [si]
```

will move a word at the offset given by the SI register into the AX register. While there is no implicit type of [SI], AX is a word operand. Operands can have a definite type, as has AX, or they can be ambiguous, as is [SI]. The definite operands are

- registers: AH AL BH BL CH CL DH DL are bytes. The rest are words.
- variables (with or without registers or a constant modifier). The type is the declared type of the variable.

Ambiguous operands are:

- constants;
- memory operands without a variable name.

If one operand is definite and the other operand is ambiguous then the definite operand type dictates the type of the instruction.

If both operands are ambiguous or both operands are definite and different, then extra qualification of one of the operands must be provided. For example, if the variables count and char are declared as:

```
count   dw      0
char    db      0
```

The following instructions as they stand are not allowed for the reasons given:

```
mov     ah , count
```

AH is a byte and count is a word. The intention may have been to move the first byte of the word count into AH but equally the second byte of count may have been intended. A third possibility is that AH may have been intended to be AX.

```
mov     char , cx
```

CX is a word and char is a byte. The intention may have been to move into char the low (CL) or the high (CH) byte of CX but equally the intention may have been to move CX into the word starting at char – char and the byte following char.

```
mov     [si] , 9
```

The intention is to move the value 9 into a memory object addressed by the SI index register. It is not clear whether the move is intended to be to the byte or to the word addressed by SI.

A memory operand may be qualified by preceding it with either the phrase:

```
byte ptr
```

or the phrase:

```
word ptr
```

The qualification BYTE PTR means that the operand is the byte whose offset is given by the (possibly word) operand following. The qualification WORD PTR means that the operand is the word whose offset is given by the (possibly byte) operand following. The different interpretations of the above three ambiguous instructions can now be written as:

```
        mov     ah , byte ptr count
or: mov         ah , byte ptr count + 1
or: mov         ax , count
```

and:

```
        mov     char , cl
or: mov         char , ch
or: mov         word ptr char , cx
```

and:

```
        mov     byte ptr [si] , 9
or: mov         word ptr [si] , 9
```

There is one final problem which can occur when the destination operand is a byte and the source operand is a constant larger than 255. This value is too large to fit into a byte and such an attempt will give rise to an assembly error.

It may be felt that a constant larger than 255 could be deemed to be a definite word operand and so no qualification of an ambiguous destination operand would be necessary. This interpretation can be extremely insecure and so is not given.

The many forms of operand possible and the qualifications sometimes required can be overwhelming at first but take heart as they will soon, by example, become second nature. The more complex variations will not be needed for some time yet.

### 5.2.6   System function calls

The operating systems DOS and CP/M-86 provide an environment for the raw 8086 processor which makes the computer more convenient to use. In addition to interpreting commands to list files or to assemble and run programs the system can also be called upon by a program to perform several functions.

Most of these functions concern input and output. The reading and writing of data from and to peripheral devices such as the console, printer and disks is a complicated process. Peripheral devices such as these operate largely independently of the processor. Before reading data, a program would need to check that a key had been pressed on the keyboard or that the required sector of the disk were currently underneath the reading heads. Before printing data, a program would have to check whether the printer had finished printing the last character that it was sent. Most of the problems involved are those of synchronization between the processor and the peripheral or the human operator. In addition the system will permit special interpretation of certain characters or character sequences. Some characters cause the erazure of the current line typed so far or the erazure of the last character. Other characters may have screen graphical functions.

Fortunately the system takes care of all these possibilities and provides a set of **function calls** which permit the assembly language programmer to read and write data in an unhindered manner.

There are many such function calls but for our purposes we shall concentrate on just eight of them. A function call is achieved by obeying a special instruction – the interrupt instruction `INT`. The two systems DOS and CP/M-86 have slightly different conventions for this interrupt instruction but these are taken care of by a part of the skeleton program introduced in the next section. All our programs will be written using the skeleton program and a function call is achieved by the instruction:

```
call    dobdos
```

`Dobdos` is the label of a small part of the skeleton program which actually obeys the interrupt instruction. When the required function has been performed the system will return to the next instruction following the `call dobdos` instruction.

The label is called `dobdos` to mean 'do a Bdos function'. `Bdos` is the name used for the part of the system which is responsible for the coordination of input and output. It stands for Basic Disc Operating System.

Information is passed between the program and the system via some of the registers. In particular the `AX` and `DX` registers are commonly used. Other registers may be altered by a function call on a CP/M-86 system. They are left unchanged under DOS systems. The function required is given by a number from zero upwards. This number must be in the `AH` register immediately prior to the function call. Other information passed is dependent upon the function call made. The function calls that we shall first encounter are shown in Table 5.1.

Functions 9 and 10 require a little more explanation. They perform multiple character input and output.

**Table 5.1**    Function calls.

| Function (value in AH) | Action |
| --- | --- |
| 1 | Read a character from the console keyboard and return its value in register AL. |
| 2 | Write the character contained in the DL register onto the console screen. |
| 3 | As function 1 but read from the auxiliary device. |
| 4 | As function 2 but write to the auxiliary device. |
| 5 | As function 2 but write to the printer. |
| 9 | Print the string of characters, at the offset given in the DX register, on the console. |
| 10 | Read a string of characters, into memory given by the offset in the DX register, from the console. |
| 11 | Check whether a character has been typed (but not yet read) on the console keyboard. If there is no character, return zero in register AL. If there is a character ready, return a non-zero value in register AL. |

Function 9 prints characters starting with the character whose offset is given in the DX register and continuing with the characters in successively higher offsets until a dollar character $ is found. The dollar sign is not printed and the call then returns. If the first character is a dollar sign then nothing at all is printed.

Function 10 reads characters from the console into memory. When reading these characters the usual editing keys such as Delete Character and Delete Line will work. The byte with offset given by register DX contains a value placed there by the programmer and this is the maximum number of characters that will be read. Reading will continue until either this maximum is reached or the Enter key is pressed. The next byte at offset given by the value in DX plus one will have placed in it by the system the actual number of characters read. The character values are placed in successive bytes beginning at the byte with offset given by the value in DX plus two. These three sections are shown in Figure 5.2.

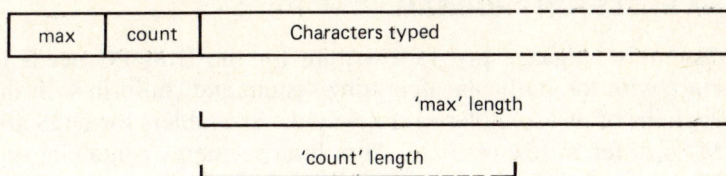

**Figure 5.2**    Function 10 data layout.

There is, unfortunately, a slight difference in the way in which DOS and CP/M-86 treat the case where too many characters are typed. DOS will not return to the program until the Enter key is pressed. The Enter key is included as one of the characters. If too many characters are typed DOS will sound the audible alarm and ignore further characters until the Enter key is pressed or earlier characters are deleted. CP/M-86 does not include the Enter key as one of the characters and when the maximum number of characters has been typed, CP/M-86 returns immediately without waiting for the Enter key to be pressed. This should not be a problem as long as the maximum number of characters requested and the corresponding memory area used to hold the typed characters are reasonably large – over 80 bytes.

Both of these function calls are described again in Section 5.5 where they are used in a complete program.

An example of using the function calls is shown in the next listing. The example is an extract of a program which repeatedly reads characters from the console and prints them on the screen. It would not normally be used as there is no way of terminating it without pressing the system reset key!

```
print_loop:
    mov     ah , 1          ;Function 1 - read char.
    call    dobdos          ;Read char into AL.

    mov     dl , al         ;Move the character into DL
                            ;ready for printing.
    mov     ah , 2          ;Function 2 - print char.
    call    dobdos
    jmp     print_loop      ;Continue indefinitely.
```

This program could be altered to print the characters on the printer instead. This would be accomplished by altering the fourth instruction from:

```
    mov     ah , 2
```

to:

```
    mov     ah , 5
```

## 5.3   A SKELETON PROGRAM

An assembly language program written for the IBM PC needs to interface with the particular operating system and conform with the conventions of its assembler(s). Luckily the assemblers for DOS and CP/M-86 differ in few respects. The three segments containing the stack, data and code are introduced in slightly different ways and there are a few slight variants in dialect. A further problem in variance between the two systems exists in the way in which a program communicates with the operating system at entry, exit and when calling upon the system to perform a function such as reading or writing data. These differences are also small but can be confusing at first.

In order to facilitate the writing of programs, a skeleton program is now given for both the DOS and CP/M-86 systems. The skeleton program introduces the segments as appropriate and establishes the interface between the program and the system.

The user can then create a program by editing a copy of this skeleton. Instructions and data declarations are inserted at the two indicated positions. When the system hands over control to the program – the program is 'run' – certain conditions or states prevail. Depending upon whether the system is DOS or CP/M-86, some of these conditions must be saved and/or altered before the program proper commences. Similarly, when the program has finished it must hand control back to the system and before doing so, some conditions or states must be restored. Instructions are included in the skeleton program for these purposes.

Three sections of code are provided in the skeleton. The first section is obeyed immediately prior to the program proper and prepares the environment for the program. Following this section the program proper is inserted. The second section follows and is tagged with the label finished. This marks the start of the instructions which return control to the system. The program may thus terminate either by encountering this section or by executing a jump to it:

```
jmp     finished
```

The third section of code provided is labelled dobdos (do a Bdos function). This provides a convenient method of asking the system to, for instance, read a character from the keyboard or write a character to the screen. The system function calls outlined in the previous section can be activated by calling this section of code:

```
call    dobdos
```

The appropriate values must first be moved into the registers concerned.

The skeleton programs for DOS and CP/M-86 are given in

Appendix C together with a detailed explanation. The explanation can be ignored for the present but it should be read at a later date.

Before proceeding with writing and running programs the appropriate skeleton must be typed into a file using the editor. Name the file either:

```
SKELETON.ASM      (for DOS)
```
or:
```
SKELETON.A86      (for CP/M-86)
```

Once the skeleton program has been typed in, print it and methodically check it line by line for typing errors. By way of an example, a very simple program can then be created. Assembling this program will also indicate any further typing errors that you had missed! The program will print a message on the screen and an appropriate name for it is 'MESSAGE'. First we must copy SKELETON into a new file called MESSAGE. This is achieved by the command:

```
COPY SKELETON.ASM MESSAGE.ASM      (for DOS)
```
or:
```
PIP MESSAGE.A86=SKELETON.A86      (for CP/M-86)
```

We now have a new file whose contents are the skeleton program and which can be edited to include the data and instructions to print our message. Never edit SKELETON itself to produce a program but always take a copy of it first because SKELETON will be the basis of most of our programs.

At the place marked for the inclusion of data insert a line containing:

```
message db        'This is our message$'
```

At the place marked for the inclusion of code insert the following three instructions, each on a separate line:

```
mov     dx , offset message
mov     ah , 9
call    dobdos
```

Inform the editor that you have finished and you should now have a file containing an assembly language program which prints out the message above. While the program is now complete (assuming no typing errors) it is not yet able to run. The program must be assembled.

The next section shows how to assemble and run the program. After reading the next section, read it again but at your IBM PC while assembling and running the message program.

## 5.4   ASSEMBLING PROGRAMS

This section describes the assembly process which converts an assembly language program into machine code.

This process was described, in general, in Chapter 2. For the 8086 the process is in two stages. These stages are commonly called **assembly** and **linking**.

Firstly the assembler translates the program by deciphering all data declarations and instructions, converting each occurrence of a name into its numerical machine code representation. While performing this task the assembler builds up a list of each data item and label. This list comprises the object's name, offset and type – whether a byte, word or label. This list can be made available to the programmer for subsequent debugging of the machine code program. The assembler also produces a list file which contains the original program together with the numerical machine code equivalent. Any errors which occurred will appear within the listing at or close to the offending line. These errors are also reported directly to the console.

The second stage of the process is called the linking of the program. This stage converts the numerical machine code representation of the program into a direct image of the program as it will appear in memory.

The reason why this process occurs in two stages is so that a large program can be written as several separate units. Each unit may be assembled separately into its numerical machine code representation. They are then all linked together into one memory image. If one of the units is altered, the first and lengthier stage of the process – assembly – is repeated on that unit alone. The intermediate assembled units are then linked together again. This eliminates the need to reassemble every unit. For our initial programs, this demarcation is an unfortunate inconvenience.

Once a program is linked, it is run by giving its name as a command. There is no need to reassemble or relink a program in order to run it again.

The two stages of assembly and linking are instigated differently under DOS and CP/M-86. Section 5.4.1, describes the process as performed with the DOS operating system. Section 5.4.2 explains the assembly and linkage stages of the CP/M-86 system.

Once the relatively simple commands to perform the assembly and linkage of a program have been mastered, you are advised to assemble, link and run the message program given in the previous section.

### 5.4.1   Assembly under DOS

DOS provides two assemblers called ASM and MASM. MASM is a larger and more versatile assembler than ASM. MASM provides many advanced facilities – notably macros. It does not matter which assembler you use for the programs shown in this book. The two are invoked in the same manner. For now, we will refer only to the assembler `ASM`.

The linking stage is performed by a program called `LINK`.

Unless specifically directed otherwise, both `ASM` and `LINK` assume certain conventions concerning the extensions of the files they process. In assembling and linking the program called message, they will assume the following:

`ASM` will expect the program called `MESSAGE` to be in a file called:

    `MESSAGE.ASM`

`ASM` will produce a file called:

    `MESSAGE.OBJ`

This file contains the numerical machine code representation of the program. `ASM` will also produce the listing of the program in the file called:

    `MESSAGE.LST`

`LINK` will accept the file `MESSAGE.OBJ` and produce a file called:

    `MESSAGE.EXE`

The program may then be run by typing its name – `MESSAGE`.

To assemble a program type:

    `ASM <program name>,,;`

followed by the Enter key. `<program name>` is the name of the assembly program without its `.ASM` extension. For our example we would type:

    `ASM MESSAGE,,;`

The assembler will report any errors that it finds in the program both to the screen and in the listing file `MESSAGE.LST`. If no errors are found, the linking stage can be performed. This stage is invoked by typing:

    `LINK <program name>;`

followed by the Enter key. For our example we would type:

    `LINK MESSAGE;`

The program may then be run by typing its name followed by the Enter key. For our `MESSAGE` example we would type:

    `MESSAGE`

Note that for this command, no semicolon is typed.

Often the listing file is not required. The file takes time to produce and can consume a large amount of disk space. When the listing is not required then the assembly stage is accomplished by omitting the two commas and typing:

```
ASM <program name>;
```

For our example we would type:

```
ASM MESSAGE;
```

### 5.4.2   Assembly under CP/M-86

The CP/M-86 assembler is called `ASM86`. The linking stage is performed by a program called `GENCMD`.

Unless specifically directed otherwise, both `ASM86` and `GENCMD` assume certain conventions concerning the extensions of the files they process. In assembling and linking the program called `MESSAGE`, they will assume the following:

`ASM86` will expect the program called `MESSAGE` to be in a file called:

```
MESSAGE.A86
```

`ASM86` will produce files called:

```
MESSAGE.H86
```
and:
```
MESSAGE.SYM
```

The first file contains the numerical machine code representation of the program. The second file contains the list of all the names used in the program. `ASM86` will also produce the listing of the program in the file called:

```
MESSAGE.LST
```

`GENCMD` will accept the file `MESSAGE.H86` and produce a file called:

```
MESSAGE.CMD
```

The program may then be run by typing its name – `MESSAGE`.
To assemble a program type:

```
ASM86 <program name>
```

followed by the Enter key. `<program name>` is the name of the assembly program without its `.A86` extension. For our example we would type:

```
ASM86 MESSAGE
```

The assembler will report any errors that it finds in the program, both to the screen and in the listing file `MESSAGE.LST`. If no errors are found, the linking stage can be performed. This stage is invoked by typing:

```
GENCMD <program name>
```

followed by the Enter key. For our example we would type:

```
GENCMD MESSAGE
```

The program may then be run by typing its name followed by the Enter key. For our message example we would type:

```
MESSAGE
```

Often the listing file is not required. The file takes time to produce and consumes a large amount of disk space. When the listing is not required, the assembly stage is accomplished by including the symbols $PZ and typing:

```
ASM86 <program name>  $PZ
```

For our example we would type:

```
ASM86 MESSAGE  $PZ
```

The symbol file can also be eliminated in this way. We will not use this file and its production is inhibited by following the symbols $PZ with the symbols SZ. For example:

```
ASM86 MESSAGE  $PZ SZ
```

The dollar symbol here introduces assembler options such as PZ and SZ. Other similar options are described in the assembler manual.

## 5.5   A PALINDROME PROGRAM

A palindrome is a word or phrase which is unaltered if written backwards. For example, 'MADAM' and 'MADAM I'M ADAM' are palindromes. Our program to detect palindromes will apply to words or phrases with no punctuation or spacing. This allows a fairly simple algorithm to be used. The phrase is checked by comparing the first character with the last character. Then the second character is compared with the last-but-one character and so on until either a mismatch occurs or we reach the middle of the palindrome.

In order to write a program to test whether words and phrases are palindromes we first need to formulate a plan of action. A suitable description of the algorithm to be used may be:

Read in a phrase and state whether or not it is a palindrome.

While this description is little more than a précis of the original problem it is useful to be able to describe a program initially in a short and meaningful way. There is clearly a large gap between the English description of our algorithm and the 8086 instructions which will form our final program. With any programming language, it is unwise to attempt an early bridging of this gap. It is all the more important to resist this temptation when using such a low-level programming language as an assembly language.

The gap is bridged slowly by refining our algorithm into more primitive steps. Three such steps can be found:

1. Read in a potential palindrome.
2. Test whether or not the input is palindromic.
3. Print a suitable message.

Each of these stages can now be dealt with individually and, almost independently. For steps one and three we are largely at the mercy of the operating system's input and output functions. There exist suitable function calls for reading in lines of input and writing out messages and so we shall concentrate first on the major task of step two.

### 5.5.1    Step two – test for a palindrome

If we restricted our program to handling potential palindromes of, say, exactly eight characters then a solution of the following form would suffice:

```
compare character 1 with character 8
 if not equal - exit as NO
compare character 2 with character 7
 if not equal - exit as NO
compare character 3 with character 6
 if not equal - exit as NO
compare character 4 with character 5
 if not equal - exit as NO
exit as YES
```

where exit as NO and exit as YES mean 'enter stage three to print out a negative or positive response respectively'.

Such a solution is rejected for two reasons. Firstly it applies only to potential palindromes of eight characters and as such is of very little practical use. Secondly it is inelegant and unnecessarily repetitive. Each of the four steps differs only by the two numbers of the characters being compared. Instead, we can abstract this algorithm to a form such as:

```
let x be the first character
 and y be the last character

repeat
   compare character x with character y
```

```
        let x be the next character up
        let y be the next character down
    until an unequal comparison,
     or x and y have crossed over
```

This solution permits potential palindromes of any length to be examined but new problems have been introduced. We need to represent x and y in our assembly program. x and y are mechanisms for accessing two characters within our potential palindrome. We can assume that this potential palindrome exists in store somewhere as a result of our input step one. At this point we should examine the ways in which store may be accessed by the 8086. An 8086 instruction which accesses store requires an offset of the operand. This offset may be given directly or it may be calculated using a combination of store values and/or registers. The addressing mode which is most suitable for our purposes here is the indirect mode using two of the addressing registers to represent x and y. If we use the registers SI and BX then our algorithm can be rewritten as:

```
    place in SI the offset of the start of the potential
       palindrome
    place in BX the offset of the end of the potential
       palindrome

    repeat
        compare the byte at SI with the byte at BX
        increase SI by one
        decrease BX by one
    until the comparison is unequal or SI is greater than
     or equal to BX
```

We may picture SI and BX as pointers within our potential palindrome as shown in Figure 5.3.

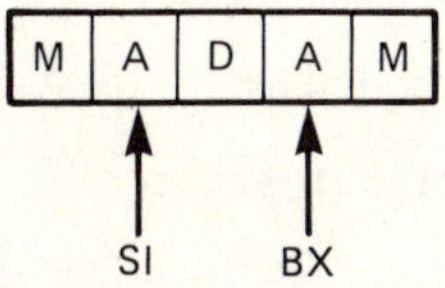

**Figure 5.3**    Representation of the potential palindrome.

At each step in our algorithm we compare the character (stored as a byte) pointed at by SI with the character pointed at by BX. SI is then increased by one and BX is decreased by one ready for the next comparison. If our comparison is unsuccessful then our phrase is not a palindrome. If our two pointers meet in the middle then our phrase is a palindrome.

Before continuing with this solution, we need to know how and where our potential palindrome is stored and its length. This information will be provided by our input step one and our attention is now turned there.

### 5.5.2   Step one – input

A suitable operating system facility for the input of our potential palindrome is provided as function call 10. This function reads in characters from the keyboard, placing each in successive bytes of memory until the Enter key is pressed. It also handles the Delete Line and Delete Character keys. The function call requires the offset of an area of data memory within the program. The memory at this offset is used by the function call as illustrated in Figure 5.2 earlier.

The first section (the first byte) must contain a number between 0 and 255. The operating system will not accept more than this number of characters. The second section (the second byte) is set by the operating system to the actual number of characters typed. The third section (bytes three onwards) will contain the characters as typed. We must reserve an area of store of suitable length for this input data structure which is often referred to as an input 'buffer'. Let us assume that our palindrome is at most 80 characters long. The value 80 would be required in the first byte. The third section would need to be at least 80 bytes long. This can be accomplished in assembly language by the following being placed in the data segment:

For DOS:

```
buf_start        db        80
buf_length       db        0
buf              db        80 dup (0)
```

For CP/M-86:

```
buf_start        db        80
buf_length       db        0
buf              rb        80
```

Our step one can now be coded as:

```
mov      dx , offset buf_start
mov      ah , 10
call     dobdos
```

Following these three instructions we now have a potential palindrome starting at buf and whose length is contained in buf_length. Step two can now be completed by initializing SI with the offset of buf and by initializing BX with that same value plus the value in buf_length less one.

### 5.5.3 Step three – output

This step simply prints out either a positive or negative message. The decision as to which message is printed has been made within step two and the simplest way of linking the two steps is to provide two entries into step three: one which will be jumped to if step two finds a palindrome, and another which will be jumped to if step two finds that the phrase is not a palindrome. These two entries will be labelled is_a_palindrome and not_a_palindrome. Step three prints one of two messages. The relevant function call to print a message is function 9. This function call expects the offset of the start of the message to be in register DX. It will print each character from that offset onwards until it finds the dollar sign character '$' (which it does not print). Our messages will be written within the data segment as follows:

```
yes_mess    db    'That was a palindrome.',cr,lf,'$'
no_mess     db    'That was not a palindrome.',cr,lf,'$'
```

The constants cr and lf are equated with the ASCII codes for carriage return and line feed. This equate is performed in the skeleton program.

Step three can be written as:

```
is_a_palindrome:
        mov     dx , offset yes_mess
        mov     ah , 9
        call    dobdos
        jmp     finished

not_a_palindrome:
        mov     dx , offset no_mess
        mov     ah , 9
        call    dobdos
        jmp     finished
```

An alternate and shorter way of coding step three would be:

```
is_a_palindrome:
        mov     dx , offset yes_mess
        jmp     print_mess

not_a_palindrome:
        mov     dx , offset no_mess
print_mess:
        mov     ah , 9
        call    dobdos
        jmp     finished
```

### 5.5.4 Final program

The three steps of the palindrome program can now be linked together and placed in our skeleton program ready for execution. Two small refinements have been made to the final program. Firstly, before waiting for the user to type in a potential palindrome a prompt message is printed. It is always wise to inform the user of what is expected. Secondly, the program repeats itself. After a potential palindrome is entered, tested and a message displayed, the program returns to step one to ask for another potential palindrome. The process continues until a blank line is typed when the program then finishes. This is achieved by altering step three so that it jumps back to step one instead of the label finished and by altering step two such that if it finds a blank line (buf_length being zero) it jumps to the label finished. The final program is for DOS. It contains many comments in order to explain its behaviour. There is only one line which needs to be altered in order to use this program with CP/M-86. The data declaration:

```
buf        db        80 dup (?)
```

should be altered to:

```
buf        rb        80
```

```
;Below are the data declarations for the palindrome program
;These are inserted in the skeleton program after the comment:
;INSERT DATA HERE

prompt_mess     db       cr,lf,'Type in a potential palindrome'
                db       cr,lf,'$'

yes_mess        db       cr,lf,'That was a palindrome!'
                db       cr,lf,'$'

no_mess         db       cr,lf,'That was not a palindrome'
                db       cr,lf,'$'

buf_start       db       80            ;Max of 80 chars accepted.
buf_length      db       0         ;Bdos will place the number
                                   ;typed in here.
buf             db       80 dup (?)    ;Reserve space for
                                       ;80 characters.
```

```
;Below are the code instructions for the palindrome program.
;They are inserted in the skeleton program after the comment:
;INSERT CODE HERE

nextline:
    mov     dx , offset prompt_mess    ;DX contains the offset of
                                       ;the start of the message.
    mov     ah , 9                     ;Function 9 - print.
    call    dobdos                     ;Print it.

    mov     dx , offset buf_start ;Buf_start is the start of
                                  ;the area into which the
                                  ;palindrome is read.
    mov     ah , 10                    ;Function 10 - read.
    call    dobdos                     ;Read the palindrome.

    mov     si , offset buf            ;SI will point into the
                                       ;palindrome from the left
                                       ;hand side. Initially it is
                                       ;set to point at the first
                                       ;character - in buf.
    mov     bl , buf_length            ;BL - the low order byte of BX
                                       ;now contains the number of
                                       ;characters in the palindrome.
    cmp     bl , 0                     ;Test whether no characters
                                       ;were typed.
    je      finished                   ;None typed - finish.

    mov     bh , 0                     ;BH - the high order byte of BX
                                       ;is set to zero so that, as BL
                                       ;contains the No. of characters
                                       ;the whole of BX now has that
                                       ;value.
    add     bx , si                    ;Add onto this count SI which
                                       ;contains the offset of the
                                       ;start of the palindrome. BX
                                       ;now points to the character
                                       ;after the last one read.
    dec     bx                         ;Decrement BX by one. BX now
                                       ;points to the last character
                                       ;typed.

compare_loop:
 ;The following instructions compare the character pointed at
 ;by SI with that pointed at by BX.
```

```
;They are repeated for each pair.

    cmp     si , bx             ;Are we now in the middle of
                                ;palindrome?
    jae     is_palindrome       ;YES - we have a palindrome.
    lodsb                       ;Move into AL the byte pointed
                                ;at by SI and increment SI.
    cmp     al , [bx]           ;Compare this character with
                                ;the one pointed at by BX.
    jne     not_palindrome      ;Mismatch - this is not a
                                ;palindrome.

    dec     bx                  ;Decrement BX to point at the
                                ;next character down from the
                                ;right hand side. Note that SI
                                ;has already been incremented
                                ;to point at the next character
                                ;up from the left hand side by
                                ;the 'lodsb' instruction above.
    jmp     compare_loop        ;Go back and try the next pair.


is_palindrome:
    mov     dx , offset yes_mess ;The affirmative message.
    jmp     print_mess          ;Go print it.


not_palindrome:
    mov     dx , offset no_mess  ;The negative message.

print_mess:
    mov     ah , 9              ;Function 9 - print.
    call    dobdos              ;Print it.
    jmp     nextline            ;Jump back and try another.
```

# 6 | Subroutines and the Stack

## 6.1 INTRODUCTION

A subroutine is a self-contained section of a program which performs a specific task or set of tasks. Once written, the subroutine may be invoked at any place within the program. This invocation is performed by a **call** instruction. The call instruction has the same format as the jump instruction. A label heralding the start of the subroutine is the operand of the call instruction. The effect is to jump to that label but, before doing so, to store away the position of the next instruction following that call. When the subroutine has finished its tasks it returns to the instruction following the original call instruction. This is performed by a **return** instruction. The effect of the return instruction is to jump to the position which was stored away by the call instruction. Exactly where this position is stored varies with different processors. As we shall see in the next section, the 8086 stores this information on the stack.

Once a subroutine has been written, it may be called from anywhere within the program. Effectively, this produces a new machine code instruction. For example, we can write a subroutine comprising the half dozen or so instructions which print out a greetings message and label the start of these instructions with the label `greetings`. The subroutine will terminate with the return instruction. The instruction:

```
call     greetings
```

will now print out the message just as though a single instruction to perform this task already existed within the 8086.

The exact mechanism is that the call instruction stores away on the stack the offset of the next instruction following and then jumps to the label `greetings`. The subroutine will terminate with the instruction:

```
ret
```

The return instruction fetches the offset from the stack and jumps to it – back to the instruction following the call.

A subroutine is a self-contained sequence of instructions. The subroutine has a single entry point which is labelled. The name of that label is the name of the subroutine. At any point within the subroutine a return instruction may be placed and its effect is to return to the caller. The subroutine should be regarded as an indivisible unit. While there is nothing to stop a program from performing a jump to a subroutine or even a jump to a label within a subroutine this would be a very unwise practice. Without an extant call instruction the return instruction would not jump to any sensible offset.

It is good practice to isolate subroutines by placing them at the end of the main program. They should only ever be entered with a call instruction and only ever left by a return instruction.

There are three main uses for subroutines:

1. Saving space.

2. Improving readability.

3. Recursion.

The first covers those occasions where a particular task performed by a group of instructions is to occur at more than one position within a program. By writing this group of instructions as a subroutine they may be called upon instead. The repetition of this group of instructions is avoided, thus saving space. As the instructions are only written once, the chances of one of the otherwise several occurrences of the instructions containing an error are eliminated. This feature makes the program more secure. A modification to the instructions is also confined to only one place within the program. Examples of such subroutines are given in the next section.

The second use of subroutines is that of improved readability. A lengthy program can be written as a monolithic sequence of instructions spanning several pages of the listing. Alternatively each logically distinct section of the program may be written as a subroutine. Each subroutine may then be read separately and its name then becomes synonymous with its actions. The main program is now a smaller and more easily read unit. It is more than twice as difficult to read and retain the contained information of two pages than it is to read and retain the information of one page. Within reason, the smaller a program or subroutine is made, the better. This improved readability aspect of subroutines will be returned to in Chapter 10.

The third and final use of subroutines is to permit a very powerful programming facility called **recursion**. Recursion is a concept where the definition of a task involves the task itself. For example, the task of printing a family tree starting at a particular ancestor consists of following the links of each offspring. Each of these links may produce further links and is a family tree in its own right. Alternatively a link may terminate as a leaf of the tree. This task can be defined as:

```
Trace family tree(ancestor) is defined as:

      Print name of ancestor.
      For each offspring:
                  trace family tree(offspring).
```

This is a concise definition of an otherwise complicated procedure. As we shall see in Section 6.3 of this chapter, subroutines may be used recursively in order to program such recursive tasks.

## 6.2   8086 SUBROUTINES AND THE STACK

The subroutine call and return mechanism saves a return address on the stack. The stack is an area of memory within the stack segment which is accessed by the stack pointer (SP) register. Words are stored on the stack in a 'last in, first out' or LIFO manner. The stack can be viewed as shown in Figure 6.1.

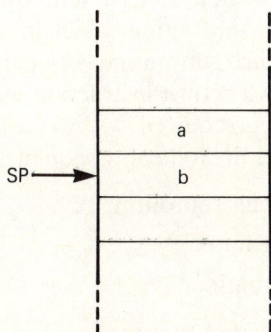

**Figure 6.1**    The stack.

The stack pointer holds the offset of the most recent word pushed onto the stack. In the above example this word is labelled as b. Objects are stored on the stack by the PUSH instruction and removed from the stack by the POP instruction. Both of these instructions have a word operand which must be a memory or register word. The exact effect of the PUSH and POP instructions is:

```
PUSH    <word>
        Decrement SP by 2.
        Store <word> in offset given by SP.

POP     <word>
        Retrieve the word at the offset given
```

```
by SP and store in <word>.
Increment SP by 2.
```

In both cases the offset is within the stack segment. The stack then grows downwards from the highest address in the stack segment. The only object directly accessible on the stack is the most recent word pushed onto the stack.

The subroutine call and return instructions use the stack to save the code offset of the instruction to return to. The `CALL` instruction firstly pushes the offset of the next instruction onto the stack and then jumps to the label given. The `RET` instruction pops this offset off the stack and jumps to it. If such a variant of the `POP` instruction existed then the `RET` instruction would be equivalent to:

```
pop      ip
```

where `IP` is the instruction pointer: the current instruction offset.

The benefits of using the stack to hold the return offset are many. Firstly it is not necessary for the 8086 to reserve a word object to hold this offset. Secondly it is possible to nest subroutine calls. That is, a subroutine may call another subroutine, which in turn may call a third subroutine and so on. As each subroutine is called the return offset is pushed onto the stack. Each return instruction uses the most recent offset which is exactly what is required.

As an example consider the following sequence of events:

The main program M calls subroutine A.

Subroutine A calls subroutine B.

Subroutine B calls subroutine C.

While subroutine C is activated the stack will contain three offsets. These are the return offsets for the main program M, subroutine A and subroutine B. When a return instruction in subroutine C is obeyed it will use the most recent value on the stack and return to subroutine B. Similarly when a return instruction in subroutine B is encountered the offset now at the top of the stack will be the return offset for subroutine A. Finally when subroutine A returns it will return to the offset placed on the stack by the original call instruction in the main program M.

It should be clear now that one constraint placed on a subroutine is that, while it is free to use the stack for storing temporary values, it must ensure that the stack is restored to the state it held at the beginning of the subroutine, before the return instruction is obeyed. If a subroutine pushed a value onto the stack and returned before popping this value off the stack, then this value would be used as the return offset causing a jump to a nonsensical location. While this feature can provide some interesting programming effects its use is not recommended to the beginner. A subroutine is, or should be, a self-contained object and it is therefore natural that its use of the stack is self-contained also. It would not therefore normally make sense for a subroutine to push a value onto the stack without later popping that value off the stack, and the programmer should take great care to ensure that the stack is treated consistently on these occasions.

One subroutine has already been used several times. It is the dobdos subroutine in the skeleton program. The remainder of this section gives two subroutines which may be of use to some programs.

### 6.2.1   A yes or no program
A program that interacts with its user may require the ability to ask questions which request a 'yes or no' answer. Within the program, a sequence of events to achieve this might be:

1. Print a message of the form 'Answer Y or N'.
2. Read a character.
3. If the character is 'Y' then proceed to the yes section.
4. If the character is 'N' then proceed to the no section.
5. Go back to step 1.

The effect is repeatedly to request a character until either a Y or an N is typed. The program then branches to one of two labels depending upon which response was given. Such a sequence of instructions is a prime candidate for a subroutine. As the subroutine is only written once, it saves space. We can make the subroutine reasonably sophisticated as its size is not as imperative as it might be if this sequence of instructions existed in many positions throughout the program. A further important benefit of making this sequence into a subroutine is that if, at a later date, we wish to permit a third response such as 'Q' to quit the program we need only alter one section of the program. If it were not a subroutine we would have to alter painstakingly each of its occurrences.

The subroutine can repeatedly demand a character until either a Y or an N is typed. When the subroutine returns, the calling program must be able to determine which response was given. Rather than just leave the character in a register which would require the calling program always to perform a comparison, the subroutine can return with the zero (equal) flag set if the answer was Y and return with the zero flag clear if the answer was N. The zero flag is set if the last arithmetic or logical instruction produced a zero result or if the last comparison instruction compared two equal values. Otherwise the zero flag is clear.

The subroutine returns from one of two places. If the response was a Y a return is made with the zero flag set and if the response was an N then a return is made with the zero flag clear.

A suitable 'yes or no' subroutine is presented in the next listing. It requires one data declaration – the prompt message. The code for subroutines should be placed after the main program immediately before the bdos subroutine.

*Yes or no subroutine*

*In the DATA segment*

```
    Yes_or_No_message        db      cr,lf,'Answer Y or N : $'
```

*In the CODE segment*

```
    Yes_or_No:
            mov     dx , offset Yes_or_No_message
            mov     ah , 9         ;Print message.
            call    dobdos

            mov     ah , 1         ;Function 1 - read character.
            call    dobdos         ;Character is returned in AL.

            cmp     al , 'Y'       ;Compare it with 'Y'.
            je      Yes_answer     ;If equal, jump to this label.

            cmp     al , 'N'       ;Compare it with 'N'.
            jne     Yes_or_No      ;If not 'N' either then
                                   ;return to the start and ask
                                   ;again.

            cmp     al , 'Y'       ;Answer is 'N' so perform a
                                   ;compare which will UNSET the
                                   ;zero (equal) flag
            ret                    ;and return.

    Yes_answer:
            ret                    ;Return - the zero flag is
                                   ;already set by the compare
                                   ;with 'Y'.
```

Note that if the

```
    cmp     al , 'Y'
```

instruction is true then the zero flag is already set and the subroutine simply returns. If the

```
    cmp     al , 'N'
```

instruction is true then the zero flag is set and the following jump if not equal instruction will not jump. The subroutine must now clear the zero flag before returning. It does this by, knowing that register AL contains N, comparing AL with Y. Any value other than N would have sufficed here.

An example of using this subroutine is now given. The main program, after printing a suitable and specific message, calls the subroutine and then jumps to a label No_branch if the response was N. Otherwise the program continues in the knowledge that the response was Y.

```
mov     dx , offset some_message
mov     ah , 9                    ;Print message.
call    dobdos

call    Yes_or_No
jne     No_branch
        .
        .
        .
        .
```

### 6.2.2    A number print subroutine

The yes or no subroutine performs the same particular task whenever it is called. It returns a result in the zero status flag. Other subroutines, such as the dobdos subroutine in the skeleton program, require the calling program to provide information. The actions of the subroutine depend upon this information. The dobdos subroutine requires a value in the AH register to determine which particular function is required and, depending upon the function, other registers are expected to contain meaningful values. Information may be passed into a subroutine and a subroutine may return information. The objects which are passed to and from a subroutine are called parameters. Often the parameters are held in registers. The bdos function 10, which reads a line of characters from the keyboard, requires parameters which are probably larger than the available registers. In this case the parameter is a reserved area of memory and the offset of this parameter is passed to the subroutine in a register. Often the registers are the most convenient choice for subroutine parameters but any consistent alternative carriers can be employed.

The next example subroutine will print out a positive number in decimal. There is no obvious correspondence between the bit pattern used internally to represent a number and the decimal digits used externally to represent that same number. A subroutine to accomplish this transformation will be of great use to any program concerned with numerical manipulations.

The subroutine will require one parameter, which is the number to be printed. It does not need to return a result. There are several methods of calculating the decimal digits which represent a number. The method used here makes use of the 8086 divide instruction. This instruction divides one integer by another producing the remainder in addition to the result after division. For example, seven divided by three produces a result after division of two with a remainder of one. If a number is divided by 10, the remainder is the least significant decimal digit. If the result after division is then divided by 10, the remainder is the next significant decimal digit. This process can be repeated to produce each decimal digit.

For example, consider the decimal number 98217. If this number is divided by 10 then a result of 9821 with a remainder of 7 is produced. This process may be continued to produce each decimal digit:

| Number | Division by 10 | Remainder |
|--------|----------------|-----------|
| 98217  | 9821           | 7         |
| 9821   | 982            | 1         |
| 982    | 98             | 2         |
| 98     | 9              | 8         |
| 9      | 0              | 9         |

When the result after division is zero, we have produced the last and most significant decimal digit of the original number.

An algorithm to print a number $n$ can be constructed as:

```
repeat
    divide n by 10
    let d be the result and let r be the remainder
    print out r
    set n to the value of d
until n equals 0
```

The problem with this algorithm is that the digits printed would be:

```
71289
```

The number has been reversed. The correct number can only be printed by storing away each digit until the first digit to be printed – the last digit to be calculated – is found. We do not know in advance how many digits will be printed. What is required is a means of storing any reasonable number of digits and then retrieving them in reverse order. The stack is ideal for this purpose. Digits can be pushed onto the stack until all digits have been calculated. They are then popped off the stack and printed individually. The order in which they will be printed in this fashion will then be the reverse of the order in which they were produced. Our algorithm can now be corrected:

```
repeat
    divide n by 10
```

```
      let d be the result and let r be the remainder
      push r onto the stack
      set n equal to the value of d
until n equals 0

repeat
      pop r off the stack
      print r
until all digits have been printed
```

As our original number 98217 is divided by 10 the digits 7, 1, 2, 8 and 9 will be pushed onto the stack. The stack will then appear as shown in Figure 6.2.

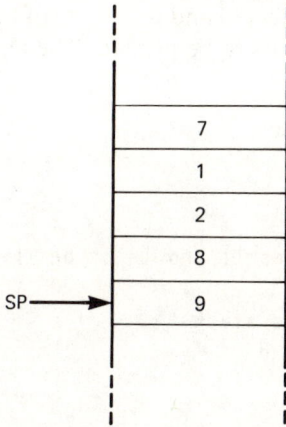

**Figure 6.2**    The stack during the number print subroutine.

The second loop in our algorithm pops each digit off the stack and prints it, resulting in the output of:

```
98217
```

There are just two problems that remain. Firstly we have calculated *digits* with values between zero and nine but we wish to print the corresponding *characters* '0' to '9'. Secondly the algorithm must be able to detect when all the digits have been popped off the stack.

The first problem is resolved by noting that characters are represented by a code. The values 0 to 127 represent the 128 characters of the ASCII character set. The correspondence between character and code is shown in Appendix B. The codes representing the characters '0' to '9' have the values 48 to 57. The digit can then be converted to the code representing the character to be printed by adding the value

48. The program will be more readable if the character constant '0' is used in the addition. The assembler will convert this constant into the value 48. The algorithm is modified by preceding the line:

```
push r onto the stack
```

with:

```
add '0' to r
```

The second problem is that of knowing when all the characters have been popped off the stack. One solution would be to count the characters as they are pushed onto the stack. A more elegant solution is to place a sentinel value onto the stack prior to the calculation of the digits. The second, printing, loop can then terminate when this sentinel value is popped off the stack. A suitable sentinel value is zero. This value is easily detected and is not one of the codes 48 to 57 which represent the characters to be printed. The algorithm can now be rewritten:

```
push 0 onto the stack

repeat
        divide n by 10
        let d be the result and let r be the remainder
        add '0' to r
        push r onto the stack
        set n equal to d
until n equals zero

pop r off the stack
while r is not equal to 0 do
        print r
        pop r off the stack
```

The algorithm can now be translated into 8086 instructions. The subroutine is called print_num. The number to be printed – the parameter – is in the register AX.

The 8086 divide instruction DIV can perform either a word or a byte division – we will use word division. This divide instruction divides the 32-bit number represented by the combination of registers DX and AX. The DX register is temporarily attached to the left hand side of the AX register. The result after division is placed in register AX and the remainder is placed in register DX. The divisor can be either a word register or a memory word but not a constant value. We will place the value 10 into the CX register and use this register as the divisor. The instruction divides the DX:AX register combination, so that calculations which involve multiplications (which produce a 32-bit answer in this DX:AX register combination) and divisions may be performed which have intermediate values outside the the range of a 16-bit word. For our subroutine this useful facility is an inconvenience. We wish to divide the AX register rather than the DX:AX register pair. This is accomplished by ensuring that the DX register contains zero prior to the division. The instruction:

```
xor     dx , dx
```

will achieve this.

The complete subroutine is given in the next listing. As the result after division is placed back into register AX by the divide instruction, the step in the algorithm which sets our n value to d is omitted. The subroutine is introduced by several comments describing the subroutine's effect, parameter details and a list of registers which are used, thereby destroying their contents.

```
print_num:
 ; A subroutine to print the decimal representation of the
 ; positive number held in register AX.
 ; The digits are calculated by repeatedly dividing AX by 10
 ; and storing the remainders on the stack. The digits are
 ; converted into their corresponding character code before
 ; they are stored. A sentinel value of 0 is placed on the stack
 ; before the first digit is produced. Each digit is finally
 ; popped off the stack and printed. This continues until the
 ; zero sentinel value is encountered.

 ; Registers on input:
 ;       AX  =  number to be printed.
 ;
 ; Registers used:
 ;       AX and DX in the division.
 ;       CX to hold the divisor of 10.
 ;       Registers used by bdos.
 ;       Status register.

        mov     cx , 10         ;Plant the divisor in CX.
        xor     dx , dx         ;Zero register DX.
        push    dx              ;Push zero onto the stack
                                ;as a sentinel.

pnum_calc_loop:
        div     cx              ;Divide DX:AX by CX.
                                ;AX = result; DX = remainder.
        add     dx , '0'        ;Convert digit to character
```

```
        push    dx                      ;and save on the stack.

        xor     dx , dx                 ;Zero DX in anticipation of
                                        ;the next division.
        or      ax , ax                 ;Set the flags according to AX.
        jne     pnum_calc_loop          ;Continue if AX is not 0.

;All digits are now on the stack - print them.
;Note that at least one digit has been placed on the stack
;following the 0 sentinel.

pnum_print_loop:
        pop     dx                      ;Fetch the next digit.
        or      dx , dx                 ;Set the flags according to DX.
        je      done_pnum               ;If 0 sentinel - finish.
        mov     ah , 2                  ;Bdos function 2 - print char
        call    dobdos                  ;in register DL
        jmp     pnum_print_loop         ;and continue.

done_pnum:
        ret                             ;Return.
```

## 6.3  RECURSIVE SUBROUTINES

The previous section of this chapter referred to three main uses of subroutines. One of these uses is to permit the programming of **recursive algorithms**. A recursive algorithm is one in which the solution to a problem is given in terms of the solution of similar but smaller problems. Such algorithms are most appropriate when the data being processed is recursive in nature. One inherently recursive object which may be familiar is an arithmetic expression. Examples of arithmetic expressions are:

$$a + b$$
$$c \star (d - e)$$
$$a \star ((b - a) \star (c + d - e) + (a/(b - c)))$$

The only concise definition of the syntax of such an expression is recursive. A typical definition of an expression might be given informally as follows.

An **expression** is:

1. a **term** or
2. a **term** + **term** or
3. a **term** − **term**.

A **term** is:

1. a **factor** or
2. a **factor** ⋆ **factor** or
3. a **factor/factor**.

A **factor** is:

1. a **variable** or
2. a bracketed **expression**.

A **variable** is:

   a , b , c ... etc.

This definition of an expression covers all the above examples. An algorithm which can interpret such an expression would be difficult to implement unless it were also recursive. A subroutine could be written to interpret an expression. When dealing with a 'factor' and an opening bracket is found the subroutine can call itself to deal with the enclosed subexpression having first saved the value of the main expression so far and the impending operator ( + − ⋆ /). In handling this subexpression the subroutine may call itself again. These nested recursive calls on the subroutine would exactly mirror the nested recursive aspects of the expression being interpreted.

Such recursive calls pose few problems. The subroutine will always return to the offset of the most recent call as held on the stack. The temporary data which must be saved before such a recursive call could also be placed on the stack. This data would then be restored from the stack when the subroutine returned. A recursive call would then take the form:

```
push each data item to be saved onto the stack
call the subroutine
pop each saved data item from the stack
```

As each nested call is enacted, the return offset and data values pertaining to each previous invocation of the subroutine are saved on the stack in a most convenient way.

In order to illustrate the use and implementation of a recursive subroutine we shall consider the problem of the Tower of Hanoi.

### 6.3.1  Tower of Hanoi

Ancient legend tells of a monastery where a process of moving the tower of Hanoi from one location to another is underway. The general problem relates to three pegs and a series of discs, each of different diameters, which are slotted onto the pegs. The tower of Hanoi consists of all the discs slotted onto one peg in order of size. The tower must be moved to another peg subject to these rules:

1. Only the top disc of a peg may be moved at a time.
2. A disc may not be placed upon a smaller disc.

Consider a tower of just three discs as shown in Figure 6.3.

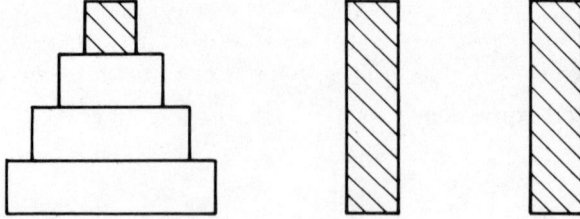

**Figure 6.3**    A tower of Hanoi with three discs.

In order to move the tower from peg one to peg three the following sequence is applied:

Move the disc from peg 1 to peg 3

Move the disc from peg 1 to peg 2

Move the disc from peg 3 to peg 2

Move the disc from peg 1 to peg 3

Move the disc from peg 2 to peg 1

Move the disc from peg 2 to peg 3

Move the disc from peg 1 to peg 3

This can be demonstrated by using three objects of different sizes as the discs and three pieces of paper to represent the pegs.

The problem to be solved is to print out the moves required to move a tower of Hanoi of any size. The key to the solution lies with the movement of the largest disc. At some stage in the movement of a tower from peg one to peg three, the largest disc must be moved from peg one to peg three. Rule one demands that only the top disc may be moved. This requires that all the other smaller discs have been moved from peg one. Rule two demands that a disc cannot be placed upon a smaller disc. As we are moving the largest disc to peg three this rule means that peg three must be empty at the time. As peg three is empty and peg one contains only the largest disc, all the other smaller discs must be on peg two at this stage. Because of rule two, these discs must exist on peg two in ascending order of size and so form a smaller tower of Hanoi. We can therefore recast the solution to moving a tower of Hanoi of size three discs as:

Move the lesser tower of Hanoi of size 2 from peg 1 to peg 2

Move the disc from peg 1 to peg 3

Move the lesser tower of Hanoi of size 2 from peg 2 to peg 3

The solution to the tower of Hanoi involves the solution to two smaller towers of Hanoi. The solution to each of the smaller towers involves the solution to two even smaller towers and so on. In other words, if we already know how to move a tower of size $n$ then we can move a tower of size $n + 1$. The general algorithm can be written as follows:

```
Algorithm Hanoi( n, a, b, c )
        n = number of discs
        a = starting peg
        b = finishing peg
        c = spare peg

call Hanoi( n-1, a, c, b )

move the disc from peg a to peg b

call Hanoi( n-1, c, b, a )
```

This algorithm is now almost complete. The remaining problem is that, as it stands, this algorithm would never terminate. It would continually enact itself for towers of size $n - 1, n - 2, n - 3 \ldots$ and so on. As with any recursive algorithm we need to write the solution in two forms. These two forms are the recursive one and a non-recursive solution to a simple case. The algorithm above could be replaced by a known solution for a trivially small sized tower and rewritten as:

```
Algorithm Hanoi( n, a, b, c )

if we know the solution for size n then do it

otherwise:
        call Hanoi( n-1, a, c, b )
        move the disc from peg a to peg b
        call Hanoi( n-1, c, b, a )
```

The algorithm may now be completed by deciding at what size $n$ we present a known solution. We know the solution for a size of three discs as given earlier in this section. This could be printed out whenever Hanoi is called with a size of three. This is, however, unnecessarily cumbersome and, in any case, the algorithm would then never terminate if called for a tower of size two, one or even zero. The temptation may be to stop at size $n = 1$. A tower of one disc has a trivial solution – move the disc from $a$ to $b$. We can, however, go one step further and stop at $n = 0$. A tower consisting of no discs requires no solution. The final algorithm can now be written as:

```
Algorithm Hanoi( n, a, b, c )

if n=0 then return doing nothing

otherwise:
        call Hanoi( n-1, a, c, b )
        move the disc from peg a to peg b
        call Hanoi( n-1, c, b, a )
```

As can be seen, the solution of a tower of size one will proceed as:

```
call Hanoi( 0, a, c, b )
move the disc from peg a to peg b
call Hanoi( 0, c, b, a )
```

Both of the calls of Hanoi will return immediately, resulting in the solitary move of the disc from peg *a* to peg *b*. The tower of Hanoi problem has at first sight a highly complex solution. By using the technique of recursion we have found a very simple solution. It is a very worthwhile exercise to attempt to find a non-recursive algorithm to solve this problem.

The above algorithm must now be translated into an 8086 subroutine. The subroutine will be called Hanoi and requires four parameters – *n*, *a*, *b* and *c*. We shall use the registers DX, AX, BX and CX to represent these parameters. Parameter *n* in register DX is a positive number. Parameters *a*, *b* and *c* will each be one of the characters 1, 2 or 3. The first line of the algorithm can be translated fairly easily:

```
        cmp     dx , 0          ;Compare n with zero.
        jne     have_a_tower    ;If not zero then continue.
        ret                     ;Otherwise return.
have_a_tower:
```

The remainder of the algorithm comprises two calls and the printing of the move. The first call of Hanoi must be written in four stages:

1. Save *n*, *a*, *b*, and *c* on the stack.
2. Alter *n*, *a*, *b*, and *c* to *n* − 1, *a*, *c* and *b*.
3. Call Hanoi.
4. Restore *n*, *a*, *b* and *c* from the stack.

Stages one and four consist of four PUSH instructions and four POP instructions respectively. Stage three is a single CALL instruction. Stage two consists of decrementing register DX (n) and exchanging the contents of registers BX and CX (b and c).

The second call of Hanoi differs only in stage two. In this case stage two consists of decrementing register DX and exchanging the contents of registers AX and CX (a and c).

The printing of the move can be accomplished by printing a message on the screen of the form:

```
Move disc from peg A to peg B
```

where A and B are the characters contained in registers AX and BX in the lower order bytes AL and BL. The message can be created in the data segment as:

```
Hanoi_message    db       'Move disc from peg '
from_peg         db       ' '
                 db       'to peg '
to_peg           db       ' '
                 db       cr,lf,'$'
```

Note that a single-line message can be split onto several lines in its definition. This has been done so that we can refer to the two bytes within the message, which we need to alter, using the names from_peg and to_peg. The printing of the message is achieved by the following instructions:

```
mov     from_peg , al       ;Plant A char in message.
mov     to_peg , bl         ;Plant B char in message.
mov     dx , offset Hanoi_message
mov     ah , 9              ;Function 9 - print
call    dobdos              ;string.
```

In printing this message we have used registers AH and DX. The routine dobdos may also corrupt other registers. As with the recursive call of Hanoi, we need to save our registers DX, AX, BX and CX before embarking on this set of instructions. We then need to restore them. The algorithm may now be written in almost its complete form as:

```
Hanoi:                          ;Subroutine Hanoi.
        cmp     dx , 0          ;Size 0 ?
        jne     have_a_tower
        ret

have_a_tower:
        SAVE REGISTERS          ;First call of Hanoi.
        dec     dx              ;Set n to n-1.
        xchg    bx , cx         ;Exchange b and c.
        call    Hanoi
        RESTORE REGISTERS
                                ;Print message.
        SAVE REGISTERS
        mov     from_peg , al   ;Plant A char.
        mov     to_peg , bl     ;Plant B char.
        mov     dx , offset Hanoi_message
```

```
              mov     ah , 9              ;Function 9 - print.
              call    dobdos
              RESTORE REGISTERS
                                          ;Second call of Hanoi.

              SAVE REGISTERS
              dec     dx
              xchg    ax , cx             ;Exchange a and c.
              call    Hanoi
              RESTORE REGISTERS

              ret
```

SAVE REGISTERS represents:

```
              push    dx
              push    ax
              push    bx
              push    cx
```

RESTORE REGISTERS represents:

```
              pop     cx
              pop     bx
              pop     ax
              pop     dx
```

Before writing out the complete program, two cosmetic improvements can be made. Firstly register DX, representing the size of the tower, is decremented for each of the two recursive calls of Hanoi. It is not used anywhere else in the subroutine. We could decrement register DX before the registers are first saved – immediately after the label have_a_tower. This replaces the two decrement instructions prior to each call. Secondly the registers are unnecessarily saved prior to the second call of Hanoi as, following this call, no further action is taken by the subroutine. As the registers' contents are no longer required then they need neither be saved nor restored at this stage. The full subroutine is now written as:

*In the DATA section*

```
    Hanoi_message    db        'Move the disc from peg '
    from_peg         db        ' '
                     db        ' to peg '
    to_peg           db        ' '
                     db        cr,lf,'$'
```

*In the CODE section*

```
    Hanoi:
              ;Subroutine Hanoi.
              ;Registers set on entry:
```

```
;           DX  = Number of discs.
;           AX  = Starting peg - '1', '2' or '3'.
;           BX  = Finishing peg        "
;           CX  = Intervening peg      "

        cmp     dx , 0          ;Tower of 0 discs ?
        jne     have_a_tower    ;No - proceed.
        ret                     ;Yes - return.

have_a_tower:
        dec     dx              ;Decrement the size in
                                ;anticipation of the
                                ;two calls of Hanoi.

        push    dx              ;Save registers.
        push    ax
        push    bx
        push    cx

        xchg    bx , cx         ;Exchange b and c.
        call    Hanoi           ;Move smaller tower to
                                ;the intervening peg.
        pop     cx              ;Restore registers.
        pop     bx
        pop     ax
        pop     dx

        push    dx              ;And save them again.
        push    ax
        push    bx
        push    cx

        mov     from_peg , al   ;Plant from_peg and to
        mov     to_peg , bl     ;peg into the message.
        mov     dx , offset Hanoi_message
        mov     ah , 9          ;Function 9 - print
                                ; string.
        call    dobdos

        pop     cx              ;Restore registers.
        pop     bx
        pop     ax
        pop     dx

        xchg    ax , cx         ;Exchange a and c
                                ;for the second call
                                ;of Hanoi.
```

```
call    Hanoi
ret
```

The subroutine should be placed in the code segment of a copy of the skeleton program immediately before the subroutine dobdos. The Hanoi_message should be placed in the program at the point marked for data. The main program, at the point marked for code, simply needs to set up the registers DX, AX, BX and CX appropriately and then call Hanoi. This can be achieved for a tower of three discs with the following instructions:

```
mov     dx , 3
mov     ax , '1'
mov     bx , '3'
mov     cx , '2'
call    Hanoi
jmp     finished
```

The program may be altered to deal with larger towers by altering the instruction which moves 3 into register DX. You may wish to write a program which asks for the number of discs and then reads a character using function call 2. In this case it is important to remember that the value returned by this function call is the code for the character typed – the digits have codes 48 to 57. This code must be converted to the corresponding number by subtracting 48 (or better still '0') from it. The instructions to read the digit and convert it to a number between 0 and 9 are:

```
mov     ah , 2          ;Function 2-read a character.
call    dobdos          ;Character returned in AL.
xor     ah , ah         ;Zero the high byte of AX.
sub     al , '0'        ;Convert code to number
mov     dx , ax         ;and place the final result
                        ;in register DX.
```

It would be wise to include a check which ensures that the character typed was in fact a digit. Finally, a word of warning is given. The recursive nature of the subroutine means that the stack can grow in size quite quickly. Each level of call increases the stack usage by five words. Calling this subroutine with large values in register DX can result in the stack being exhausted and the program failing. Towers of up to eight discs should be quite acceptable. When a program runs out of space in this way it can 'hang' the system, requiring the system to be reset. If need be, a larger area of memory could be allocated to the stack.

## 6.4   AN ALTERNATIVE SUBROUTINE MECHANISM

The above examples of subroutines do not make any substantial connection between the subroutine and its data. The subroutine's data are global – they can be accessed by any other part of the program. Additionally, the data must be saved prior to a recursive call. An alternative approach can be used which allocates a subroutine's data space upon entry to that subroutine. On exit from the subroutine the data space is relinquished. This has the advantage that only the subroutine may access its own data and no other, possibly erroneous, part of the program may interfere. This can be a great advantage in writing a program one subroutine at a time, as each subroutine can be tested individually and, when perfected, used in the knowledge that it will stay correct no matter what new subroutines are added.

A recursive call to a subroutine presents no new problems under this system. When the call is made a new area of data space is created and the calling subroutine's data are saved and temporarily unavailable until this call returns. This approach has as its main disadvantage the fact that any values in a subroutine's data space are lost when the subroutine returns.

Such a mechanism is typically that used by a high-level programming language. It involves allocating data space on the stack. As the stack is in a separate segment, the data must be accessed in an unconventional manner. For that reason this approach has not been used.

# 7 | Control Structures

## 7.1 INTRODUCTION

Computer programs consist of a set of instructions along with the associated data. The instructions make up the algorithm. The algorithm can be built out of five basic constructs:

1. Sequence.
2. Exception jump.
3. Subroutine.
4. Selection.
5. Loop.

The first construct is a series of instructions obeyed sequentially. It is a construct which is fundamental to the computer because, in the absence of any jump instructions, each instruction in turn is fetched from memory and obeyed. An example of a sequence is:

> Read in a number
> Double that number
> Print the result

The second construct is, or certainly should be, rare in most programs. It is a conditional jump which is used when an unexpected or erroneous situation occurs and a section of the program or the whole program is aborted. For example, during the processing of some data an illegal value could be read and the continuation of processing the data may not be meaningful. In that case an appropriate error message could be printed and a jump made to either the end of the program or the end of the containing subroutine.

The third construct is the subroutine where a section of the program is called. This subroutine later returns control to the instruction following the call. This construct was explained in the preceding chapter.

The fourth construct is the selection. One or more different sets of instructions is selected depending upon a calculated value. The common forms of selection are examined in Section 7.2.

The fifth construct is the loop. A set of instructions are obeyed over and over again, either a known number of times or while a certain condition persists. The common forms of loops are examined in Section 7.3.

## 7.2  SELECTIONS

There are three common kinds of selection. They are typically provided in high-level programming languages in the forms:

```
1. if <condition> then <action> end_of_if.
2. if <condition> then <action_1>
                    else <action_2> end_of_if
3.  case <value> of
        <value_1> : <action_1>
        <value_2> : <action_2>
                .
                .
                .
                .
        <value_n> : <action_n>
    end_of_case
```

In the first form, an action – a set of instructions – is performed if and only if a certain condition is true. For example, a program could be written which keeps track of the time as expressed in hours, minutes and seconds. A section of this program which incremented the time by one second may be written as:

```
increment seconds

if seconds > 59
        then seconds := 0
                increment minutes
end_of_if
```

The action of this algorithm is to reset the value of seconds to zero and to increment the value of minutes at the instance of a new minute. This section should, of course, be followed immediately by a similar construct which checks for a new hour:

```
if minutes > 59 then .....
```

Note that the language used to describe this algorithm is loosely based on the Pascal programming language. In particular the symbol := is used to denote assignment in order to avoid confusion with the = symbol which is used as a test for equality.

The second form of selection is similar to the first but has an alternative action to be taken when the condition is false. For example, a teaching program could be written which asks the user questions, reads the answers and then prints suitable messages. The program could take the form of a series of question and answer steps each having the form:

```
print 'What result does the following calculation
        produce ?
                    25 * 10 - 3 '

        read answer

        if answer = 247
                then print 'That is correct'
                else print 'No. The answer is 247'
        end_of_if
```

The user is asked a question, the user's answer is then read and compared with the correct answer. Depending upon the correctness of the read answer one of two possible messages is printed.

The third form of selection, the case construct, permits one of many possible actions to be performed depending upon some computed value. A list of possible values is given, each value followed by an appropriate action. A value is computed and, if that value is among the list provided, the corresponding action is undertaken. Usually the list of values is given in order and often the values are consecutive numbers. However, such ordering is not mandatory and the translation into assembly language may be less straightforward.

As an example, a routine could be written to 'verbalize' numbers. Instead of printing numbers in the form:

123

the spoken form could be printed:

one hundred and twenty three

There are several aspects within an algorithm to perform this conversion, one of which is to print out the name of a digit. The value to be printed is placed in a data object called digit. The selection of which name is to be printed is accomplished by the following case construct:

```
case digit of
        1 : print 'one'
        2 : print 'two'
        3 : print 'three'
                    .
                    .
                    .
        9 : print 'nine'
end_of_case
```

A case construct can be given an additional action to be performed if the value presented is not one of the values in the given list. This is, however, performed by a combination of the case construct and the if-then-else construct:

```
if digit > 0 and digit < 10
        then case digit of
                1 : print 'one'
                2 : print 'two'
                        .
                        .
                        .
                9 : print 'nine'
            end_of_case
        else print '???'
    end_of_if
```

In practice it is always wise to cater for such a possibility.

## 7.2.1  The if-then construct

This construct consists of a test and an action to be performed if that test yields true. This is coded by jumping over the instructions which perform the action if the test yields false. The example given earlier would become:

```
test seconds > 59
        if not, goto skip_label
        seconds := 0
        increment minutes
    skip_label:
```

The conditional jump is performed by one of the many branch instructions. The branch instructions test the status flags of the processor as described in Chapter 4. The flags are usually set by obeying the compare (CMP) instruction. This instruction sets the flags by performing a subtraction of the source operand from the destination operand without altering either. Once set, the branch instruction is used to test the result. In our example the test was:

```
seconds > 59
```

The variable seconds is compared with 59 and a branch performed over the action if the condition is 'less than or equal to'. The full set of instructions are then written as:

```
            cmp     seconds , 59
            jle     skip_label
            mov     seconds , 0
            inc     minutes
    skip_label:
```

The label `skip_label` has no significance to the program as a whole. It would not normally be referred to anywhere else in the program. For each such construct a different label name must be chosen and this, unfortunately, leads to a proliferation of labels, often with unimaginative and uninformative names, reducing the readability of the program. A system of choosing such names should be devized and suitable comments should be inserted around the construct in order to lessen this problem.

The above comments apply even more so to the next two constructs which result in several labels each. The readability of a program can be enhanced by also adopting a convention regarding the layout of such constructs. All instructions between the test and the final label could be indented further than normal, for example. This makes the set of instructions comprizing a construct more readily visible as a single construct.

### 7.2.2 The if-then-else construct

This construct is simply an extension of the if-then construct and it is coded accordingly. The form of the if-then-else construct is:

```
if <condition>
        then <action_1>
        else <action_2>
```

This is coded as:

```
perform the test
if false, goto skip_label_1

        <action_1>
        goto skip_label_2

skip_label_1:
        <action_2>

skip_label_2:
```

The example given earlier where an answer was compared with the correct result could then be coded as:

```
cmp     answer , 247          ;247 is correct.
jne     skip_label_1          ;Not equal - perform the
                              ;'else' action.

mov     dx , offset yes_mess  ;THEN.
mov     ah , 9                ;Test was equal - Perform
                              ;the 'then' action by
```

```
                                              ;printing the 'correct'
            call      dobdos                  ;message.
            jmp       skip_label_2            ;Then finish.

   skip_label_1:                              ;ELSE.
            mov       dx , offset no_mess     ;Print the 'incorrect'
            mov       ah , 9                  ;message.
            call      dobdos

   skip_label_2:                              ;END_OF_IF.
```

For the same reasons given in connection with the if-then construct, suitable indentation of the above instructions is suggested.

The more efficiency-minded reader may well notice that of the three instructions comprizing each alternative action only the first instruction is different. In such a case it is possible to move the common ending instructions to the end of the construct:

```
            cmp       answer , 59             ;TEST.
            jne       skip_label_1

            mov       dx , offset yes_mess    ;THEN.
            jmp       skip_label_2            ;Print 'correct' message.

   skip_label_1:                              ;ELSE.
            mov       dx , offset no_mess

   skip_label_2:                              ;END_OF_IF.
            mov       ah , 9                  ;But the printing is
            call      dobdos                  ;still to be done.
```

## 7.2.3  The case construct

This construct takes one of many possible actions depending upon some calculated value. The simplest form will be examined first. One of $N$ different actions will be performed depending upon a value between 0 and $N - 1$. Each action terminates with an unconditional jump to the end of the case construct. So far we have a structure as shown:

```
   action_0:                                  ;Action for 0.
                     <instructions for action 0>
            jmp       end_of_case
```

```
action_1:                                    ;Action for 1.
              <instructions for action 1>
       jmp    end_of_case

                      .
                      .
                      .

action_9:                                    ;Action for 9.
              <instructions for action 9>


end_of_case:
```

Here, there are 10 different actions listed. Now we require an ability to jump to the requisite label. The offset of each label must be stored in a table and the required offset is then selected by looking into the table at the appropriate position. The table is declared immediately preceding the first action label:

```
table:
       dw     offset  action_0
       dw     offset  action_1
       dw     offset  action_2
                .
                .
                .
       dw     offset  action_9
```

Note that this creates 10 words in the code segment which are not instructions but constant data. It would not be sensible to jump to the label table! This table is placed amongst the code for reasons of clarity. The data is not cluttered by it and it helps to keep related objects together.

The value which controls the case statement, once calculated, is placed into a convenient register – BX is suggested. The case construct is completed by the following four instructions which, using the value in register BX, locate the required offset within table and jump to it. These instructions are placed immediately before table:

```
shl    bx , 1            ;Multiply the value in BX by
                         ;2 as each table entry is 2
                         ;bytes long.
add    bx , offset table
                         ;Add the offset of the
                         ;start of the table. BX now
                         ;contains the offset of the
                         ;word in table which has the
                         ;required label offset value!
mov    bx , cs:word ptr [bx]
```

```
                              ;Move into BX the required
                              ;offset from the table.
jmp        bx                 ;Jump to the required action
                              ;label.
```

The first instruction multiplies the value in the BX register by two as each table entry contains two bytes.

The offsets of the 10 action labels are stored within table at offsets table, table+2, table+4 ... table+18. By adding the offset of table to the BX register the required word is found.

The third instruction moves the contents of the word addressed by the BX register – the selected table entry – into the BX register. The CS: simply ensures that the code segment is used and not the data segment. The use of such a segment override is explained in Chapter 12. Normally the data segment is assumed for data manipulation operations. The prefix CS: overrides this assumption.

Finally the jump instruction jumps to the offset contained in the BX register.

The mechanics of jumping to the required action label have been described for completeness but such knowledge is not necessary in order to make a case construct. The method of coding case constructs is summarized as:

1. For each required action, starting at the action for the value zero, write a suitably labelled set of instructions to perform the action. Each set of instructions ends with a jump to a common end label.

2. Write a table containing each action label in order. The table is labelled with a unique name and each entry is of the form:
   ```
   dw         some_label
   ```
   Place the table before the first action.

3. The start of the whole case construct is then written. It consists of the four instructions:
   ```
   shl        bx , 1
   add        bx , offset <table name>
   mov        bx , cs:word ptr [bx]
   jmp        bx
   ```
   Where <table name> is the label chosen to identify the table constructed in (2).

All that remains is to ensure that the calculated value to control the case construct is placed into the BX register beforehand.

The example of a case construct which was given earlier would then be coded as follows:

```
        mov        bx , digit          ;Controlling value.

        ;CASE construct.
```

```
        shl     bx , 1
        add     bx , offset digit_case_table
        mov     bx , cs:word ptr [bx]
        jmp     bx

        ;CASE table.

digit_case_table:

        dw      offset    digit_0
        dw      offset    digit_1
        dw      offset    digit_2
        dw      offset    digit_3
        dw      offset    digit_4
        dw      offset    digit_5
        dw      offset    digit_6
        dw      offset    digit_7
        dw      offset    digit_8
        dw      offset    digit_9

        ;CASE actions.

digit_0:
        mov     dx , offset digit_mess_0
        mov     ah , 9
        call    dobdos
        jmp     end_digit_case

digit_1:
        mov     dx , offset digit_mess_1
        mov     ah , 9
        call    dobdos
        jmp     end_digit_case

digit_2:
        mov     dx , offset digit_mess_2
        mov     ah , 9
        call    dobdos
        jmp     end_digit_case

digit_3:
        mov     dx , offset digit_mess_3
        mov     ah , 9
        call    dobdos
        jmp     end_digit_case
```

```
digit_4:
        mov     dx , offset digit_mess_4
        mov     ah , 9
        call    dobdos
        jmp     end_digit_case

digit_5:
        mov     dx , offset digit_mess_5
        mov     ah , 9
        call    dobdos
        jmp     end_digit_case

digit_6:
        mov     dx , offset digit_mess_6
        mov     ah , 9
        call    dobdos
        jmp     end_digit_case

digit_7:
        mov     dx , offset digit_mess_7
        mov     ah , 9
        call    dobdos
        jmp     end_digit_case

digit_8:
        mov     dx , offset digit_mess_8
        mov     ah , 9
        call    dobdos
        jmp     end_digit_case

digit_9:
        mov     dx , offset digit_mess_9
        mov     ah , 9
        call    dobdos


end_digit_case:

        ;END_OF_CASE.
```

Note that the final action does not need to include the jump to the end of the case construct. In practice, much space would be saved if the two common ending instructions for each action which perform the printing were moved to the end of the case construct rather than repeated for each action.

Four final points are now made which remove the current restrictions on the values which are permitted.

Firstly the construct as shown does not check that the value in the BX register is between zero and nine. An if-then or an if-then-else construct should first be used to check the value. The programmer may then choose to ignore the case statement if a value is out of range or an error message could be printed.

Secondly we may wish to ignore certain discrete values within the encompassing range. In this case, such actions are not declared and the corresponding entry in the case table uses the end of the case construct label. In the above example this would consist of entries of the form:

```
dw       offset end_digit_case
```

But only if no common instructions for the actionable values were placed there on efficiency grounds! In that event a second ending label would be required.

Thirdly we may wish to consider a range that does not start at zero. We may have a range of years such as 1982 to 1985. To permit this, we simply subtract 1982 from our year and then proceed with a case construct using values in the range zero to three instead.

Finally we may wish to perform the same action for more than one particular value. For example we may wish to perform one action for the values zero, one and two but individual actions for the values three and four. In this case the three actions may be written and labelled as:

```
action_012:

action_3:

action_4:
```

The table of offsets would then have its first three entries all referring to action_012:

```
new_table:

        dw       offset  action_012
        dw       offset  action_012
        dw       offset  action_012
        dw       offset  action_3
        dw       offset  action_4
```

## 7.3 LOOPS

A loop achieves the repeated execution of a set of instructions. It is this ability to obey repetitively a sequence of instructions which gives the computer its power. For example, programs exist to process employee records in order to produce a payroll. Each record in turn is processed by the same set of instructions. In a mathematical calculation the computation of a particular value may require the execution of several iterations (repetitions) of the same mathematical operations. All but the simplest of computer programs will require the facility to loop.

There are two kinds of loop, commonly called the **deterministic** loop and the **non-deterministic** loop. As their names imply, with the deterministic loop the number of repetitions is known in advance whereas the non-deterministic loop continues until some condition arises. For example, we may need to process a series of data values to calculate their average. For each data value we would perform the same operations of adding that value into a running total and keeping track of how many items have been processed. There are two possible ways of presenting the data to the program. The data could be terminated by a special value. Alternatively the data could be preceded by a count of the number of items following.

In the first case the number of repetitions is not known in advance. The loop must continue until an event occurs – the terminating data value is found. Such a non-deterministic loop may take the form:

```
loop while data present
        process data
end_loop
```

In the second case we know in advance how many data values will be processed and hence how many repetitions are required. A deterministic loop would be used and may take the form:

```
loop X times
        process data
end_loop
```

The common forms of non-deterministic and deterministic loops are now examined.

### 7.3.1 Non-deterministic loops

A non-deterministic loop repetitively obeys a series of instructions until some event occurs. There are two popular forms of such a loop. Both forms comprise a test and a set of instructions. The instructions are obeyed under the control of the test. If the test is performed before the instructions this produces a loop called the **while** loop. If the test is performed after the instructions a loop called the **repeat** loop is produced. These two forms are represented as:

```
while <condition> do
        .
    <instructions>
```

```
                       .
        end_while_loop
```

and:

```
        repeat
                       .
            <instructions>
                       .
        until <condition>
```

The while loop tests a condition and, if that condition is true, the instructions are obeyed. The test is then performed again and, if it is still true, the instructions are performed a second time. This continues until the test yields false.

The repeat loop obeys the instructions and then tests the condition. If the condition is true then the loop terminates. Otherwise the instructions are obeyed again and again until the test yields true.

The two distinctions between these two forms of looping are:

1. The while loop need not obey the instructions at all whereas the repeat loop will obey the instructions at least once.
2. The while loop continues whilst a condition prevails. The repeat loop continues until a condition occurs.

These loops are constructed as follows:

*WHILE loop*

```
        while_loop_start:
                          test the condition
                          if false - jump to end_loop
                                     .
                            <instructions>
                                     .
                          jump to while_loop_start
        end_loop:
```

*REPEAT loop*

```
        repeat_loop_start:
                                     .
                            <instructions>
                                     .
                          test the condition
                          if false - jump to repeat_loop_start
```

The main difference between these two loops is that the while loop executes its instructions zero or more times whilst the repeat loop executes its instructions one or more times. In the previous section, the example given was to read in numbers and calculate their average. The data are terminated by a value of, say, zero. It is quite possible, albeit unlikely, that there are no data. In this case the terminal value of zero is encountered immediately. A while loop is therefore the appropriate choice. Such a program could be written as:

```
total := 0
items := 0

while ( read a number and that number is not zero ) do
        total := total + number
        items := items + 1
end_while_loop
```

Following this loop we would need to test for the possibility that no data items were processed:

```
if items = 0
        then print 'No data given'
        else print 'Average = '  total / items
end_of_if
```

The loop shown would translate into 8086 assembly code as follows. A suitable routine called read_num is assumed to exist. It reads a number from the keyboard and returns its value in the BX register.

```
        mov     total , 0           ;Zero the running total.
        mov     items , 0           ;Zero the count.

while_loop_start:
        call    read_num            ;Read a number.
        cmp     bx , 0              ;Test for terminator.
        je      end_loop            ;Finish if zero read.

        add     total , bx          ;Add it into the total.
        inc     items               ;Increment the count.

        jmp     while_loop_start    ;Go back and continue.

end_loop:
```

A common use for the repeat loop is within an interactive program which asks a question and then reads a reply. If the reply given is not understood then the most sensible course of action is to repeat the question and read a new answer. This process will continue until a recognizable answer is read. A typical example is:

```
repeat
        print 'Please answer Y or N'
        read answer
until answer = 'Y' or answer = 'N'
```

In this way, typing errors are largely accounted for and an unambiguous response is assured. This repeat loop could be coded in 8086 assembly code as shown:

```
repeat_loop_start:
        mov     dx , offset question_message
        mov     ah , 9                  ;Print the question.
        call    dobdos


        mov     ah , 1                  ;Read a character from
        call    dobdos                  ;the keyboard.


        cmp     al , 'Y'                ;Is it 'Y' ?
        je      end_loop                ;Yes - terminate.


        cmp     al , 'N'                ;Is it 'N' ?
        jne     repeat_loop_start       ;No - repeat.

end_loop:

        ;AL now contains either 'Y' or 'N'.
```

### 7.3.2  Deterministic loops

A deterministic loop is obeyed a certain known number of times. Often that number is known at the time of writing the program but it may be calculated prior to the loop start. The most general form of deterministic loop is typically provided in high-level programming languages as:

```
for <variable> := <start_value> by <increment> to
                    <end_value> do
                            .

                    <instructions>

                            .

end_for_loop
```

The **for** loop initializes a variable with a starting value and obeys the instructions given. After obeying the instructions the variable is augmented by the increment value and the instructions obeyed again. This continues until the variable exceeds the ending value. If the starting value is greater than the ending value then the loop terminates immediately without obeying the instructions at all. This algorithm is summarized as:

1. Assign `<start_value>` to `<variable>`.
2. If `<variable>` is greater than `<end_value>` then terminate.
3. Obey `<instructions>`.
4. Add `<increment>` to `<variable>`.
5. Go back to step 2.

This very general structure permits the variable to be used within the instructions. Such a loop will be seen to be most valuable in Chapter 9 when operating on arrays. A variant of this loop permits the variable to count downwards from its starting value to a smaller ending value. In this case the increment is subtracted each time. Most commonly the increment value is one. This value is assumed if no increment is provided.

Often this loop is used to obey a set of instructions a given number of times. In this case the existence of the variable, which is not used within the instructions, is actually an inconvenience. The example examined earlier to process a series of numbers and produce an average shows this point clearly. The total number of items to be processed is first read. That number of items is then read and a total accumulated:

```
total := 0
read n

for i:= 1 to n do
        read x
        total := total + x
end_for_loop

if n > 0 then average := total / n
```

The variable i is not required in this case. Instances where the variable is required occur when the action within the loop is directly dependent upon the repetition count. A table of squares of numbers could be produced in this way quite conveniently:

```
for i:= 1 to n do
        print i i*i
end_for_loop
```

The different types of deterministic loop stem from the simplification of the most general for loop as given at the start of this section:

```
for <variable> := <start_value> by <increment> to
                    <end_value> do <instructions>
```

This general loop can be modified to count downwards and can alternatively be expressed as:

```
for <variable> := <start_value> by <increment> downto
                  <end_value> do <instructions>
```

In this case the starting value should be greater than the ending value.
The two common simplifications are:

1. The increment value is one.
2. The variable is not required; the start value and the increment
   are both one. The loop is performed end_value times.

The coding of such loops is now examined. The general loop
consists of four sections. Firstly the variable is initialized with the
starting value. Secondly the variable is compared with the ending
value. If the variable is greater, then the loop terminates. Thirdly the
instructions within the loop are obeyed. Finally the variable is augmented by the increment value and a jump made back to the second
section:

```
            <variable> := <start_value>

for_loop_start:


            compare <variable> with <end_value>
            if greater then jump to end_for_loop

                          .

            <instructions>

                          .


            add <increment> to <variable>
            jump back to for_loop_start

end_for_loop:
```

This can be coded in 8086 assembly code as follows. The lines are
numbered for reference in the ensuing discussion:

```
    1:              mov     ax , start_value
    2:              mov     variable , ax

    3:      for_loop_start:

    4:              mov     ax , variable
    5:              cmp     ax , end_value
    6:              jg      end_for_loop

                    <instructions>

    7:              mov     ax , variable
```

```
 8:              add       ax , increment
 9:              mov       variable , ax
10:              jmp       for_loop_start

11:      end_for_loop:
```

There are many improvements possible here depending upon the nature of the variable, the increment, and the start and end values. It has been assumed above that all are memory words and therefore direct single operations between them are not possible. The initialization of the variable requires two instructions (lines one and two) because one memory word cannot be moved directly into a second memory word. If the start value were a constant or if the variable were a register then a single instruction could be used. Similarly, the comparison (lines four and five) requires two instructions because one memory word cannot be compared directly with a second memory word. If the variable were a register or if the end value were a constant then, again, a single instruction would suffice. The last section (lines seven to ten) is particularly clumsy. The variable is to be increased by the increment value. If the increment value were a constant then lines seven to nine could be replaced by:

```
add       variable , constant_increment_value
```

Similarly, if the variable were a register then a single instruction would be available. Finally note that in the most general case given, line four is redundant. At that place the variable's value is already contained in the AX register. The for loop is at its simplest if the variable is a register. If we use the AX register as the variable then the for loop simplifies to:

```
         mov       ax , start_value

for_loop_start:

         cmp       ax , end_value
         jg        end_for_loop
                      .
         <instructions>
                      .
         add       ax , increment
         jmp       for_loop_start

end_for_loop:
```

The loop is made to count backwards by changing two instructions. The jump following the comparison becomes JL – jump if less than – and the ADD instruction is replaced by a SUB instruction. In the simpler case where the increment is one, the final section of the loop in all cases would simplify to:

```
inc     variable            ;Or 'DEC' for backwards count.
jmp     for_loop_start
```

This applies whether the variable is a register or a memory word.

The program section referred to earlier to print a table of squares from one to a particular value can now be written. The routine print_num introduced in Chapter 6 is used by this program section:

```
;To print a table of squares from one to a value
;in the variable 'end_value'.

        mov     ax , 1            ;Start at one.

for_loop_start:

        cmp     ax , end_value   ;Finished ?
        jg      end_for_loop     ;Yes - terminate.

        push    ax               ;Save AX.
        call    print_num        ;Print it.
        pop     ax               ;Restore AX.

        push    ax               ;Save AX again.
        mul     ax               ;Square AX.
        call    print_num        ;Print the square.

        pop     ax               ;Restore original AX.

        inc     ax               ;Increment to
                                 ;next value
        jmp     for_loop_start   ;and continue.
end_for_loop:
```

The final form of deterministic loop is the simplest case where a certain number of repetitions are required. The 8086 provides specialized instructions for this type of construct. The CX register is typically used for counting and two instructions special to that register are:

```
jcxz    <label>
```

and:

```
loop    <label>
```

The JCXZ instruction jumps to its destination label if the CX register contains zero. The setting of the zero status flag is neither consulted nor altered. The LOOP instruction first decrements the value in the CX register by one. A jump is then made to the destination label if the result is not zero. The status flags again are neither consulted nor altered. The simple loop can be expressed as:

```
loop 'number' times

          .
<instructions>
          .

end_loop
```

This can be expressed in 8086 assembly language as:

```
        mov     cx , number     ;Count down from
                                ;number to zero.
        jcxz    end_loop        ;Stop now if
                                ;number is zero.
loop_start:

                .
        <instructions>
                .

        loop    loop_start

end_loop:
```

The JCXZ instruction is required in case the number of iterations is zero. If this instruction were omitted and if number were zero then 65 536 iterations would be performed. This is because the LOOP instruction decrements the CX register and then checks for it being zero. Firstly zero is decremented to produce $-1$, i.e. the CX register would contain all 1s, which has the all-positive integer interpretation of 65 535. This would then be counted down to zero. If the number of iterations is known to be non-zero or if the above effect is desired then the JCXZ instruction should be left out.

Earlier, the program section which calculated the average of a series of numbers was shown. If the approach is taken whereby the number of items to be processed in calculating the average is first read as input then the above form of loop is the most efficient and elegant solution. The existence of a routine called read_num, which does not modify the contents of the AX register, is again assumed. This routine reads a number typed at the keyboard and returns the value in register BX. The program section is:

```
            mov       ax , 0          ;Use AX to accumulate total.
            call      read_num        ;Read No of items to process
            mov       cx , bx         ;and plant it into CX.

            jcxz      end_loop        ;None to read.
            push      bx              ;Save the number of items
                                      ;for the calculation later.

cx_loop_start:

            call      read_num        ;Read next number.
            add       ax , bx         ;Add it into the total
            loop      cx_loop_start   ;and continue if more to do.
            ; AX is now the total.
            ; The original count is still on the stack.

            pop       bx              ;Restore the count.
            mov       dx , 0          ;DX will be used in the
                                      ;following 32 bit division.
            div       bx              ;Divide DX:AX by BX.

end_loop:
```

Note that the label end_loop has been moved down over the instructions which perform the calculation to avoid a division by zero should the number of items to process be zero.

Finally, two variants of the LOOP instruction should be explained. They are LOOPE (loop while equal) and LOOPNE (loop while not equal). They can also be written as LOOPZ and LOOPNZ. They permit a loop construct which combines the features of the deterministic and the non-deterministic loops. Both instructions decrement the CX register by one but only jump if both the CX register is not yet zero *and* the zero flag is set (LOOPE) or clear (LOOPNE). In this way, a loop is terminated by reaching a certain count (CX is decremented to zero) or by a certain condition arising. The LOOPE and LOOPNE instructions would therefore normally be preceded by an instruction (such as compare) which affects the zero status flag. Which of the two events was responsible for terminating the loop can be ascertained by testing the zero flag but note that the CX register could have reached zero coincidentally at the same time that the condition first arose!

As an example we could modify our averaging program to stop prematurely if a zero value is read:

```
        mov     ax , 0
        call    read_num
        mov     cx , bx
        jcxz    end_loop
        push    bx

cx_loop_start:

        call    read_num
        add     ax , bx
        cmp     bx , 0
        loopne  cx_loop_start

        ;We arrive here either because all items have
        ;been read or because the zero flag is set.
        ;We could find out using a JE or a
        ;JNE instruction.

        pop     bx              ;Count
        sub     bx , cx         ;Less those remaining
        mov     dx , 0
        div     bx

end_loop:
```

Note that the terminating zero is included in the averaging. This is probably not desired and the loop should be followed by a JE instruction which will branch to an alternative calculation of the average.

# 8 | Data Manipulation

One of the advantages of writing programs in assembly language is the ability to manipulate data efficiently in the central processing unit. Efficiency in this context is usually a measure of program execution speed or, perhaps, economy of memory. Skilled choice of the most appropriate machine code instructions and data structures can lead to outstanding improvements in speed over a program written in a high-level language, for example. In some applications, this efficient use of basic resources makes all the difference between a convenient, usable program and a lumbering giant.

The key to writing efficient routines lies initially in the correct choice and definition of data structures for a given application, so that they may be manipulated conveniently by the available range of machine instructions. In this section we examine some of the basic operations that may be performed on various data representations.

## 8.1 BIT OPERATIONS

In many applications we can take advantage of the assembly language programmer's ability to manipulate individual bits of data in an MPU register: an ability denied to most high-level language programmers. For example, this added flexibility allows a programmer to use different bits of a data word to represent different things and to extract or alter them at random, without affecting surrounding bits. A number of standard techniques are used in this bit manipulation process and some of these are introduced later in this chapter.

### 8.1.1 Masking

Masking is the process of selectively identifying particular bit positions in a register in order to perform an operation on these bits alone. Only the selected bits are affected; the remainder are untouched – they are effectively hidden during the operation, hence the use of the term 'mask' in this context. In practice, bits may be masked 'in' or 'out' of a pattern, and examples of both are considered later.

**Masking out** is used to force selected bits in a register to zero. One example of this was introduced in Section 3.5.1 as a way of converting lower-case ASCII alphabetic characters to upper-case. It was recognized that lower-case characters from 'a' to 'z' inclusive differ from their upper-case counterparts by one bit only: bit 5 is a 1 for lower-case and a 0 for upper-case. When reading characters typed by a user with the intention of recognizing them as commands, for example, it is usually more 'friendly' to ignore case altogether, accepting either an upper or lower-case command. We may then prefer to zero bit 5 of the register containing the character in order to perform subsequent comparisons against upper-case characters only. As mentioned in Section 3.5.1, assuming that the character is read into AL, we can do this by a single logical AND instruction:

```
and     al , 0dfh
```

The mask in this case is the constant binary pattern 11011111 written as a hexadecimal constant. The AND operation performs the masking out of bit 5; all other bits are ANDed with 1 and, hence, unaffected by the operation. This operation is illustrated as:

| 7 | 6 | 5 | 4 | 3 | 2 | 1 | 0 | bit |
|---|---|---|---|---|---|---|---|-----|
| 1 | 1 | 0 | 1 | 1 | 1 | 1 | 1 | mask |
| AND | AND | AND | AND | AND | AND | AND | AND | AND |
| X | X | X | X | X | X | X | X | data |
| ↓ | ↓ | ↓ | ↓ | ↓ | ↓ | ↓ | ↓ | |
| X | X | 0 | X | X | X | X | X | result |

where X, in the result, represents a 0 or a 1 in the original data which has been carried through unaltered. Note that it does not matter whether bit 5 is a 0 or a 1 beforehand; it will certainly be 0 after the AND. The masking is in this case equivalent to subtracting 32 (20h) from a lower-case character while leaving untouched a character that is already upper-case. To improve readability, we may prefer to define the mask beforehand as a constant in order to give it a sensible name, as in:

```
upper_case_mask      equ  0dfh


        ..
        ..
        and     al , upper_case_mask
```

In a similar way, we often wish to 'remove' the most significant bit of a character held in eight bits. ASCII makes use of only the least significant seven bits in a byte (128 patterns). Especially in input and output, the eighth bit is frequently used as a parity bit. Parity was introduced briefly in Chapter 3 but for our purposes here we note that for some characters this bit may be set to 1. In making comparisons against character constants this can give unexpected results when the parity bit is not set correctly in the constant. It is usual to mask out the parity bit on a character as soon as it has been read:

```
parity_mask      equ   7fh

        ..
        ..
        and       al , parity_mask
```

assuming, again, that the character is read into AL. This process is often referred to as **parity stripping**.

Conversely, we may wish to set particular bits in a word to 1 rather than force them to 0 as above. This setting of bits, or **masking in** can be performed by a logical OR operation. In the first example above, for instance, we may opt to convert all alphabetic characters read in to lower case rather than to upper case. To do this, bit 5 must be coerced into a 1. A suitable mask is 00100000:

```
lower_case_mask        equ   20h

        ..
        ..
        or        al , lower_case_mask
```

A logical OR of a bit with 0 will not change the original bit. An OR with 1 in bit 5 position will produce 1 regardless of the original bit value, forcing the character to lower case.

Note that in both examples of case conversion the masking is only sensible for alphabetic characters. One possible test would be to mask bit 5 of a character out (or in) and then subtract the ASCII code for A (or a). If the result lies outside the range 0–25 then the original character was not alphabetic and should be restored from a saved copy, since there is then no way of working out the original setting of bit 5. Alternatively, one could check for lower-case characters before performing a conversion to upper case. The following subroutine reads a character from the console keyboard, strips parity and converts any lower-case alphabetic characters to upper case.

```
read_keys:
        mov       ah , 1              ;System function
                                      ;call 1
        call      dobdos              ;reads from the
                                      ;keyboard into AL.
        and       al , parity_mask    ;Strip parity.

        cmp       al , 'a'
        jb        notlc               ;Character < 'a'
        cmp       al , 'z'
        ja        notlc               ;Character > 'z'
```

```
        and      al , upper_case_mask   ;Convert lower-
                                        ;case
                                        ;to upper-case.
notlc:
        ret
```

In this particular case the upper-case masking instruction could be replaced by an arithmetic subtraction of 32.

Note the use of 'jump if above (below)' instructions in the above, following the compare instructions. These are based on the setting of the C (carry) flag (and the zero flag in the case of JA). One may be tempted to use the sign flag in these circumstances, by means of a JL (jump if less than) or JS (jump if sign is negative) instruction, for example. In general this would be unwise since the setting of the sign flag assumes that values in a comparison are signed two's complement numbers, which clearly they are not in this application. In this particular case we would 'get away' with using the sign flag on the grounds that stripping the parity bit will ensure that the 'numbers' are all positive before the comparison. Reserving use of the sign flag for true two's complement operations is by far the most sensible policy, however. When using conditional jumps after an INC or DEC note that neither of these instructions affects the carry flag but they do affect the other flags. Thus, to increment the CX register and jump if CX is less than or equal to zero we can use:

```
inc     cx
jle     label
```

but the JBE instruction would not work correctly here.

## 8.1.2  Sets and Boolean operations

A set is a collection of values of one type which are related in some way. The set of all students taking a particular examination and the set of all characters that may be used in a computer program are two examples of sets. The potential use of sets and their operations is introduced here by way of an example. Consider the task of reading two hexadecimal numbers and determining:

a) How many of the hex digits 0–F are present in both numbers?

b) How many of them are present in neither number?

c) How many of them are present in one number but not both?

For example, given the two hexadecimal numbers:

```
9CB31
```

and:

```
3D6FC3
```

then the answers to the above questions (with the actual hex digits in brackets) would be:

a) 2 (C,3)
b) 8 (0,2,4,5,7,8,A,E)
c) 6 (1,6,9,B,D,F)

We may approach this problem by considering the hex digits to be the 16 elements of a set: the set of hex digits. Thus, for each of the two hexadecimal numbers we may write a representation of the digits contained in the number in terms of membership of this set. To mark the presence or absence of a digit in the possible set of 16 digits we can use a row of 16 bits; one bit for each possible hex digit. A bit is set to a 1 if the corresponding digit appears one or more times in the number and to a 0 otherwise, giving representations for the two examples above of:

```
                           hex digit
               F E D C B A 9 8 7 6 5 4 3 2 1 0
   9CB31       0 0 0 1 1 0 1 0 0 0 0 0 1 0 1 0
   3D6FC3      1 0 1 1 0 0 0 0 0 1 0 0 1 0 0 0
```

The value of this representation now becomes apparent when we consider the three questions to be answered. Firstly, the number of digits that are present in both numbers can be determined by looking for columns in which a 1 appears in both numbers (C and 3). More usefully, we can produce a third set – the set of digits present in both numbers – from the other two by a logical AND operation:

```
               F E D C B A 9 8 7 6 5 4 3 2 1 0
   set A       0 0 0 1 1 0 1 0 0 0 0 0 1 0 1 0
   set B       1 0 1 1 0 0 0 0 0 1 0 0 1 0 0 0
   ─────────────────────────────────────────────
   set C = A AND B   0 0 0 1 0 0 0 0 0 0 0 0 1 0 0 0
```

Thus, the answer to question a) is the number of 1s in this third set and, if required, we can identify which digits are present in both numbers as well as how many there are. Set C is called the **intersection** of sets A and B since it identifies the elements that are common to both sets.

The set required to calculate the answer to question b) can be determined by similar means, first using a logical OR operation. A OR B gives the set of digits which are present in either number. This is the **union** of sets A and B such that a digit is a member of this set if it appears in A or B or both. In fact, we require the inverse of this set; the **complement** of set A union B. This we can generate by negating the union:

| | F E D C B A 9 8 7 6 5 4 3 2 1 0 |
|---|---|
| set A | 0 0 0 1 1 0 1 0 0 0 0 0 1 0 1 0 |
| set B | 0 0 1 1 0 0 0 0 0 1 0 0 1 0 0 0 |
| A OR B | 1 0 1 1 1 0 1 0 0 1 0 0 1 0 1 0 |
| NOT (A OR B) | 0 1 0 0 0 1 0 1 1 0 1 1 0 1 0 1 |

There are eight '1' bits in this result and, again, the actual digits present in neither number are readily identifiable in this representation.

The digits present in either number but not both are elements of the set called the **symmetric difference** of A and B. This is generated by the exclusive OR operation on A and B:

| | F E D C B A 9 8 7 6 5 4 3 2 1 0 |
|---|---|
| set A | 0 0 0 1 1 0 1 0 0 0 0 0 1 0 1 0 |
| set B | 1 0 1 1 0 0 0 0 0 1 0 0 1 0 0 0 |
| A XOR B | 1 0 1 0 1 0 1 0 0 1 0 0 0 0 1 0 |

In order to generate the two sets A and B in the first place, and to count bits in the new sets, we need to manipulate bits in a rather different way to the above. Two further processes are considered next and we shall use this example as an illustration of their use.

### 8.1.3 Shifting and rotating

As described in Section 4.3.2, there are eight instructions that cause the bits of a word to be moved left or right. These include two instructions for shifting bits left or right (SHL and SHR) and two for rotating bits within the word (ROL and ROR). In these latter two, bits shifted out of one end of the word are shifted back in at the other end. A further two rotate instructions (RCL and RCR) include the carry bit in the rotation cycle. In all cases, the number of places through which to move the bits may be specified in the instruction as 1 or as CL, in which case the shift count is taken from this register.

We may use a variable shift left instruction to generate the set patterns in the example above. Each of the sets A and B is created by reading separately the hexadecimal digits in the numbers and by setting the corresponding bits in the 16-bit words representing the sets. In the example given, the first hex digit of the first number is 9, thus we wish to set bit 9 in the word representing this set. By creating a mask in which only bit 9 is set we may mask this into the set pattern (which is initially all zero). Masks for the remaining digits are used in a similar manner:

|                                  | F E D C B A 9 8 7 6 5 4 3 2 1 0 |
|----------------------------------|---------------------------------|
| first hex number (9CB31)         |                                 |
| initial set                      | 0 0 0 0 0 0 0 0 0 0 0 0 0 0 0 0 |
| digit '9' mask                   | 0 0 0 0 0 0 1 0 0 0 0 0 0 0 0 0 |
| result after OR operation        | 0 0 0 0 0 0 1 0 0 0 0 0 0 0 0 0 |
| digit 'C' mask                   | 0 0 0 1 0 0 0 0 0 0 0 0 0 0 0 0 |
| result after OR operation        | 0 0 0 1 0 0 1 0 0 0 0 0 0 0 0 0 |
| digit 'B' mask                   | 0 0 0 0 1 0 0 0 0 0 0 0 0 0 0 0 |
| result after OR operation        | 0 0 0 1 1 0 1 0 0 0 0 0 0 0 0 0 |
| digit '3' mask                   | 0 0 0 0 0 0 0 0 0 0 0 0 1 0 0 0 |
| result after OR operation        | 0 0 0 1 1 0 1 0 0 0 0 0 1 0 0 0 |
| digit '1' mask                   | 0 0 0 0 0 0 0 0 0 0 0 0 0 0 0 1 |
| result after OR operation        | 0 0 0 1 1 0 1 0 0 0 0 0 1 0 0 1 |
| ( = set A)                       |                                 |

The variable shift count comes in useful for creating the digit masks during this process. A 1 is placed in the least significant bit of an otherwise empty word and shifted left $n$ places to produce the mask for the hexadecimal digit n. In the above example, the digit is read as an ASCII character and must first be converted to a binary number. This number is the shift count to be placed in the CL register before issuing the SHL instruction.

A further use of the shift instruction is illustrated at the end of this example as a means of counting the number of 1s in a word. This is required to count the members of the resulting sets. Consider a 'shift left' (SHL) instruction applied to the word containing the 1s to be counted. Shifting one place left moves the bit representing the F digit of the set into the carry flag. We could test for a 1 here using, for example, the 'jump if carry' (JC) instruction. An alternative method is used in the next program. A second shift to the left of one place moves the bit representing the E digit into the carry, where it too may be tested. A cycle of 16 shifts will allow us to accumulate a count of the number of 1s in the word.

A complete algorithm and program for this exercise can now be presented. Separate subroutines are written for the individual operations on the sets and these should be studied carefully as examples of the bit manipulation processes introduced above.

```
make set A (representing the first hex number)
make set B (representing the second hex number)

intersection = A AND B                    ; a)
count bits in intersection
```

```
complemented union = NOT (A OR B)     ; b)
count bits in complemented union

symmetric difference = A XOR B        ; c)
count bits in symmetric difference
```

make set may be broken down into:

```
create an empty set
read the first digit in the hex number

Repeat
  make mask for this digit
  OR it into the set
  read the next digit
Until the end of the number
```

Two locations can be defined to hold the sets A and B:

```
setA      dw        0
setB      dw        0
```

Some ASCII constants are also used in the program:

```
space     equ       ' '
cr        equ       13
lf        equ       10
```

cr and lf are defined in the skeleton program (Appendix C) which should be used with this program.

### Program

The program makes use of the routine print_num introduced in Section 6.2.2 to print the results as decimal numbers on the screen:

```
exercise_entry:
        call    make_set                ;Make the set A.
        mov     setA , ax

        call    make_set                ;Make the set B.
        mov     setB , ax

        mov     ax , setA
        and     ax , setB               ;Intersection.
        call    count_bits
        call    print_num               ;Print the answer to a).
        call    newline
```

```
        mov     ax , setA
        or      ax , setB               ;Union
        not     ax                      ;complemented.
        call    count_bits
        call    print_num               ;Print the answer to b).
        call    newline


        mov     ax , setA
        xor     ax , setB               ;Symmetric difference.
        call    count_bits
        call    print_num               ;Print the answer to c).
        call    newline


        jmp     finished                ;Exit.


;---------------------------------------------------------------
;
;
;Subroutines
;
;---------------------------------------------------------------



make_set:
        ;Creates a 1 word set representing the hex digits
        ;contained in the next number at the input.
        ;
        ;Skips spaces to locate the start of the next number.
        ;Numbers must be terminated by a space or cr, and a
        ;newline is printed on the screen.
        ;
        ;On exit,
        ;    AX contains the 1 word set.
        ;
        ;Affects registers used in dobdos calls.
        ;

        mov     ax , 0                  ;Create an empty set
        push    ax                      ;on the stack.

read_char:
        mov     ah , 1                  ;Console read function.
        call    dobdos                  ;Read a char into AL.
        cmp     al , space
        je      read_char               ;Skip spaces.
```

```
mask_loop:
        call    make_mask               ;Get a mask for the digit
                                        ;in AX.

        pop     bx                      ;Retrieve set from stack.
        or      ax , bx                 ;Mask in the new bit.
        push    ax                      ;Save set on stack again.

        mov     ah , 1
        call    dobdos                  ;Read the next digit.
        cmp     al , space
        je      mdone
        cmp     al , cr
        je      mdone                   ;Stop if a space or cr
                                        ;is encountered.
        jmp     mask_loop               ;Otherwise, repeat for
                                        ;the next digit.
mdone:
        call    newline
        pop     ax                      ;Exit with the set in AX.

        ret

;-----------------------------------------------------------


make_mask:
        ;Converts the hex digit in AL (in ASCII) into a bit mask.
        ;On entry,
        ;   AL contains an ASCII code.
        ;On exit,
        ;   AX contains the corresponding bit mask.
        ;
        ;Affects registers used in dobdos calls.
        ;

        cmp     al , '0'                ;Look for a digit 0-9.
        jb      error
        cmp     al , '9'
        ja      hex_A_to_F

        sub     al , '0'                ;Convert it to binary.
        jmp     hex_ok

        ;Not a 0 - 9 digit, look for A - F or a - f.
```

```
hex_A_to_F:
        and     al , 0dfh               ;Change char to upper-case.
        cmp     al , 'A'
        jb      error                   ;Fail if the character is
        cmp     al , 'F'                ;not a valid hex digit.
        ja      error

        sub     al , 'A'-10             ;Convert the A-F character
        jmp     hex_ok                  ;to the corresponding
                                        ;binary number.

error:
        jmp     finished                ;A recovery routine might
                                        ;be better here.

        ;The binary code of the hex digit 0-F is in AL.
        ;Use this as the shift count to create the mask.

hex_ok:
        mov     cl , al                 ;Place shift count in CL.
        mov     ax , 1                  ;The initial bit pattern.
        shl     ax , cl                 ;Shift left by 'count'
                                        ;places to create the one-
                                        ;bit mask.
        ret                             ;With the mask in AX.


;-------------------------------------------------------------


count_bits:
        ;Counts the number of 1's in the word in AX.
        ;On entry,
        ;   AX contains the word to count.
        ;On exit,
        ;   AX contains the count.
        ;
        ;Affects registers BX and CX.
        ;

        mov     cx , 16                 ;The loop count.
        mov     bx , 0                  ;Zero BX to hold the count.

shift_loop:
        shl     ax , 1                  ;Shift 1 place left and
        adc     bx , 0                  ;add the carry flag to BX.
```

```
        loop    shift_loop              ;Repeat CX times.

        ;Move the count to AX and exit.

        mov     ax , bx

        ret

;------------------------------------------------------------


print_num:
        ;See Section 6.2.2

;------------------------------------------------------------


newline:
        ;Outputs a carriage return and line feed character.
        ;
        ;Affects registers used by dobdos calls.
        ;

        mov     ah , 2                  ;Output char DOS function.
        mov     dl , cr                 ;Carriage return code.
        call    dobdos

        mov     ah , 2
        mov     dl , lf                 ;Line feed code.
        call    dobdos

        ret

;------------------------------------------------------------
```

## 8.1.4  Register and flag setting

The logical operators are sometimes useful for initializing registers and for setting flags. These features are well-illustrated in the print_num subroutine of Section 6.2.2 where an eXclusive-OR operation is used as a means of zeroing a register:

```
xor     dx , dx
```

To examine why this sets DX to zero, consider the XOR at a bit-by-bit level. Each bit of DX is XORed with itself. Thus, we have only the possibilities of 0 XOR 0 or 1 XOR 1 which, in both cases, yields 0. However, since this is considerably more obscure than:

```
mov      dx , 0
```

we need to justify the use of such a devious technique over and above the trivial saving of one clock cycle. In fact, the two instructions do not have quite the same effect, since MOV does not affect the status flags whereas XOR does. Thus, we can guarantee that the zero flag will be set after the XOR case but not after the MOV instruction. And, vital to routines in which arithmetic is being performed, the carry will be set to zero by the XOR operation.

Sometimes the lack of effect on the flags of a MOV instruction can be used to advantage: in order to load a register before making a jump conditional on a previously set flag, for example. At other times this same policy is a nuisance. For example, suppose we wish to load the accumulator with an integer stored in memory and to make a jump depending on whether its value is zero or not. The problem here is that:

```
mov      ax , anumber
```

is not sufficient alone to set the zero flag according to the value of anumber. The general solution which will work for comparisons with any value is to follow the MOV with a compare instruction:

```
cmp      ax , 0
```

This will set all relevant flags correctly. In the special cases of testing for positive, zero or negative contents, however, a commonly used alternative is a logical OR of the register with itself:

```
or       ax , ax
```

A logical AND is equally effective: neither has any effect on the register contents but both set the relevant flags. An example of this use of logical operations is also shown in the print_num subroutine in Section 6.2.2.


## 8.2  ARITHMETIC

As introduced in Section 4.3.2, there are instructions defined in the 8086 for addition and subtraction of 8-bit and 16-bit integers, with two's complement representation for negative numbers. Instructions to multiply two integers of 8 or 16 bits, or to divide integers of 16 or 32 bits are also provided. This section considers extensions to these basic instructions to permit arithmetic on multiple length integers; to examine the 8086 facilities for binary-coded decimal handling; and to consider arithmetic on floating-point fractions.

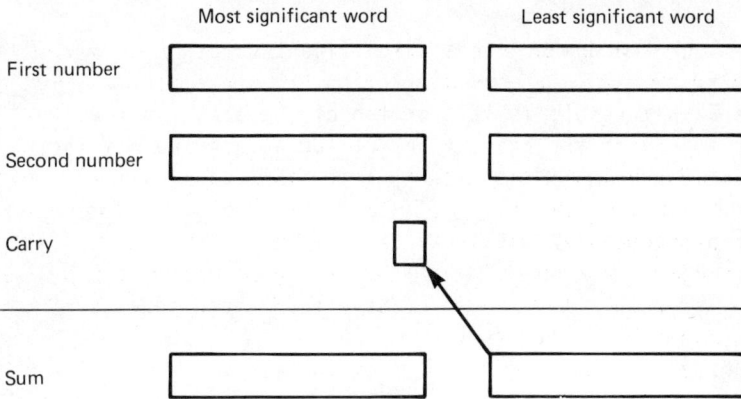

**Figure 8.1**  Addition of 32-bit signed integers.

### 8.2.1   Multiple-length binary integers

It was explained in Section 3.2 that the range of two's complement integers in a word is $-2^{n-1}$ to $2^{n-1}-1$, where n is the wordlength. Thus, using 16-bit arithmetic, a range of $-32\,768$ to $32\,767$ is possible. In many circumstances this range is too small and we may wish to use perhaps 3- or 4-byte integers. A 4-byte integer has a two's complement range of about plus or minus $2 \times 10^9$, for example. The following algorithms are developed to perform arithmetic on 2-word (32-bit) integer values. Whenever such integers are stored on the stack the most significant 16-bit word of the integer is stored on top of the least significant word.

Addition and subtraction of 32-bit signed integers is quite straightforward on the 8086. Addition is carried out by adding the least and most significant words of the numbers separately, remembering to pass over the carry from the least to the most significant sums as shown in Figure 8.1.

The instruction set contains the operations needed to perform both the least significant word sum (ADD) and the add with carry in the most significant word position (ADC). A subroutine to perform this double word addition is:

```
double_add:
        ;A 32-bit add subroutine.
        ;On entry,
        ;  the two 32-bit numbers to add are on top of the stack
        ;  in the order
        ;           1st number, most significant word (m.s.w.)
        ;           1st number, least significant word (l.s.w.)
        ;           2nd number, most significant word
```

```
;                 2nd number, least significant word.
;On exit,
;   the 32-bit result is left on top of the stack, m.s.w.
;   on top, with the carry flag set for a carry out of the
;   32-bit sum.
;
;Affects registers AX, BX, CX, DX, SI.

pop     si                      ;Save the return address.

pop     ax                      ;1st no. m.s.w.
pop     bx                      ;1st no. l.s.w.
pop     cx                      ;2nd no. m.s.w.
pop     dx                      ;2nd no. l.s.w.

add     bx , dx                 ;Add the l.s. words.

adc     ax , cx                 ;Add m.s. words with carry.

push    bx
push    ax                      ;Save the result on stack.

push    si                      ;Restore the return address

ret
```

Subtraction of 32-bit signed integers is performed in an identical manner except that the subtract (SUB) and subtract with borrow (SBB) instructions replace ADD and ADC respectively. The above routine can be extended to cater for triple word integers, and so on, using 'add with carry' instructions on all pairs of words except the least significant pair.

Multiplication of $n$-word integers requires a slightly more complicated translation to make use of the 16-bit MUL instruction. Two 32-bit integers will in general produce a 64-bit (4-word) result when multiplied together. An algorithm is derived as follows:

Consider two 32-bit numbers $a$ and $b$, each made up of two words such that:

$$a = 2^{16}a_1 + a_0$$

and:

$$b = 2^{16}b_1 + b_0$$

Thus:

$$a \star b = (2^{16}a_1 + a_0)(2^{16}b_1 + b_0)$$
$$= 2^{32}a_1b_1 + 2^{16}(a_1b_0 + a_0b_1) + a_0b_0$$

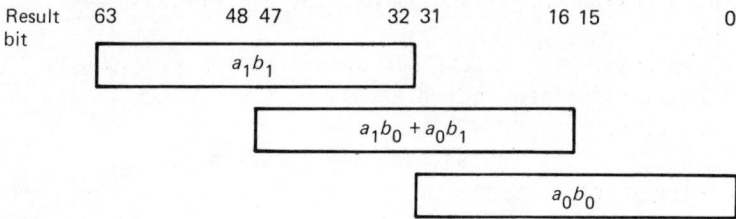

**Figure 8.2** 2-word multiply by partial products.

From this it can be seen that a 2-word multiply can be generated from a set of four partial products, each of which can be produced using the unsigned 8086 multiply instruction. This can be represented by Figure 8.2.

A correction is needed to handle signed two's complement multiplication in two words, according to the rules:

if $a$ is negative, subtract $b \times 2^{32}$ from the result
if $b$ is negative, subtract $a \times 2^{32}$ from the result

A subroutine to perform 32-bit signed multiplication on stack based operands is:

```
double_mult:
        ;32-bit multiplication, producing a 64-bit result.
        ;On entry,
        ;   the two 32-bit operands are on the stack
        ;   (most significant word first).
        ;On exit,
        ;   the 64-bit result is left on the stack.
        ;
        ;Affects registers AX, BX, CX, DX, BP, SI, DI.
        ;

        pop     si                      ;Save the return address.

        ;Unstack the operands.

        pop     bx                      ;a1
        pop     cx                      ;a0
        pop     di                      ;b1
        pop     bp                      ;b0

        push    si                      ;Restore return address.
```

```
            ;Make up the sign correction from a and b in DX:AX.

            xor     ax , ax
            xor     dx , dx         ;Zero DX:AX.


            or      bx , bx         ;Set the sign flag for a.
            jge     try_b

            ; a is negative, move   b to DX:AX.

            mov     dx , di
            mov     ax , bp

try_b:
            or      di , di         ;Set the sign flag for b.
            jge     signout

            ; b is negative, add a to DX:AX.

            add     ax , cx
            adc     dx , bx

            ;Save the correction on the stack.

signout:
            push    ax
            push    dx

            ;Form the partial products.

            mov     ax , bx
            mul     di              ;a1b1
            push    ax
            push    dx              ;Save on the stack.

            mov     ax , cx
            mul     bp              ;a0b0
            push    ax
            push    dx              ;Save on the stack.

            mov     ax , bx
            mul     bp              ;a1b0
            push    ax
            push    dx
```

```
         mov     ax , cx
         mul     di               ;a0b1
         push    ax
         push    dx


         call    double_add       ;a1b0 + a0b1, on stack.


;Now form the total product in four words in DI:BX:CX:DX
;(DI most significant).

         pop     bx               ;a1b0 + a0b1 m.s.w.
         pop     ax               ;a1b0 + a0b1 l.s.w.


         pop     cx               ;a0b0 m.s.w.
         pop     dx               ;a0b0 l.s.w.


         pop     di               ;a1b1 m.s.w.
         jnc     skip_inc         ;If it is set, add in
         inc     di               ;the carry from the above
                                  ;double add.
skip_inc:
         add     cx , ax          ;a0b0 m.s.w+(a1b0+a0b1) l.s.w.


         pop     ax               ;a1b1 l.s.w.
         adc     bx , ax          ;+(a1b0+a0b1) m.s.w.


;DI already contains a1b1 m.s.w., but add
;in any carry from the above.


         jnc     sign_correction
         inc     di


;Now subtract the sign correction on top of the stack
;from the two most significant words (DI:BX).


sign_correction:
         pop     bp               ;Correction m.s.w.
         pop     ax               ;Correction l.s.w.
         sub     bx , ax
         sbb     di , bp


;Stack the result, m.s.w. on top.


         pop     si               ;Save the return address.
```

```
        push    dx
        push    cx
        push    bx
        push    di

        push    si              ;Restore return address.

        ret
```

Division of a 64-bit numerator by a 32-bit denominator is considerably more difficult than the multiplication case above since we are not able to make use of partial divisions from DIV in the same simple way. An algorithm that is easier to write involves performing the division by repeatedly subtracting the denominator from the numerator as many times as possible, after which the count is the quotient.

### 8.2.2  Binary coded decimal arithmetic

BCD arithmetic was introduced in Section 3.4 as an attractive alternative to binary arithmetic in some circumstances. It is supported in the 8086 with two special instructions which take note of the carry (and auxiliary carry) flag setting in order to make the necessary decimal adjustments following an add or subtract operation. BCD digits, packed two to a byte, can be added together using the normal ADD (or ADC) instruction but the destination register should be AL in order to use the adjust instruction. All the necessary BCD adjustments referred to in Section 3.4 are performed by this one instruction (DAA). A 4-digit BCD add subroutine is:

```
bcd_add:
        ;A 4-digit BCD add subroutine (positive integers only).
        ;On entry,
        ;   BX:CX contain the 4-digit packed BCD integers.
        ;on exit,
        ;   DX contains the BCD sum.
        ;
        ;Affects AX.
        ;

        ;Sum the least significant pairs of digits first.

        mov     al , bl
        add     al , cl
        daa                     ;Decimal adjust.
```

```
        mov     dl , al

        ;Sum the most significant pairs.

        mov     al , bh
        adc     al , ch                 ;Remembering the carry.
        daa                             ;Adjust.

        ;(We could test the carry flag here for overflow)

        mov     dh , al                 ;Leave the result in DX.

        ret
```

Exchanging the ADD and ADC instructions for SUB and SBB, and replacing the decimal adjust for addition (DAA) by decimal adjust for subtraction (DAS) is sufficient to convert the above into a BCD subtract routine.

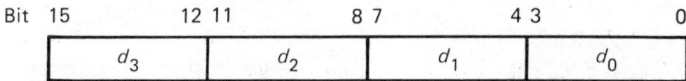

Bit   15            12 11          8 7          4 3          0

| $d_3$ | $d_2$ | $d_1$ | $d_0$ |
|---|---|---|---|

**Figure 8.3**  Packed BCD digits.

A representation of an integer number based on several BCD digits held in a single word is an example of a **packed** data structure. In the above subroutine, four BCD digits are assumed to be packed into a word in the organization shown in Figure 8.3, where $d_0$ is the least significant BCD digit. Packing BCD digits is a convenient way of reducing storage requirements and of keeping the digits of a number together, rather than spread across separately addressed bytes or words. The main penalty paid is the packing and unpacking time, which is not usually a barrier in BCD working, where the emphasis is usually on numerical simplicity rather than raw execution efficiency. Packing is normally carried out by using a combination of mask and shift instructions. The next example is for reading and packing a 4-digit BCD number.

```
get_packed_bcd:
        ;Reads a 4-digit BCD number and packs into a single word.
        ;If more than 4 digits are entered, only the last 4 are
        ;packed.
```

```
        ;The number must be terminated by a space.
        ;Other non-decimal characters are skipped.
        ;On exit,
        ;   AX contains the packed BCD number.
        ;
        ;Affects BX, CX & other registers used in dobdos calls.

        xor     bx , bx             ;Clear BX ready to receive
                                    ;packed digits.
read_digit_loop:
        push    bx

read_a_digit:
        mov     ah , 1
        call    dobdos              ;Read one character.

        and     al , 7fh            ;Strip parity.

        cmp     al , ' '            ;Look for terminating
        je      read_done           ;space.

        sub     al , '0'
        jb      read_a_digit        ;not 0-9
        cmp     al , 9
        jg      read_a_digit        ;not 0-9

        ;The BCD digit is in AL.

        pop     bx                  ;The packing word.
        mov     cl , 4              ;Set up the shift count.
        shl     bx , cl             ;Shift pattern 4 bits left
        or      bl , al             ;and mask in the new digit.

        jmp     read_digit_loop     ;Pack the next digit.

read_done:
        pop     ax                  ;Exit with the packed
                                    ;word in AX.

        ret
```

Note that replacing the constant count specified SHL instruction (SHL BX , CL) by four single-bit shifts of the form SHL BX , 1 could be preferred on efficiency grounds since the total shift would then take eight CPU cyles instead of 24 for the variable shift. This significant increase in speed is due to the lack of machine cycles to fetch the shift count in the CL register. It is not possible to make such a substitution, of course, in cases where a calculated value for the shift count is set in CL prior to a shift operation.

### 8.2.3  Unpacked decimal arithmetic

The 8086 also provides instructions to allow arithmetic to be performed on decimal digits held in unpacked format (i.e. one per byte). Similar 'adjust' instructions to the packed case above permit corrections to be made following addition or subtraction of two such digits. However, in this case, only single-digit numbers are added or subtracted rather than the pair of packed BCD digits considered above. We can perform multi-digit addition and subtraction by using the carry flag.

The instructions provided are called **ASCII adjust instructions** as opposed to the **decimal adjust instructions** used in packed BCD arithmetic. This stems from their potential use in performing arithmetic on single-character representations of decimal digits. The ASCII character codes for the digits range from 30hex to 39hex and addition may be performed directly on two such codes, with the result corrected by the ASCII adjust for addition (AAA) instruction, as in the three examples shown in Figure 8.4:

|  | $3+4$ |  | $3+8$ |  | $8+9$ |
|---|---|---|---|---|---|
| ASCII codes of | | 33 | | 33 | | 38 |
| digits to add | | 34 | | 38 | | 39 |
| After ADD | 0 | 7 | 1 | 1 | 1 | 7 |
| After AAA | AH | AL | AH | AL | AH | AL |

Filler of 6 added to AL and carry of '1' (auxiliary flag) added to AH.

**Figure 8.4**   ASCII adjust for addition.

Note that the result of the ADD must end up in AL for correction and that a 2-digit decimal result is produced in AH (tens digit) and AL (units digit). AH must be zero initially. It is also apparent that there is no need to convert the digits from ASCII codes to binary decimals before addition (by masking with 0fh or subtracting the code for 0, for example) since one action of AAA is to blank out the upper four bits of the corrected result in AL. The equivalent instruction for correcting a subtraction is ASCII adjust for subtraction (AAS).

In fact, the 8086 goes one step further and provides correction instructions for single-digit multiplication and for division of a 2-decimal-digit number (single-digit result). For multiplication, the ASCII adjust for multiply (AAM) instruction is issued following a multiplication of two, single unpacked decimal digits (*not* ASCII coded). MUL is used between two single-byte operands to produce a 16-bit result in AX (AH:AL). The action of AAM is to extract the tens digit of the result out of AL and to place this in AH, leaving the units digit in AL, as shown in Figure 8.5.

|  | exampie 1 $2 \times 3$ | example 2 $4 \times 6$ |
|---|---|---|
| single unpacked decimal digit operands | 3 2 | 6 4 |
| After MUL | 0    6 | 0    18 (hex) |
| After AAM | 0    6 | 2    4 |
|  | AH  AL | AH  AL |

**Figure 8.5**   ASCII adjust for multiplication.

Note that the correction will not work in the multiply case if ASCII coded operands are used. In division, the adjustment process is slightly different in that the ASCII adjust for division (AAD) is issued *before* the division takes place. Its action is to reverse the process described for AAM: to recombine the tens digit with the units digit of the numerator to give the correct binary pattern in AX for subsequent division by DIV, as in Figure 8.6.

|  | 24/4 | | 27/4 | |
|---|---|---|---|---|
| numerator (in AH:AL) | 2 | 4 | 2 | 7 |
| After AAD (in AH:AL) | 0 | 18 (hex) | 0 | 1B (hex) |
| denominator (in, e.g. BL) |  | 4 |  | 4 |
| After DIV | 0 | 6 | 3 | 6 |
|  | AH | AL | AH | AL |

Remainder

**Figure 8.6**   ASCII adjust for division.

The integer result of the division is returned in AL (upper four bits zero), with the remainder placed in AH.

### 8.2.4    The 8087 Numeric Processor

Commercial software and hardware packages are available on some computer systems to provide arithmetic facilities, particularly in respect of floating-point arithmetic. A particularly relevant component in the 8086 family is the 8087 Numeric Processor Extension.

This powerful piece of hardware may be added to computer systems based on the 8086 or 8088 the processor and it is designed to be interfaced to this CPU. It provides a comprehensive range of arithmetic operations on numbers defined in the formats shown in Table 8.1.

**Table 8.1**    8087 Data types.

| Data type | Bits | Significant digits | Approximate range |
|---|---|---|---|
| Word integer | 16 | 4 | $-32\,768 < X < 32\,767$ |
| Short integer | 32 | 9 | $-2 \times 10^9 < X < 2 \times 10^9$ |
| Long integer | 64 | 18 | $-9 \times 10^{18} < X < 9 \times 10^{18}$ |
| Packed decimal | 80 | 18 | $-99...99 < X < 99...99$ (18 digits) |
| Short real | 32 | 6–7 | $8.43 \times 10^{-37} < |X| < 3.37 \times 10^{38}$ |
| Long real | 64 | 15–16 | $4.19 \times 10^{-307} < |X| < 1.67 \times 10^{308}$ |
| Temporary real | 80 | 19 | $3.4 \times 10^{-4932} < |X| < 1.2 \times 10^{4932}$ |

The data formats include multi-word integer representations as well as a choice of floating-point reals (see Section 3.3.2). The presence of an 8087 chip enhances the programming model of the CPU; it adds new data types, new registers and new instructions while still appearing to be a single processor. Internally, the 8087 provides eight further registers, each of 80 bits. All internal computations are performed between numbers in temporary real (80-bit) format and converted to the chosen type, normally without the programmer being aware of the switch. The internal registers are used by some instructions as a register stack, with operands stripped from the top of this stack. Other instructions address specific registers directly. A list of the principal operations provided by the 8087 is given in Table 8.2.

In programming these arithmetic functions, the user may not need to be aware of the separate existence of a numerical processor. We may use the additional instructions as if they were normal CPU instructions. Under favourable circumstances, however, we may take advantage of its separate existence in order to perform an arithmetic operation in parallel with normal CPU activity – in other words, to initiate a computation but leave it to complete autonomously on the 8087 while we perform some other process in the CPU. Built-in facilities provide the necessary coordination between the two processes.

**Table 8.2**    Principal 8087 instructions.

| Class | Instructions |
|-------|--------------|
| Data Transfer | Load (all data types), Exchange |
| Arithmetic | Add, Subtract, Multiply, Divide, Subtract Reversed, Square Root, Scale, Remainder, Integer Part, Change Sign, Absolute Value, Extract |
| Comparison | Compare, Examine, Test |
| Transcendental | Tangent, Arctangent, $2^x - 1$, $Y.Log_2(X + 1)$, $Y.Log_2(X)$ |
| Constants | $0, 1, \pi, Log_{10}2, Log_e2, Log_210, Log_2e$ |
| Processor control | Load Control Word, Store Control Word, Store Status Word, Load Environment, Store Environment, Save, Restore, Enable Interrupts, Disable Interrupts, Clear Exceptions, Initialize |

Most importantly, the 8087 monitors all operations in an attempt to detect errors and to provide exception handling procedures for sensible treatment of such errors.

For some systems it may be possible to obtain a software arithmetic package which will provide similar or identical facilities to the 8087 except, of course, in execution speed. A typical performance improvement of between 10 and 100 times will be evident when using an 8087, but precise differences will vary wildly depending on the application.

# 9 | Block Data Operations

## 9.1 STRUCTURED DATA OBJECTS

Data used in programs so far have consisted of bytes, which are used typically to represent characters, and words, which are used typically to represent numbers. Often a representation is required of a larger object which may consist of several smaller components. We have already encountered a simple example of such an object. The bdos function 9, which prints a message on the screen, recognizes a series of bytes as a character string terminated by the dollar character. The 8086, in common with many processors, has little in-built conception of data beyond bytes and words. Any higher structure is in the mind of the programmer and a representation of this structure in terms of bytes and words must be created within the program. Most high-level programming languages provide abstract data objects which assist in the creation of customized structures. Typical of such provisions are strings, arrays and records. A **string** is a sequence of characters with an indication of its length. An **array** is a table of like objects, each being identified by a number showing its position within the table. A **record** is a group of objects (called fields), often of different sizes. Each field is identified by a name which locates its position relative to the start of the record.

Each of these three structures can be used to represent an item of data composed of many parts but conveniently considered to be one unit. This chapter describes how these three structures may be simulated in assembly language. Before they are dealt with individually, a group of 8086 instructions called the string instructions are described. Despite their name, they are used for all three structures and could more aptly be named the block data instructions.

## 9.2 THE STRING INSTRUCTIONS

The string instructions make use of the following registers:

| | |
|---|---|
| SI | The source byte/word |
| DI | The destination byte/word |
| AL/AX | The alternative source or destination byte/word |
| CX | The repetition count |

The five string instructions make use of the SI and DI registers, or one of these two registers plus the AL or AX register. Each instruction may be repeated a number of times as specified by the CX register. Each of the five string instructions has two forms. The first form operates on a byte and the second form operates on a word. The two forms are indicated to the assembler by adding either the letter B or the letter W to the mnemonic.

The five string instructions are:

| Mnemonic | Meaning | Registers used |
|----------|---------|----------------|
| MOVS | Move | SI DI |
| CMPS | Compare | SI DI |
| LODS | Load | SI AL/AX |
| STOS | Store | AL/AX DI |
| SCAS | Scan | AL/AX DI |

The SI and DI registers contain the offset of the byte or word operand involved. When involved in a string instruction, the SI register points to the source operand and the DI register points to the destination operand. Additionally the SI and/or DI registers are altered as appropriate. The registers are altered by one if the string instruction was a byte operation and they are altered by two if the string instruction was a word operation. The next such string instruction will then operate on the next byte or word in sequence.

The registers SI and DI can be altered either by being incremented or by being decremented. The status flag D (direction) can be set or cleared by the instructions STD and CLD. If the D flag is clear then the SI and/or DI registers are automatically incremented by one or two. If the D flag is set then the SI and/or DI registers are automatically decremented by one or two. Throughout this chapter it is assumed that the D flag is clear. When mention is made of either the SI or the DI register being incremented by a string instruction, it should be read that they would have been decremented instead if the D flag were set at the time. The skeleton program ensures that the D flag is clear before the main program starts.

The individual instructions are now examined in detail.

### MOVS   Move string   (Move source to destination)

This instruction moves one byte or word from the offset given by the SI register to the offset given by the DI register. Both registers are then incremented.

For example:

SI contains 100

DI contains 200

The instruction:

```
movsb
```

copies the byte at offset 100 into offset 200 and then increments SI and DI by one to become 101 and 201 respectively.

The instruction:

```
movsw
```

copies the word at offset 100 (bytes 100 and 101) into the word at offset 200 (bytes 200 and 201) and then increments SI and DI by two to become 102 and 202 respectively. No other register is affected.

### CMPS  Compare string  (Compare the source operand with the destination operand)

This instruction compares the source operand addressed by SI with the destination operand addressed by DI. The status flags are set accordingly. The two registers are then incremented by one for the CMPSB instruction and by two for the CMPSW instruction.

### LODS  Load string  (Load source operand into AL or AX)

This instruction loads the source operand addressed by SI into the AL register in the case of LODSB and into the AX register in the case of LODSW. The SI register is then incremented accordingly. Neither the DI register nor the operand addressed by it is altered by this instruction.

### STOS  Store string (Store AL or AX into the destination operand)

This instruction stores either the AL register (STOSB) or the AX register (STOSW) into the destination operand addressed by the DI register. The DI register is then incremented accordingly. Neither SI nor the source operand addressed by SI is affected.

### SCAS  Scan string  (Compare AL or AX with the destination operand)

This instruction compares the AL register (SCASB) or the AX register (SCASW) with the destination operand addressed by DI. The relevant status flags are then set by the result and the DI register is incremented accordingly. Neither the SI register nor the source operand addressed by it is affected.

### Repeated string instructions

As described so far, the string instructions do not appear to perform operations on strings – multiples of bytes or words. The string instructions may, however, be prefixed by the special instruction REP (repeat). This prefix has two forms, REPE and REPNE which stand for 'repeat while equal' and 'repeat while not equal' respectively. The distinction between the two only arises when prefixing one of the two compare string instructions CMPS or SCAS. By convention, the other three string instructions are prefixed by REPE. The assembler will recognize the mnemonic REP as being equivalent to REPE.

The effect of prefixing a string instruction by the repeat instruction is to obey that string instruction repeatedly. For the string instructions MOVS, LODS and STOS, the number of times that the instruction is obeyed is given by the CX register. The CX register is decremented by one each time the string instruction is obeyed. Note that the CX register is always decremented whether the D flag is set or clear. When the value in the CX register becomes zero, the repetition ceases and execution of the program continues with the instruction following the string instruction. If the CX register contains zero when the repeat prefix is encountered for the first time, the string instruction is not obeyed at all.

For example:

```
mov     cx , 200              ;Load the count 200.
mov     si , offset table1    ;Table1 is the source.
mov     di , offset table2    ;Table2 is the
                              ;   destination.
rep     movsb                 ;Move CX (200) bytes.
                              ;CX is now zero.
```

The above instructions will copy 200 bytes from table1 into table2. The MOVSB instruction is obeyed 200 times and each time the CX register is decremented by one. After the above instructions have been obeyed, the CX register will contain zero, the SI register will contain the offset of table1 plus 200 and the DI register will contain the offset of table2 plus 200.

When the prefixed string instruction is either one of the compare instructions CMPS or SCAS the repetition is governed by two factors. As before, the CX register is decremented on each repetition and the repetitions cease when this register contains zero. The instruction is not obeyed at all if CX contains zero at the start. With the compare string instructions, the repetition may cease prematurely if the comparison is not equal. If the prefix used is REPNE then the comparison will cease prematurely if an equal comparison is found. The testing of the equal status flag is performed after the comparison and so its initial value is not important. The prefix REPE (or REP) should be read as 'repeat while equal (zero flag is set) but no more than CX times'. The prefix REPNE should be read as 'repeat while not equal (zero flag is clear) but no more then CX times'.

The effect of prefixing a string instruction by either REPE or REPNE is summarized next. Note that for the first three instructions there is no distinction between REPE and REPNE – the setting of the zero flag is not examined. This fact is made more apparent by using the mnemonic REP instead. This is equivalent to REPE.

MOVS, LODS or STOS prefixed by REP (e.g. REP MOVSB)

1. If CX = 0 then skip to next instruction.
2. Decrement CX by one.
3. Perform the string instruction.

4. Go back to step 1.

CMPS or SCAS prefixed by REPE

1. If CX = 0 then skip to next instruction.

2. Decrement CX by one.

3. Perform the string instruction.

4. If status is equal (zero flag is set) then go back to step 1.

CMPS or SCAS prefixed by REPNE

1. If CX = 0 then skip to next instruction.

2. Decrement CX by one.

3. Perform the string instruction.

4. If status is not equal (zero flag is clear) then go back to step 1.

The practical uses of repeating a string instruction are as follows:

### REP MOVS
Move (copy) CX bytes or words from the source offset in SI to the destination offset in DI. A large area of memory can be quickly copied in this way.

### REP LODS
Load into AL or AX the CX bytes or words at the source offset in SI. As each load into either AL or AX will overwrite the previous value the net effect has no practical use.

### REP STOS
Copy the value in AL or AX into the CX bytes or words at the destination offset in DI. A large number of bytes or words can quickly be set to one value.

### REPE CMPS
Compare the CX bytes or words at the source offset in SI with their counterparts at the destination offset in DI, stopping prematurely if an unequal pair of bytes or words is found. After this repeated instruction the equal flag will be set if all CX operands were equal and the CX register will contain zero. If the equal flag is not set then a pair of operands was found to be unequal. In the latter case the CX register will indicate the position of the unequal pair. The relative position of the pair is calculated by subtracting the value in the CX register from its original value. This produces the number of comparisons made including the first mismatch.

### REPNE CMPS
Compare the CX bytes or words at the source offset in SI with their counterparts at the destination offset in DI, stopping prematurely if an equal pair of bytes or words is found. After this repeated instruction the equal flag will be clear if all CX operands were unequal and

the CX register will contain zero. If the equal flag is set then a pair of operands was found to be equal. In the latter case the CX register will indicate the position of the equal pair.

### REPE SCAS

Compare the AL or AX register with each of the CX bytes or words starting at the destination offset in DI, stopping prematurely if a mismatch is found. After this repeated instruction the equal flag will be set if all CX bytes or words were equal to the value in AL or AX. The CX register will contain zero. If the equal flag is clear then one of the bytes or words was unequal and the value in the CX register will indicate its position.

### REPNE SCAS

Compare the AL or AX register with each of the CX bytes or words starting at the destination offset in DI, stopping prematurely if a match is found. After this repeated instruction the equal flag will be clear if all CX bytes or words were unequal to the value in AL or AX. The CX register will contain zero. If the equal flag is set then one of the bytes or words was equal and the value in the CX register will indicate its position.

As an example the CMPSB instruction, prefixed firstly by REPNE and then by REPE, will be used to locate an equal substring within two strings and at the same location in each string:

```
mov     cx , length_of_strings
mov     si , offset string1
mov     di , offset string2

repne   cmpsb                   ;Compare until a match.

jne     no_match                ;None matched.

mov     bx , cx                 ;Save CX in BX
mov     ax , cx                 ;and in AX.
repe    cmpsb                   ;Continue until a
                                ;mismatch.
sub     bx , cx                 ;The number of bytes
                                ;progressed.
                                ;If the substring ends at
                                ;the end of the main strings
                                ;then CX will not have been
                                ;decremented over the
                                ;last character. In this case
                                ;CX will be 0 and BX must be
                                ;incremented.
```

```
        or    cx , cx        ;Check CX.
        jne   match_found    ;BX is correct.
        inc   bx             ;Correct BX.

match_found:
        ;BX is the length of the substring.
        ;The substring is located at:
        ;(length_of_strings - AX - 1 + offset string)

                    .
                    .
                    .
                    .
                    .

no_match:

        ;No match was found.
        ;*******************
```

## 9.3  STRINGS

A string is a data object comprizing a sequence of characters. The
length of this sequence may vary. In practice, there is usually a
maximum length to this sequence chosen by the programmer. There
exist techniques to alter dynamically the number of bytes associated
with a data object but those methods are beyond the scope of this
chapter.

The simpler and more common representations of a string will be
used here. A string will always occupy a fixed space – the maximum
length that a string may be. The number of bytes within that space
which are occupied by the string will be indicated in some way. There
are two popular approaches to indicating this length. The first
approach is to include an extra byte or word within the string, at the
start, which contains the string's length. The second approach is to
terminate the string with a special value – typically zero. This terminator byte is also called a **sentinel**. For example, if the maximum
length of a string were decided upon as 80 bytes, the string
This is a string could be represented by these two approaches as
shown in Figure 9.1.

Note that the count of 16 and the terminator 0 refer to a word or
byte with that value and not to the values of the characters 1, 6 or 0.

These two representations have already been encountered in
connection with the bdos functions 9 and 10 which print and read
sequences of characters. Function 9 prints characters starting at a
given offset until a terminator character is found. The terminator

character in that case is the dollar character $, which is an unfortunate choice as it disallows that character from being part of the string. Function 10 reads characters into successive offsets in store and returns with a count of the characters inserted into the string.

| 16 | This is a string | | |
|----|------------------|--|--|

(a)

| This is a string | 0 | |
|------------------|---|--|

(b)

**Figure 9.1**    (a) Count of characters (b) Terminator.

The choice between these two representations is governed by a combination of the sorts of operations that are to be carried out and personal preference. Some operations on strings are so common that many programming languages provide them as simple functions. Routines to perform some such operations on strings using the terminator representation now follow. A program using these routines must include the following declarations in the data segment:

For DOS

```
max_string_length      equ      200  ;For example.
string_size            equ      max_string_length+1

string_input_buf       db       max_string_length , 0
                       db       string_size dup (0)
```

For CP/M-86

```
max_string_length      equ      200  ;For example.
string_size            equ      max_string_length+1

string_input_buf       db       max_string_length , 0
                       rb       string_size
```

The constant max_string_length is the size of the largest string available and may be altered as appropriate. The constant string_size is the length that a complete string will occupy and is one larger in order to allow room for the terminator of a maximum sized string.

Strings may then be declared, for example, as follows:

For DOS

```
new_string      db      string_size dup (0)
```

For CP/M-86

```
new_string        rb        string_size
```

The routines presented are:

```
copy_string
input_string
print_string
length_string
compare_string
sub_string
left_string
right_string
cat_string
```

Their operation is explained by comments within the listings and illustrates several useful techniques for manipulating string structures. Most of these routines will alter several registers and care should therefore be taken to save registers as required before calling the routine. Any routine requiring SI or DI to be set on entry will, however, save and restore those two registers.

```
copy_string:
                ;On entry SI contains the offset of the source string
                ;and DI contains the offset of the new string.
        call    length_string   ;Get length of SI string in CX.
        inc     cx               ;Add 1 to include the terminator.
        rep     movsb            ;Perform the copy.
        ret


;***********************

input_string:
                ;On entry DI has offset of new string to be read.
        mov     ah , 10                     ;Bdos 10 - read.
        mov     dx , offset string_input_buf    ;Area to read to.
        call    dobdos
        xor     ch , ch          ;zero CH
        mov     cl , string_input_buf+1     ;The length read.
        mov     si , offset string_input_buf+2  ;Start of string.
        rep     movsb                       ;Copy the string.
        xor     al,al                       ;Zero AL.
```

```
        stosb                               ;Store at the end.
        ret


;***********************

print_string:
            ;On entry SI has the offset of the string to print.
            ;Bdos function 9 cannot be used as the string
            ;may contain its dollar terminator.

        push    si                      ;Save SI
        lodsb                           ;Fetch byte of string.
        or      al , al                 ;Set flags according to AL.
        jz      done_print_string       ;Found terminator - stop.

        mov     dl , al                 ;Place char in DL.
        mov     ah , 2                  ;Print one char in DL.
        call    dobdos
        jmp     print_string            ;Continue.

done_print_string:
        pop     si                      ;Restore SI.
        ret


;***********************


length_string:
            ;On entry SI has the offset of the string to be
            ;measured.
            ;On exit CX contains the length, SI has been restored.
        push    si          ;Save SI.
        xor     cx          ;Zero CX to start with.
ls_loop:
        lodsb               ;Load the next char.
        or      al , al     ;Set flags according to AL.
        jz      done_length ;Found the terminator.
        inc     cx          ;Increment the counter.
        jmp     ls_loop     ;Continue.

done_length:
        pop     si          ;Restore SI.
        ret


;***********************
```

```
string_lengths:
                ;This routine is used by several of the following
                ;routines. It returns the length of the string in SI
                ;in BX and the length of the string in DI in AX.
        push    si              ;Save SI.
        call    length_string   ;Length of SI string.
        push    cx              ;Save it.
        mov     si , di         ;Prepare to get length of DI string.
        call    length_string   ;Get the length.
        mov     ax , cx         ;Put length of DI string in AX.
        pop     bx              ;Pop the saved length of SI string
                                ;into BX.
        pop     si              ;Restore SI.
        ret


;************************

compare_string:
                ;On entry SI has the offset of the string to be
                ;compared with the string with offset in DI.
                ;Because the terminator byte is zero, a correct
                ;(less than) comparison will occur if one string
                ;is shorter than the other.
        push    si              ;Save SI.
        push    di              ;Save DI.
        call    length_string   ;Get length of one string.
        inc     cx              ;Compare one extra byte.
        repe    cmpsb           ;Compare strings and set flags.
        pop     di              ;Restore DI.
        pop     si              ;Restore SI.
        ret


;************************

sub_string:
                ;On entry SI and DI contain offsets to strings.
                ;On exit the flags are set equal or not equal
                ;according to whether the SI string is within the
                ;DI string.
                ;Both SI and DI are preserved.
        push    si              ;Save SI.
        push    di              ;Save DI.
        call    string_lengths  ;Get both lengths.
        sub     ax , bx         ;Difference in length.
```

```
        jl        end_substring       ;Negative - substring is larger
                                       ;than the main string. The flags
                                       ;are already set not equal - return.
        inc       ax                  ;AX now contains the maximum
                                       ;number of tests required.
        xor       dx , dx             ;Zero counter DX. This will contain
                                       ;the start of the substring in the
                                       ;main string.

sub_string_loop:
        push      si
        push      di                  ;Save SI and DI.
        mov       cx , bx             ;Length of substring.
        repe      cmpsb               ;Compare it in main string.
        pop       di
        pop       si                  ;Restore SI and DI.
        je        end_sub_string      ;If CMPSB was equal return.
        inc       dx                  ;Now try one byte further in
                                       ;and so increment the counter
        inc       di                  ;and increment the starting point
                                       ;for the comparison.
        dec       ax                  ;Decrement count of maximum number
                                       ;of tries.
        jne       sub_string_loop     ;Continue if there are more to try.

        ;No match was found. The flags currently are set equal
        ;so any instruction which will set them unequal is required.

        inc       ax                  ;Increment AX to 1 - clear equal flag.

end_sub_string:
        pop       di                  ;Restore original DI.
        pop       si                  ;Restore original SI.
        ret


;************************

left_string:
                  ;On entry SI has the offset of a string. DI has the
                  ;offset of the destination string. CX is a count.
                  ;The DI string will become the first CX chars of
                  ;the SI string.
        cmp       cx , max_string_length
        jbe       cx_within_range         ;Don't permit a string above
                                          ;the maximum catered for.
        mov       cx , max_string_length  ;Only transfer the maximum.
```

```
cx_within_range:
    push    si
    push    di                  ;Save SI and DI.
    rep     movsb               ;Copy CX chars.
    xor     al , al             ;Zero AL and plant it at
    stosb                       ;the end of the new string.
    pop     di
    pop     si                  ;Restore SI and DI.
    ret


;************************

right_string:
            ;This function is similar to left_string except
            ;that the DI string becomes the last CX chars of the
            ;SI string.
    push    si
    push    di                  ;Save SI and DI.
    push    cx                  ;Save the count.
    call    length_string       ;Find length of source string.
    pop     ax                  ;Pop the saved count into AX.
    cmp     ax , cx             ;Compare this count with the
                                ;length of the main string.
    jbe     ok_right_string     ;Continue if this is within
                                ;the actual length.
    mov     ax , cx             ;Put into AX the length of the
                                ;main string.
ok_right_string:
    ;AX now contains the number of characters to move.
    ;CX contains the number of characters in the SI string.
    sub     cx , ax             ;This is the starting position
                                ;in SI for the move.
    add     si , cx             ;Add to SI.
    mov     cx , ax             ;Put the count into CX.
    inc     cx                  ;Add one so that the terminator
                                ;byte in the main string is
                                ;also moved.
    rep     movsb               ;Move the right string.
    pop     di
    pop     si                  ;Restore SI and DI.
    ret


;************************

cat_string:
            ;On entry SI and DI both contain string offsets.
```

```
                ;A copy of the SI string is copied to the end of
                ;the DI string. If there is not enough room, then
                ;as much as possible is copied.
        push    si
        push    di              ;Save SI and DI.
        call    string_lengths  ;SI length in BX, DI in AX.
        add     di , ax         ;DI now points to the 0
                                ;terminator in the DI string.
        add     ax , bx         ;Find the length of total new
                                ;string.
        sub     ax , max_string_length  ;Is it too large ?
        jle     copy_cat_string ;NO - continue.
        sub     bx , ax         ;Subtract the difference.

copy_cat_string:
        mov     cx , bx         ;Move the count into CX.
        inc     cx              ;Add one to include the 0
                                ;terminator.
        rep     movsb           ;Copy.
        pop     di
        pop     si              ;Restore SI and DI.
        ret
```

## 9.4  ARRAYS

An array is a table of data objects of which each has the same size. The objects are referred to by number, starting at zero, indicating their positions within the array. This number is called the object's **index**. The simplest form of array is where the objects are bytes or words. This form of array will be dealt with here. Objects which are larger than words would themselves be either arrays or records. This combination is dealt with in the next section.

The common operations on arrays are:
- declare;
- copy;
- compare;
- move through the array examining each object in turn;
- locate a particular object.

### Declaring an array
To declare an array the name, type (byte or word) and size is required. An array called numbers consisting of 10 words would be declared as:

For DOS

```
        numbers         dw      10 dup (?)
```

For CP/M-86

```
numbers          rw       10
```

For an array of bytes, the DW and RW are replaced with DB and RB respectively. Note that DOS permits each item to be initialized to a particular value. The declaration:

```
numbers          dw       10 dup (5)
```

would initialize all 10 words of the array to the value 5. Each word or byte of an array can be initialized to a particular individual value by listing those values. In both DOS and CP/M-86 the declaration:

```
numbers          dw       0,10,20,30,40,50,60,70,80,90
```

would create an array of 10 words, each word being initialized to the value shown.

Conceptually we would refer to the 10 words of the array numbers as numbers [0], numbers [1], ..., numbers [9]. The array has the *name* numbers, the *size* 10 and its *type* is word.

### Copying an array
The values in one array can be copied into another array of the same or larger size using the MOVS string instruction. To copy the array numbers as declared above into another like array called values, the following instructions could be used:

```
mov     si , offset numbers     ;Source array.
mov     di , offset values      ;Destination array.
mov     cx , 10                 ;Size of array.
rep     movsw                   ;Move CX words.
```

If the arrays concerned had been arrays of 10 bytes rather than 10 words, then the only change required would be that the MOVSB instruction be used instead of the MOVSW instruction.

### Compare two arrays
The comparison of two arrays is performed in the same manner as the above copy, except that the CMPS string instruction with a prefix of REPE is used. For example, we could compare the array numbers with the array values as follows:

```
mov     si , offset numbers     ;Source array.
mov     di , offset values      ;Destination array.
mov     cx , 10                 ;Size of array.
repe    cmpsw                   ;Compare a maximum
                                ;of CX words.
```

Following the comparison the flags will be set according to the last two words compared. If all 10 values are the same then the equal flag will be set – JE will jump. The JA, JB and JG, JL instructions can be used to jump according to the comparison of the first unequal pair of words.

### Move through an array

Often each object within the array is required in turn. For example, we may wish to print out the value of each object. In this case, the LODS string instruction is used. The CX register will again contain the size of the array but it will be decremented by the LOOP instruction. This form of loop was introduced in the last chapter. Assuming the existence of a routine print_num that prints out the value in the AX register and preserves the values held in the SI and CX registers, the following instructions would print out all 10 words in the array numbers:

```
            mov     si , offset numbers     ;Source array.
            mov     cx , 10                 ;Size of array.

    print_loop:
        lodsw                               ;Load word into
                                            ;AX from array.
            call    print_num
            loop    print_loop              ;Decrement CX and
                                            ;jump if CX is
                                            ;not yet zero.
```

For an array of bytes, the LODSB instruction would be used instead. Another example of this kind of array access is to examine each object of the array and perform some calculation on it. The result is then placed in the corresponding object of a second array. A second array called squares is created in this manner by the next listing. Each word in the squares array is the square of the value in the corresponding word in the numbers array.

```
    mov     si , offset numbers ;Source array numbers.
    mov     di , offset squares ;Destination array squares.
    mov     cx , 10             ;Size of the arrays.

square_loop:
    lodsw                       ;Fetch next word into AX.
    mul     ax                  ;Square it.
    stosw                       ;Store result in squares.
    loop    square_loop         ;Decrement CX and jump back
                                ;if more words to process.
```

As a final example we shall construct an array of 10 words whose values are calculated by adding together the corresponding words in two other 10-word arrays. The two source arrays are called arrayA and arrayB. The destination array is called arrayC. As there is only one string source register SI the register BX is used to access arrayB.

```
        mov     si , offset arrayA  ;Source 1 array.
        mov     bx , offset arrayB  ;Source 2 array.
        mov     di , offset arrayC  ;Destination array.
        mov     cx , 10             ;Size of the arrays.

add_loop:
        lodsw                       ;Fetch next arrayA word into AX.
        add     ax , word ptr [bx]  ;Add to AX the next arrayB word.
        stosw                       ;Store the result into arrayC.
        inc     bx                  ;Increment BX twice so that it
        inc     bx                  ;points to the next word in
                                    ;arrayB.
        loop    add_loop            ;Continue until all 10 are done.
```

The register BX is used to hold the successive offsets of each word in arrayB. While the LODSW instruction automatically increments the SI register by two, the BX register must be incremented twice explicitly. If the arrays are byte arrays, the program becomes:

```
        mov     si , offset arrayA  ;Source 1 array.
        mov     bx , offset arrayB  ;Source 2 array.
        mov     di , offset arrayC  ;Destination array.
        mov     cx , 10             ;Size of the arrays.
add_loop:
        lodsb                       ;Fetch next arrayA byte into AL.
        add     al , byte ptr [bx]  ;Add to AL the next arrayB byte.
        stosb                       ;Store the result into arrayC.
        inc     bx                  ;Increment BX so that it points
                                    ;to the next byte in arrayB.
        loop    add_loop            ;Continue until all 10 are done.
```

In such dealings with word arrays it is important to remember that all offsets are byte offsets and while string instructions such as LODSB and LODSW will increment SI as required, care must be taken when using other instructions on other registers.

### Locating a particular object

In order to locate a particular word or byte within an array, the offset of that word or byte must be calculated. If the index of the required word or byte is known at the time of writing the program then the calculation can be performed by the assembler. The array `numbers` consists of words called `numbers [0]` up to `numbers [9]`. `Numbers [3]` consists of bytes 6 and 7 within the array. The offset of `numbers [3]` is given as:

```
numbers + 6
```

or slightly more meaningfully:

```
numbers + 3*2
```

For a byte array no multiplication by two is required. If we wish to move the value between one of the array words and a register then the `MOV` instruction is used. If we wish to load the offset itself into a register then the `LEA` (load effective address) instruction is used.

For example:

```
mov     ax , numbers + 3*2
mov     numbers + 3*2 , dx
lea     bx , numbers + 3*2
```

If the index of the required word or byte is to be calculated within the program then one of the index registers `BX`, `SI` or `DI` should be used. The index is calculated and placed into one of these registers – say `BX`. The offset of the array can now be indexed by this register in order to address the required object. Supposing an array of bytes exists called `table`. The index of the required byte is calculated and placed in register `BX`. The offset of this byte is:

```
table [bx]
```

For an array of words one further manipulation is required. The byte offset of a particular index must be doubled to produce the offset of the required word. Doubling a value is accomplished easily in a binary representation. The value is shifted left by one bit position. The `SHL` instruction is thus applied to the `BX` register:

```
shl     bx , 1
```

After this instruction the `BX` register contains the correct byte offset to locate the required word. If `J` is the name of a memory word in which the required index of a word in the numbers array exists then the following instructions will locate that word:

```
mov     bx , J
shl     bx , 1
```

The value of that word may be moved between registers `AX` and `CX` and its offset can be loaded into register $I by the following instructions:

```
mov     ax , numbers [bx]
mov     numbers [bx] , cx
lea     si , numbers [bx]
```

Finally the special instruction XLAT (translate) should be considered in the context of arrays. It is an instruction which can be applied to byte arrays which are no larger than 256 bytes. Such arrays' indices will themselves fit into a byte. Individual values of such an array can be loaded into the AL register in a very straightforward manner. The XLAT instruction adds to the offset found in the BX register the value in register AL. The value of the byte with that resulting offset is then loaded into that same register AL. Assuming the existence of a byte array called table which is less than 257 bytes long then table [I] (where I is assumed to be a byte containing the required index) can be loaded into register AL by the following three instructions:

```
mov     bx , offset table
mov     al , I
xlat
```

## 9.5  RECORDS AND COMBINATION TYPES

A record is a data object which consists of several smaller data objects which may be of different sizes. Each such object within the record is called a field of that record and is identified by a unique name – known as the field-name. For example, a simple personnel record might list a person's surname, sex and age. One such record could be called Asst_Manager and is shown in Figure 9.2.

The entire structure is called Asst_Manager. Within this structure are three fields called Surname, Sex and Age. Other similar records could exist called, for example, Manager, Clerk, Typist etc. Each record would be of the same type – Personnel – and would contain three fields called Surname, Sex and Age. In order to identify a field of a record we need two items of information. First, we must identify the record – Clerk for example. Second, we specify the field's name within that record – Surname for example. The clerk's surname is identified by these two names and a common convention for writing this description is:

```
Clerk.Surname
```

The benefits of the record structure are twofold. Firstly, all information concerning one person can be referred to by one name – records may be copied and compared as a whole. Secondly, the same meaningful names – Surname, Sex and Age – can be used in many different records without confusion.

**Figure 9.2**  Asst_Manager record.

The way in which records can be represented in 8086 assembly language is now described.

### 9.5.1  Representation of records

A record is represented as each of its fields in order. The ordering of the fields is irrelevant as long as it is kept the same for each instance of such a record. The above personnel record has three fields which we could represent as follows:

1. Surname: 20 bytes containing characters.

2. Sex: One byte containing either M or F.

3. Age: One word containing a number.

If we envisage the fields in that order then the record can be drawn as shown in Figure 9.3.

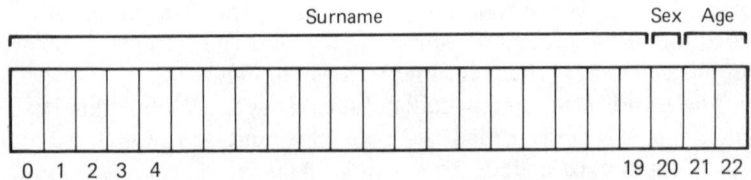

**Figure 9.3**  Personnel record.

Each field has then the following attributes:

| Name | Starting position | Length | Type |
|---|---|---|---|
| Surname | 0 | 20 | Byte |
| Sex | 20 | 1 | Byte |
| Age | 21 | 2 | Word |

Note that, while most people's age will comfortably fit into a byte, a word has been used in order to illustrate the manipulation of different sized objects within one record.

The whole record has a size of 23 bytes. In our program we could define several constants which are then used to declare records and access the fields of those records:

```
;Personnel record

;Relative field positions

Surname equ    0
Sex     equ    20
Age     equ    21

Personnel_size equ    23
```

Records can then be defined as occupying Personnel_size bytes:

For DOS
```
Clerk   db      Personnel_size dup (?)
Manager db      Personnel_size dup (?)
```

For CP/M-86
```
Clerk   rb      Personnel_size
Manager rb      Personnel_size
```

In both cases we can include initial values for each field:
```
Clerk   db      'Harrison            '
        db      'M'
        dw      42

Manager db      'Beatie              '
        db      'M'
        dw      45
```

Records may be copied using the string instruction MOVS:
```
mov     si , offset Clerk       ;Promotion of clerk
mov     di , offset Manager     ;to manager.
mov     cx , Personnel_size     ;No. of bytes to move.
rep     movsb                   ;Perform the copy.
```

Similarly records may be compared using the string instruction CMPS.

The individual field offsets are referred to by specifying the record offset and the field name:
```
offset Clerk + Surname
offset Manager + Age
```

The byte field Sex and the word field Age may be accessed as:

```
byte ptr Clerk + Sex
word ptr Manager + Age
```

Such fields may then be manipulated:

```
inc    word ptr Manager + Age          ;Birthday.
cmp    byte ptr Clerk + Sex , 'M'      ;Male ?
je     Male_Clerk
```

As the records were declared with byte attributes, the BYTE PTR prefix for the Sex byte is optional. The word ptr prefix must, however, be present.

Sometimes it is convenient to use one of the registers BX, SI or DI to contain the offset of a record. If this offset is placed in the BX register, the three fields may be referred to as:

```
byte ptr Surname [bx]
byte ptr Sex [bx]
word ptr Age [bx]
```

The next routine will print out the three fields of a personnel record. The record's offset must be present in register BX upon entry to the routine. The routine calls the print_num routine given in Chapter 6. The information is annotated by planting the fields' values into a message in the data segment declared thus:

```
Pmessage       db      'Name : '
Pm_Surname     db      '                       ',cr,lf
               db      'Sex : '
Pm_Sex         db      ' ',cr,lf
               db      'Age : $'

Pm_end         db      cr,lf,'$'
```

The routine is:

```
Personnel_print:
    ;BX contains the offset of a personnel record.
    ;Each field of this record is printed out.

    lea    si , byte ptr Surname [bx]  ;Move offset of the

                                       ;surname into SI.
    mov    di , offset Pm_Surname      ;Position in Pmessage
                                       ;to plant Surname.
    mov    cx , 20                     ;No. bytes in Surname.
    rep    movsb                       ;Copy into message.
```

```
        mov     al , byte ptr Sex [bx]      ;Fetch sex byte
        mov     Pm_Sex , al                 ;and place in message.

        mov     dx , offset Pmessage        ;Print out the message
        mov     ah , 9                      ;so far.
        call    dobdos

        mov     ax , word ptr Age [bx]      ;Fetch the age word.
        call    print_num                   ;Print out the value.

        mov     dx , offset Pm_end          ;Finish off with a
        mov     ah , 9                      ;new line.
        call    dobdos

        ret
```

### 9.5.2   Record representation in DOS

There is a facility available in the DOS macro assembler MASM only which assists considerably with the use of records. The structure of a record may be defined using the assembler pseudo-op STRUC. The personnel record could be defined as:

```
Personnel       struc
                Surname db 20 dup (' ')
                Sex     db 'M'
                Age     dw 0
Personnel       ends
```

Note that the name chosen for this record type – Personnel – must appear both at the beginning and at the end of the definition. Following the above declaration, the name Personnel may be used to declare some records:

```
Clerk   Personnel
Manager Personnel
```

The names Clerk and Manager may be used as before. The fields will be initialized to the values given in the definition of Personnel. The fields may be initialized to other discrete values in certain circumstances. Refer to the MASM manual for details of this facility. The fields are referred to by following a record name with a dot and then the field-name. No byte or word attribute need be given as this is deduced from the structure definition.

For example:

```
mov     al , Manager.Sex
lea     si , Manager.Surname
```

Alternatively, if the offset of a record is placed in a base or index register such as BX then the fields are referred to as:

```
mov     [bx].Sex , al
inc     [bx].Age
```

This facility in the MASM assembler greatly enhances the readability of programs using records and increases the convenience to the programmer considerably.

### 9.5.3  Combination types

An array is a table of data objects of the same type. A record is a list of data objects of different types. Both are themselves data objects. A record has already been described which contains as one of its fields an array. In general records may contain records and/or arrays. Arrays may have as their elements objects which are records or arrays. A two dimensional array is in fact simply an array where each element is an array. For example, a two dimensional array of words can be represented as follows. The first dimension – the rows – is indexed from zero to nine. The second dimension – the columns – is indexed from zero to four. The array is called matrix. The array matrix is an array of 10 elements indexed from zero to nine. Each of these 10 elements is itself an array of five words which are indexed from zero to four. In order to locate a particular word, the following procedure is adopted.

To locate matrix(X,Y):

1. Locate the offset of row X.
   Each row is five words long. The byte offset is therefore:
   ```
   matrix + (X * 10)
   ```
2. Locate the relative offset of word Y in row X.
   The byte offset of word Y within its row is:
   ```
   Y * 2
   ```
3. The final offset is the sum of these two:
   ```
   matrix + (X * 10) + (Y * 2)
   ```

The size of the array matrix is 50 words, as it is 10 arrays each of five words. This array could then be declared as:

For DOS

```
matrix  dw      50 dup (?)
```

For CP/M-86

```
matrix  rw      50
```

The instructions to locate the word matrix(X,Y) are now given. It is assumed that values of X and Y are contained in registers AX and BX.

```
shl     bx , 1              ;Multiply BX (Y) by 2.
mov     cx , 10             ;Prepare to multiply AX by 10.
mul     cx                  ;Multiply AX (X) by CX (10).
add     bx , ax             ;Compute final result into BX.
add     bx , offset matrix  ;Add the main offset.

;BX now contains the offset of the word matrix(X,Y)

mov     ax , word ptr [bx]  ;AX now contains matrix(X,Y).
```

In the same way, where the array is an array of records, the offset of a particular record is calculated as:

index ∗ size of the record + offset of the array

This offset is then used in the same way as the offset of a single record.

Similarly where a field of a record is an array, all that is required to access that array is its offset. This is calculated as the offset of the record plus the relative offset of the array field.

Such complex structures are rarely needed in most programs but in certain contexts their use can be most convenient. It is a worthwhile exercise to invent a complicated structure and then discover how you would access each elementary data item within it.

# 10 | Programming Methodology

## 10.1 INTRODUCTION

The purpose of this chapter is to suggest programming methods which result in programs that perform as they were intended to. This aim may appear simple and obvious but there are many instances of programs which seem to work correctly until a certain set of circumstances arises and the program fails. The outcome is usually that of varying degrees of embarrassment and expense, but life itself has been endangered by program errors. Amongst the more common classic 'computer errors' is the invoicing program which sends final demands for payment of 0.00. A more subtle error was found in the program which controlled a particular Venus space probe. The error occurred in a section of code designed to adjust the final approach of the craft. Instead the probe was sent several million miles from its target.

Such errors are commonly called 'bugs'. There are established methods of writing programs so that bugs are less likely to exist. These methods are described in the following section. Unfortunately bugs will sometimes appear no matter how careful the programmer tries to be. Tools exist to assist the location of such bugs and these are described later in this chapter.

## 10.2 PROGRAMMING METHODS

The intention of this section is to examine common approaches to writing correct and understandable programs. A program that is easily understood is easily maintained. During the construction of such a program, the mind is not overburdened with trying to understand the rest of the program and can concentrate on writing correct algorithms. Programs written in an undisciplined manner which mutate rather than evolve into their final form are not likely to be easily understood. Without a good understanding of a program, errors are more likely to be present and not easily detected.

Programs must be readable in order to be understood. A program is considered readable if it can be read easily. This implies that the program should wherever possible reflect the problem in hand. A program is made more readable by the lavish use of comments. Comments should precede each major section of the program and describe that section's function. Comments should also be used following most instructions in order to make the algorithm quite clear. The assemblers provide the facility to equate names with values using the EQU directive as described in Chapter 5. Meaningful names are usually preferable to numbers. Numbers which are essentially parameters to the program should be expressed as names equated with the relevant values. Not only is their alteration made simpler but the subsequent appearance of the name within the program assists the programmer in understanding the program. The EQU directive is in fact more powerful than has been described. In general a name may be equated with a string of symbols such as an instruction or an address. Expressions such as:

```
[bx+di]100
```

can be replaced by meaningful names declared as, for example:

```
name_field       equ       [bx+di]100
```

There are two well-appreciated methods of determining whether a program is behaving correctly. The first approach is **testing**. The program is run several times with different data and the results produced are checked against those expected. The second approach is called program **proving**. A detailed and formal mathematical statement is made concerning all data values at each junction in the program. This statement is called an **assertion**. As each program unit is encountered, its effect on the preceding assertion is calculated and a new assertion is written. In this way, the final assertion should include the original program specification. During the construction of the program proof inconsistencies and logical flaws can be found. The construction of the proof assists in locating errors as well as providing a final 'stamp of approval'.

Program testing is clearly desirable – nobody should write a program and sell it without at least trying it first! Testing by itself, however, cannot guarantee to locate all errors unless it is exhaustive. Exhaustive testing requires the running of the program with every possible combination of data values. For even a trivial program the number of such combinations will run into the millions. Exhaustive testing is not practical for this reason.

Program proving, on the other hand, claims to locate every potential error. It does have its drawbacks. Firstly the construction of the proof is very time consuming. Secondly the proof itself may have its own hidden errors. There exist several systems designed to automate the construction of program proofs and thereby reduce these disadvantages but such systems are still in their infancy.

Many programmers adopt a style of 'informal proving' of a program's correctness. This is performed by reading through the program as it would be obeyed. The programmer plays the part of the processor interpreting each instruction and updating the values of the data variables. During this process the programmer is constantly asking 'What if ... ?' in order to find potential flaws should a particular variable have a particular value. A related process occurs when a programmer is looking for the cause of an error. A section of the program is examined in order to determine whether it could produce the fault.

Both these processes of 'hand checking' programs can be assisted if programs are written according to certain guidelines. These guidelines were formed by experience of program proving. It was found that programs could be written painlessly according to guidelines which resulted in the easier construction of a program proof. A program is easier to prove correct if the assertions which must be written at each junction in the program are simpler and therefore easier to construct. If this is the case then the informal method described above is simpler and the program as a whole is more readily understood. You will probably have experienced programs which take time to understand and other, equally powerful, programs which take little time to understand. The latter have been written in a better style.

The general term for this style is **structured programming**. Structured programming is based on the belief that programs should be written as simple units whose overall structure accurately reflects the problem in hand. Each unit is self-contained and has only one entrance and only one exit. The commonly 'approved' units have been described in Chapter 7. They include subroutines, selections and loops. The fundamental features of these units are:

1. They are completely self-contained.
2. They are small.

The first feature encapsulates the unit as a 'black box' which performs a well-defined task. This feature is destroyed if the guts of the unit are accessible to or accessed by other parts of the program. The programmer may succumb to the temptation to jump into the unit other than at its correct entrance. Should this occur then the unit has been given an extra meaning and it is doubly difficult to predict its actions. Wherever a label occurs it is possible for a jump to be made to that label. While reading the program the programmer must envisage all possible jumps to each label. In a large program there may be many possible cross-references. The proper connections between units must be clearly defined and adhered to if the programmer is to have a chance of understanding all possible actions of the program.

The second feature of a unit is that it is small. This begs the question of 'how small?' A unit should be small enough such that it can be understood as a whole. Its workings can be retained in the brain's short-term memory. In general units should be no longer than, say, a page in order to qualify as small.

The enormous advantages of using such units become appreciated when writing large programs. Any large program consists of many isolable tasks. It is each task that is to be written, read and understood rather than each physical page of the program. If each task is physically localized then the program is more readable. If each task is spread throughout the program then the program is difficult to read and understand and errors will no longer 'leap off the page' as the brain cannot accommodate such a large amount of information at one time. For example consider the following grouping of letters:

HPMITBEC

It would take some time to remember this sequence. On the other hand the grouping:

THEIBMPC

is easily remembered as three units, called words – THE IBM PC. The usefulness of words is that, once remembered individually as a sequence of letters, they can be used as a unit. The word 'THE' can be examined without reference to the other two words. Its exact spelling or constitution can be recalled when necessary but normally it is known as a whole. A word is an indivisible unit which is understood in isolation. It can be used with other words to construct sentences.

The equivalent units of programs are subroutines. A program should be written as a series of subroutines each performing a well-defined task. They should be physically small. Large tasks can be kept small by reducing them to a series of calls to subroutines performing smaller tasks. In this way a program can be written and read without ever needing to look at more than, say, one page of a listing at a time. The main program itself will probably be a simple sequence of subroutine calls reflecting for example:

- read data;
- process data;
- print results.

The subroutine representing 'process data' would typically contain calls of subroutines performing particular self-contained tasks. We can understand the program as follows.

The subroutine 'read data' is read and understood without the requirement to be aware of the rest of the program. Once that is understood, so is the occurrence of the name 'read data' also. As each subroutine is read and understood its use is synonymous with its actions. The details of its actions need not be recalled in order to understand its use in other subroutines.

The isolation of units of a program greatly enhances the readability of a program. Subroutines should include a comment describing their action. It is the comment that is then referred to rather than the details of the implementation. With this approach large programs can be constructed in small steps. Each task is implemented as a small subroutine. Each subroutine may be tested separately before being combined with the rest of the program. If subroutines are self-contained then errors associated with their actions are easier to locate. The maintenance of a large program becomes the individual maintenance of several small units each of an easily manageable size.

This methodology is assisted by the 8086 assemblers which provide facilities for the natural expression of a program as a set of units. The richness of the 8086 instruction set means that the constructs described in Chapter 7 are easily built. By using these constructs the programmer is building the program out of well-tried and tested building blocks. Like any other engineer the programmer must use well-defined building blocks in order to produce a satisfactory product. The programmer is forced to keep program units small by the short range of conditional branch instructions. While this is not the reason for the restriction on the range of these instructions, a good programmer will rarely find the range too small.

Finally reference should be made to the ability to assemble units of programs separately. The assemblers can assemble units separately and the resulting machine code modules are later combined. This facility primarily exists so that when a section of the program is altered, only the unit involved need be reassembled. This can save a considerable amount of time if the whole program is very large. A second benefit is that such program units are guaranteed to be self-contained. Their use by other units is constrained as it is only possible for such units to be entered by their correct entrances. All other local names in a unit are not public knowledge to other units. The details of separate assembly can be found in the manufacturer's documentation.

The guidelines given in this section should assist with the writing of programs which behave correctly. Errors will still, unfortunately, exist and as many as possible of these errors must be located and removed. Such errors are called **bugs** as their existence is similar to that of a virus – small and difficult to locate and identify but large in their effect. The process of removing these bugs is similarly called **debugging** and it is this painful and frustrating but, ultimately, satisfying task that we consider next.

## 10.3  DEBUGGING PROGRAMS

Finding and correcting errors in programs is an expensive activity when measured as a proportion of the cost of a complete software project. The historical lessons to be learned from this aspect of software production point very strongly to the need to reduce the incidence of programming errors in the first place. In principle, any technique aimed at producing error-free programs is likely to be worthwhile, even if it involves considerable additional overheads in the design and coding phases of a project.

In fact, it is recognized that structured programming techniques such as those considered earlier in this chapter have the benefit of reducing both the number of errors and the overall project time (including subsequent maintenance). Even more importantly, good modular structure in a program lends itself to testing of procedures in isolation so that any errors discovered will be relatively easy to locate and to correct. In the extreme case, it is entirely feasible to reject a 'rogue' procedure and to rewrite it from the original specification. For the sanity of project leaders with deadlines to meet it is salutary to note that a well-designed program split into 10 modules, nine of which have been thoroughly tested, may be deemed to be approaching 90 per cent completion. It is a brave leader who is prepared to say the same of a 'monolithic' (single-program unit) program at any stage in its creation.

From the above discussion we deduce that it is preferable not to make errors in the first place, and work on program proving may eventually provide the formal specification tools with which to guarantee error-free programs. In the meantime it has been recognized that it is in general impossible to detect the absence of bugs – only their presence. The best one can hope to achieve is to minimize their likely existence and provide the best-structured environment in which to isolate them.

In the rest of this chapter we introduce tools available for the dynamic testing of programs to locate and correct run-time errors.

## 10.4  DYNAMIC DEBUGGING TOOLS

The systems programs for monitoring other programs during execution have different names under DOS (DEBUG) and CP/M-86 (DDT86) though the facilities provided are basically similar. In both cases the debugging program resides in memory alongside the user program to be monitored. Control is passed first to the debugger whose subsequent action is dictated by a choice of mainly single-letter commands, most of which accept parameters. The full set of DEBUG and DDT86 commands is shown in Table 10.1. Detailed parameter formats and effects of these commands are contained in the relevant manual.

**Table 10.1**   DEBUG and DDT86 commands.

| DEBUG | | | DDT86 | Operation | Category |
|---|---|---|---|---|---|
| DOS 1 | DOS 2 | DOS 3 | CP/M-86 | | |
| G | G | G | G | Execute program with/without breakpoint | Transfer control |
| T | T | T | T | Trace execution with display | |
| – | – | – | U | Trace execution without display | |
| – | – | P | – | Proceed to next instruction | |
| Q | Q | Q | ^C | Quit | |
| D | D | D | D | Display memory | Display program/ data |
| U | U | U | L | Disassemble instructions | |
| E | E | E | S | Change memory contents | Change state |
| R | R | R | X | Examine/change CPU registers | |
| – | A | A | A | Assemble statements into memory | |
| F | F | F | F | Fill memory with constant values | |
| M | M | M | M | Move memory block | |
| I | I | I | QI | Read from I/O port | |
| O | O | O | QO | Write to I/O port | |
| L | L | L | E/R | Load a file into memory | File opera- tions |
| N | N | N | I | Define files | |
| W | W | W | W | Write data to disk | |

| DEBUG | | | DDT86 | Operation | Category |
|---|---|---|---|---|---|
| DOS 1 | DOS 2 | DOS 3 | CP/M-86 | | |
| C | C | C | B | Compare blocks of memory | Miscel- laneous utilities |
| H | H | H | H | Hexadecimal add/subtract | |
| S | S | S | SR | Search for characters | |
| - | - | - | V | Show memory layout of files read | |

The following description offers an overview of debugger commands with examples of their use.

### 10.4.1    Setting up

To work on a particular program it is usual to specify the file containing an assembled version of the program with the call of DEBUG or DDT86. It can be assumed in most cases that the segment registers (CS, DS, ES, SS) will be correctly initialized by default, though these can be altered: in DOS, by issuing parameters with the call, for example. When using the skeleton program outlined in this book it is not necessary to reset segment registers or the stack pointer since the skeleton program itself assigns values to these. The debugger maintains a 'current instruction' pointer which is initialized to the first instruction in the code section of the user program.

Note that program execution monitoring commands assume that address parameters are offsets in the code segment, and in the memory display commands the code or data segment is assumed, depending on whether an instruction code or a data listing command is chosen.

### 10.4.2    Program execution monitoring

Monitoring the run-time behaviour of a program is the most important feature of the debugger. The user can execute a selected part of a program while monitoring its progress by displaying register and memory contents, for example.

There are two main mechanisms used in this monitoring activity supported by the debuggers: breakpoints and single-stepping of instructions. A **breakpoint** can be set in a user program by specifying the address of an instruction at which execution should be halted. The program can then be run from the current point (or a new one) in the knowledge that control will be returned to the debugger command mode when a breakpoint is reached. Since the debugger will 'trap' this point by inserting code at the relevant point in the user program, execution will proceed at full speed.

The second technique – **single-stepping** – is equivalent to setting a breakpoint after each instruction in the program. It allows the user to step through a sequence of instructions while watching a display of information as each is obeyed.

A typical method of using the debugger is to run the program to a breakpoint set just before the region to be investigated and then to trace through this region by single-stepping. Many of the remaining debugger commands are concerned with displaying further information on register or memory contents or with altering these contents.

The two main debugger commands concerned with monitoring program execution are G (Go) and T (Trace). The G command causes the user program to be executed from the current instruction, or from a specified address, until either it completes or a breakpoint address given in the command is reached. Several such addresses may be given to insert breakpoints in various branches of a program. Thus:

```
G 205 3F6     (DOS)
G,205,3F6     (CP/M-86)
```

causes the program to be executed from the current instruction until either of the two breakpoint addresses 205 or 3F6 are reached or, failing that, the end of the program is reached. Note that address values are stated in hexadecimal to the debuggers. On reaching any breakpoint, all breakpoints are removed by the debugger and, in DOS, the current values in registers and flags are displayed on the screen.

In its simplest and often most useful form the T (Trace) command is issued without parameters:

```
T             (DOS and CP/M-86)
```

This executes the next instruction and then displays the values in MPU registers. When followed by a hexadecimal constant this command can be made to trace more than one instruction, with register and flag settings displayed after each is obeyed. The U command in DDT86 behaves similarly to T except for suppressing the display of registers after all but the first instruction in the trace.

The P (Proceed) command in DOS 3 causes execution to proceed from the current instruction literally to the instruction which follows the current one in memory. The current instruction should be a subroutine call, a loop instruction, an interrupt or a repeat string instruction, and it is single-stepped by the P command. The effect is similar to placing a breakpoint at the next instruction prior to executing, for example, the subroutine call and it is convenient to have a single command for this purpose.

Tracing through a system call in DDT86 causes the whole call to be treated as a single tracing step. The action under DEBUG is not predictable and should be avoided by using the breakpoint or 'Proceed' technique.

The debugger program is terminated by typing Q (Quit) in DOS or Control C ( ^C) in CP/M-86.

### 10.4.3    Listing data and instructions

At any time in the command mode of the debugger the user can request a display of data contained in memory or registers. A specified block of memory is displayed by the D (dump or display) command with the contents of each location shown in both hexadecimal and, if it is a printable character, in ASCII representation. This form of display is particularly useful for checking addresses and contents of locations containing program data.

Mere mortals for whom hexadecimal instruction codes are not immediately recognizable will find the alternative U (DOS) or L (CP/M-86) command more useful for displaying program instructions. These commands disassemble memory contents to display assembler mnemonics for instructions, assuming that sensible instructions are contained in the portion of memory specified. The debugger has no access to the original assembly program and is thus unable to reproduce the symbols used to represent addresses and constants (though **symbolic** debuggers exist that are designed to do just this). Instead, all addresses and literals are displayed as absolute hexadecimal values, which is normally quite sufficient to identify the relevant section of a program listing, for example.

The R (DOS) or X (CP/M-86) command is used to display the contents of registers and flags. Unlike the memory display commands, R and X also perform the function of allowing changes to be made to the register contents, as described later in this chapter.

### 10.4.4    Changing state

The commands described in the last two sections enable the user to run a program under the control of the debugger and to examine the state of a program: memory and register contents. An added dimension in program debugging is to modify this state before continuing to execute further instructions. The motivation behind this might be a desire to test a section of program with new data values or, perhaps, to change one or two instructions. If an error is discovered the user may 'patch' in a simple temporary change to the program to test its effect. Used with care this can be an effective and rapid technique.

The simplest of the commands for changing state are the E (DOS) or S (CP/M-86) commands for changing the contents of memory locations and the R or X commands introduced in Section 10.4.3 for modifying register values. Typically, the user changes one or a succession of memory locations by specifying an address with the E (enter) or S (set) command and by providing alternative values to enter into these addresses. Used on their own, the R/X commands will display the contents of registers and flags. If a specific register is named in the command its present contents are displayed and the user is given the option of entering a new value.

To assist in the calculation and insertion of 8086 instructions, CP/M-86 and the later versions of DOS provide an A (assemble) command which will accept assembly language instruction formats. The instructions are assembled and placed in memory from the absolute address provided by the user in the command. All addresses and literals must be stated as absolute hexadecimal values to this assembler and some additional information may be needed. In the absence of data definitions, for example, the assembler is unable to tell whether some operands refer to a word or a byte memory location without further information of the kind given in:

```
neg     byte ptr [128]
```

Similarly, to distinguish a memory operand from a literal operand requires adoption of a convention: memory operands are enclosed in square brackets:

```
mov     ax , 36        ;Place the value 36 in AX.
mov     ax , [36]      ;Place the contents of
                       ;offset 36 into AX.
```

Other conventions peculiar to assembly in the debugger are described in the relevant DOS or CP/M-86 manual.

Of the remaining commands which change state, two are available to perform special operations on memory contents. The first of these is the M (move) command which allows a block of memory to be copied to a new part of the memory. This is occasionally useful to save or restore a region containing data values for a program in order to restart a computation from a known memory state. Perhaps marginally more useful is the F (fill) command which allows the user to fill a block of memory with one or more of the constant values specified in the command. When examining a region of memory for insertions made by a section of program, it is easier to spot these if the whole region is set to a common value (zero, for example) prior to tracing through the program instructions in question.

Commands are also provided to read a value from any input port and to write a value to any output port. These are included in this section since they clearly change the state of any program being examined. In practice, they are probably most useful in tracing the behaviour of peripheral systems attached to the ports.

## 10.4.5  Other debugger commands

Table 10.1 contains commands shown in two further categories: file operations and miscellaneous utilities. The first of these embraces commands to load one or more files into memory for monitoring in the debugger and to write out modified data to disk files. Note that both executable (.EXE) and .HEX extension files in DOS have formats which cannot be created by DEBUG and, thus, they may not be written to disk by the W command.

In addition, the N (DOS) or I (CP/M-86) commands provide the useful function of initializing file control blocks to the file names specified in the command. The detailed behaviour of these commands varies quite considerably between the operating systems, however, and the relevant manual entries should be studied before using them.

Clearly, the execution monitoring aspects of the debuggers were designed to work on binary programs held in memory. Sometimes it is useful to load a non-binary file into memory for examination and possible alteration and the above file operation commands can be used to do this. ASCII text files studied with the memory display commands reveal non-printable characters in hexadecimal format and their end-of-line (Carriage return/Line feed) structure, for example. When operating on non-binary files it is wise to refrain from using any of the program execution commands of the debugger if chaos is to be avoided!

Very briefly, the final group of commands in Table 10.1 is called 'Miscellaneous utilities'. One of these, the V command in DDT86 only, gives the addresses of each separate file currently loaded into memory by the R or E commands of this debugger. The other three commands offer more general facilities which are occasionally useful when working with debuggers. The H command provides a quick method of adding and subtracting hexadecimal numbers which can be useful in calculating address offsets, for example. The S (DOS) or SR (CP/M-86) command is used to search a block of memory for a given value. This can save time in locating a known instruction code or, perhaps more commonly, a data value in a large buffer of data. Finally, the C (DOS) or B (CP/M-86) commands compare two blocks of memory and report any differences between their contents. One buffer of data can thus be compared to another as an aid to locating errors, for example.

## 10.5    A DEBUGGING EXAMPLE

Figure 10.1 contains a complete assembler listing and symbol table of a program similar to the palindrome program written in Chapter 5, including the skeleton program required to run this under DOS. In fact, a small change has been made to the program in order to introduce a bug for the purposes of demonstrating the use of the debugger. When the program is run it behaves correctly when given a palindrome containing an odd number of letters. It also correctly detects phrases which are not palindromes. If a palindrome containing an even number of letters is given, however, the program incorrectly states that it is not a palindrome.

Already, the astute programmer will have a rough feel for the likely cause of such symptoms in such a small program. However, as an illustration we may run the program under control of DEBUG in order to track down the error. A listing of the dialogue produced during this debugging process is given in Figure 10.2, with comments inserted to explain the actions taken and results obtained. It is left as an exercise for the reader to try the equivalent process using DDT86 under CP/M-86.

```
0000                         stack    segment para stack 'stack'
0000      64 [                         db       100 dup ('STACK ')
          53 54 41 43
          4B 20
                   ]

0258                         stack    ends

0000                         data     segment para public 'data'
0000  0000                   saveprefix       dw       0

                             ;Constants.

= 000D                       cr               equ      0dh
= 000A                       lf               equ      0ah

                             ;Program Segment Prefix data.

= 0021                       fcblength        equ      33
005C                                  org      5ch
005C      21 [               default_fcb      db       fcblength dup (?)
             ??
                   ]

0080                                  org      80h
0080      80 [               disk_buffer      db       80h dup (?)
             ??
                   ]

0100                                  org      100h

                             ;INSERT DATA HERE ........
                             ;****************
```

Figure 10.1   Palindrome program listing (with error).

```
0100   0D 0A 54 79 70 65      promptmess      db        13,10,'Type
                              in a potential palindrome',13,10,'$'

       20 69 6E 20 61 20
       70 6F 74 65 6E 74
       69 61 6C 20 70 61
       6C 69 6E 64 72 6F
       6D 65 0D 0A 24
0123   0D 0A 54 68 61 74      yesmess         db        13,10,'That
                              was a palindrome!',13,10,'$'

       20 77 61 73 20 61
       20 70 61 6C 69 6E
       64 72 6F 6D 65 21
       0D 0A 24
013E   0D 0A 54 68 61 74      nomess          db        13,10,'That
                              was not a palindrome',13,10,'$'

       20 77 61 73 20 6E
       6F 74 20 61 20 70
       61 6C 69 6E 64 72
       6F 6D 65 0D 0A 24


015C   50                     bufstart        db        80
                              ;Max 80 characters.
015D   00                     bufno           db        0
015E        50 [              buf             db        80 dup (?)
                   ??
                      ]



01AE                          data    ends

0000                          code    segment para public 'code'
                              assume  cs:code, ds:data, es:data,
                                      ss:stack


0000                          mainentry:
0000   50                             push    ax
0001   8C DB                          mov     bx , ds
                                      ;Save segment start in BX.
0003   B8   ---- R                    mov     ax , data
                                      ;Fetch data segment start.
0006   8E C0                          mov     es , ax
                                      ;Copy PSP to new data segment.
0008   33 F6                          xor     si , si
000A   8B FE                          mov     di , si
000C   B9 0080                        mov     cx , 80h
000F   F3/ A5                         rep     movsw
0011   8E D8                          mov     ds , ax
```

**Figure 10.1 (cont.)**

```
                                    ;Data segment start into DS.
0013  89 1E 0000 R                  mov     saveprefix , bx
                                    ;Save original segment start.
0017  BA 0080                       mov     dx , 80h
                                    ;Set new dta.
001A  B4 1A                         mov     ah , 1ah
001C  E8 0066 R                     call    dobdos
001F  FC                            cld
                                    ;Clear the direction flag.
0020  58                            pop     ax

                                    ;INSERT CODE HERE ......
                                    ;****************

0021                      nextline:
0021  BA 0100 R                     mov     dx , offset promptmess
0024  B4 09                         mov     ah , 9
0026  E8 0066 R                     call    dobdos

0029  BA 015C R                     mov     dx , offset bufstart
002C  B4 0A                         mov     ah , 10
002E  E8 0066 R                     call    dobdos

0031  BE 015E R                     mov     si , offset buf
0034  8A 1E 015D R                  mov     bl , bufno
0038  80 FB 00                      cmp     bl , 0
003B  74 21                         je      finished
003D  32 FF                         xor     bh , bh
003F  03 DE                         add     bx , si
0041  4B                            dec     bx

0042                      compareloop:
0042  3B F3                         cmp     si , bx
0044  74 08                         je      ispalindrome

0046  AC                            lodsb
0047  3A 07                         cmp     al , byte ptr [bx]
0049  75 09                         jne     notpalindrome

004B  4B                            dec     bx
004C  EB F4                         jmp     compareloop

004E                      ispalindrome:
004E  BA 0123 R                     mov     dx , offset yesmess
0051  EB 04 90                      jmp     printmess
0054                      notpalindrome:
0054  BA 013E R                     mov     dx , offset nomess
```

**Figure 10.1 (cont.)**

```
0057                          printmess:
0057   B4 09                          mov     ah , 9
0059   E8 0066 R                      call    dobdos
005C   EB C3                          jmp     nextline


005E                          finished:
005E   A1 0000 R                      mov     ax , saveprefix
0061   50                             push    ax
0062   33 C0                          xor     ax , ax
0064   50                             push    ax
0065                          finito  proc far
0065   CB                             ret
0066                          finito  endp


0066                          dobdos:
0066   CD 21                          int     21h
0068   C3                             ret


0069                          code    ends

                             end     mainentry
```

```
Segments and groups:

              N a m e              Size   Align  Combine Class

CODE . . . . . . . . . . . . .      0069   PARA   PUBLIC  'CODE'
DATA . . . . . . . . . . . . .      01AE   PARA   PUBLIC  'DATA'
STACK. . . . . . . . . . . . .      0258   PARA   STACK   'STACK'

Symbols:

              N a m e              Type   Value  Attr

BUF. . . . . . . . . . . . .     L BYTE  015E   DATA    Length =0050
BUFNO. . . . . . . . . . . .     L BYTE  015D   DATA
BUFSTART . . . . . . . . . .     L BYTE  015C   DATA
COMPARELOOP. . . . . . . . .     L NEAR  0042   CODE
CR . . . . . . . . . . . . .     Number  000D
DEFAULT_FCB. . . . . . . . .     L BYTE  005C   DATA    Length =0021
DISK_BUFFER. . . . . . . . .     L BYTE  0080   DATA    Length =0080
DOBDOS . . . . . . . . . . .     L NEAR  0066   CODE
FCBLENGTH. . . . . . . . . .     Number  0021
FINISHED . . . . . . . . . .     L NEAR  005E   CODE
FINITO . . . . . . . . . . .     F PROC  0065   CODE    Length =0001
ISPALINDROME . . . . . . . .     L NEAR  004E   CODE
```

**Figure 10.1 (cont.)**

```
LF . . . . . . . . . . . . . .   Number  000A
MAINENTRY. . . . . . . . . . .   L NEAR  0000   CODE
NEXTLINE . . . . . . . . . . .   L NEAR  0021   CODE
NOMESS . . . . . . . . . . . .   L BYTE  013E   DATA
NOTPALINDROME. . . . . . . . .   L NEAR  0054   CODE
PRINTMESS. . . . . . . . . . .   L NEAR  0057   CODE
PROMPTMESS . . . . . . . . . .   L BYTE  0100   DATA
SAVEPREFIX . . . . . . . . . .   L WORD  0000   DATA
YESMESS. . . . . . . . . . . .   L BYTE  0123   DATA


Warning Severe
Errors  Errors
0       0
```

**Figure 10.1**

```
A>debug palin.exe
```

{DEBUG is now entered and the user program loaded from the file palin.exe. The g command below causes the user program to be entered, with a breakpoint set at offset 21 (hex) in the code segment – the start of the user program, labelled nextline in the listing in Figure 10.1. Note that DEBUG prints a hyphen as a prompt for commands.}

```
-g21

AX=0000  BX=0E84  CX=0000  DX=0080  SP=0258  BP=0000  SI=0100  DI=0100
DS=0E9B  ES=0E9B  SS=0EB6  CS=0E94  IP=0021    NV UP EI PL ZR NA PE NC
0E94:0021 BA0001       MOV     DX,0100
```

{Having reached the breakpoint, the contents of registers are displayed and the next instruction to be obeyed (MOV DX,0100) is also given.}

```
-d15c
0E9B:0150                                      50 00 37 34           P.74
0E9B:0160  27 98 E5 FF 22 72 F6 23-85 11 00 00 48 25 FC CC  '..."r.#....H...
0E9B:0170  DC FE 5E 54 52 88 14 33-97 8A EA BC BC FF 41 66  ..^TR..3......Af
0E9B:0180  24 00 00 00 47 00 22 00-00 64 00 00 63 45 45 45  $...G."..d..cEEE
0E9B:0190  FF FF 00 00 FF FF 00 40-40 40 40 0F 0F 0F 00 00  .......aaaa.....
0E9B:01A0  00 33 33 33 33 00 00 00-33 33 33 00 00 00 48 23  .3333...333...H#
0E9B:01B0  53 54 41 43 4B 20 53 54-41 43 4B 20 53 54 41 43  STACK STACK STAC
0E9B:01C0  4B 20 53 54 41 43 4B 20-53 54 41 43 4B 20 53 54  K STACK STACK ST
0E9B:01D0  41 43 4B 20 53 54 41 43-4B 20 53 54              ACK STACK ST
```

**Figure 10.2**  A sample DEBUG dialogue.

Programming Methodology

{Using the d (dump) command, the contents of the block of 128 bytes of memory from offset 15c (hex) in the data segment is displayed. Offset 15c is the start of the buffer to be used to hold the phrase. Because it is declared as buf db 80 dup (?) the rubbish in memory from whatever process last used this part of memory is still there.}

```
-f15e,1ad,0
```

{To make future buffer contents more readable we may use the f (fill) command to place zeros in the buffer initially, being careful not to overwrite the buffer length (50 hex) in offset 15c.}

```
-d15c
0E9B:0150                                           50 00 00 00              P...
0E9B:0160  00 00 00 00 00 00 00 00-00 00 00 00 00 00 00 00    ................
0E9B:0170  00 00 00 00 00 00 00 00-00 00 00 00 00 00 00 00    ................
0E9B:0180  00 00 00 00 00 00 00 00-00 00 00 00 00 00 00 00    ................
0E9B:0190  00 00 00 00 00 00 00 00-00 00 00 00 00 00 00 00    ................
0E9B:01A0  00 00 00 00 00 00 00 00-00 00 00 00 00 00 48 23    ..............H#
0E9B:01B0  53 54 41 43 4B 20 53 54-41 43 4B 20 53 54 41 43    STACK STACK STAC
0E9B:01C0  4B 20 53 54 41 43 4B 20-53 54 41 43 4B 20 53 54    K STACK STACK ST
0E9B:01D0  41 43 4B 20 53 54 41 43-4B 20 53 54                ACK STACK ST
```

{Displaying the buffer again, as above, shows the effect of this filling with zeros.

There is no reason to suspect the first part of the program of containing an error – the program appears to read phrases correctly – and so we may risk continuing with a breakpoint set at the start of the compare loop (label compareloop in the listing).}

```
-g42

Type in a potential palindrome
redder

AX=0A0D  BX=0163  CX=0000  DX=015C  SP=0258  BP=0000  SI=015E  DI=0100
DS=0E9B  ES=0E9B  SS=0EB6  CS=0E94  IP=0042    NV UP EI PL NZ NA PE NC
0E94:0042 3BF3          CMP      SI,BX
```

{In running to this breakpoint the program has requested a phrase to be entered and redder is typed as an example of a palindrome of the kind known to cause an error. Out of interest we may now examine the buffer again to check that the phrase has been stored correctly:}

```
-d15c
0E9B:0150                                           50 06 72 65              P.re
0E9B:0160  64 64 65 72 0D 00 00 00-00 00 00 00 00 00 00 00    dder............
0E9B:0170  00 00 00 00 00 00 00 00-00 00 00 00 00 00 00 00    ................
0E9B:0180  00 00 00 00 00 00 00 00-00 00 00 00 00 00 00 00    ................
0E9B:0190  00 00 00 00 00 00 00 00-00 00 00 00 00 00 00 00    ................
```

**Figure 10.2 (cont.)**

```
0E9B:01A0  00 00 00 00 00 00 00 00-00 00 00 00 00 00 48 23   ..............H#
0E9B:01B0  53 54 41 43 4B 20 53 54-41 43 4B 20 53 54 41 43   STACK STACK STAC
0E9B:01C0  4B 20 53 54 41 43 4B 20-53 54 41 43 4B 20 53 54   K STACK STACK ST
0E9B:01D0  41 43 4B 20 53 54 41 43-4B 20 53 54               ACK STACK ST
```

{Everything looks OK so far, but the comparison loop about to be obeyed must be suspect. The loop is entered below using the t (trace) command to print out information after each instruction is obeyed. There are seven instructions in each pass through the loop and we would expect at least three iterations for redder. Observe that as the loop is obeyed three times the pointers into the phrase (held in BX and SI) behave as expected – identifying pairs of letters in the phrase – until the last two instructions traced.}

-t17

```
AX=0A0D  BX=0163  CX=0000  DX=015C  SP=0258  BP=0000  SI=015E  DI=0100
DS=0E9B  ES=0E9B  SS=0EB6  CS=0E94  IP=0044    NV UP EI NG NZ NA PO CY
0E94:0044 7408           JZ      004E

AX=0A0D  BX=0163  CX=0000  DX=015C  SP=0258  BP=0000  SI=015E  DI=0100
DS=0E9B  ES=0E9B  SS=0EB6  CS=0E94  IP=0046    NV UP EI NG NZ NA PO CY
0E94:0046 AC            . LODSB

AX=0A72  BX=0163  CX=0000  DX=015C  SP=0258  BP=0000  SI=015F  DI=0100
DS=0E9B  ES=0E9B  SS=0EB6  CS=0E94  IP=0047    NV UP EI NG NZ NA PO CY
0E94:0047 3A07          CMP     AL,[BX]                      DS:0163=72

AX=0A72  BX=0163  CX=0000  DX=015C  SP=0258  BP=0000  SI=015F  DI=0100
DS=0E9B  ES=0E9B  SS=0EB6  CS=0E94  IP=0049    NV UP EI PL ZR NA PE NC
0E94:0049 7509          JNZ     0054

AX=0A72  BX=0163  CX=0000  DX=015C  SP=0258  BP=0000  SI=015F  DI=0100
DS=0E9B  ES=0E9B  SS=0EB6  CS=0E94  IP=004B    NV UP EI PL ZR NA PE NC
0E94:004B 4B            DEC     BX

AX=0A72  BX=0162  CX=0000  DX=015C  SP=0258  BP=0000  SI=015F  DI=0100
DS=0E9B  ES=0E9B  SS=0EB6  CS=0E94  IP=004C    NV UP EI PL NZ NA PO NC
0E94:004C EBF4          JMP     0042

AX=0A72  BX=0162  CX=0000  DX=015C  SP=0258  BP=0000  SI=015F  DI=0100
DS=0E9B  ES=0E9B  SS=0EB6  CS=0E94  IP=0042    NV UP EI PL NZ NA PO NC
0E94:0042 3BF3          CMP     SI,BX

AX=0A72  BX=0162  CX=0000  DX=015C  SP=0258  BP=0000  SI=015F  DI=0100
DS=0E9B  ES=0E9B  SS=0EB6  CS=0E94  IP=0044    NV UP EI NG NZ NA PO CY
0E94:0044 7408          JZ      004E

AX=0A72  BX=0162  CX=0000  DX=015C  SP=0258  BP=0000  SI=015F  DI=0100
DS=0E9B  ES=0E9B  SS=0EB6  CS=0E94  IP=0046    NV UP EI NG NZ NA PO CY
0E94:0046 AC            LODSB
```

**Figure 10.2 (cont.)**

```
AX=0A65  BX=0162  CX=0000  DX=015C  SP=0258  BP=0000  SI=0160  DI=0100
DS=0E9B  ES=0E9B  SS=0EB6  CS=0E94  IP=0047   NV UP EI NG NZ NA PO CY
0E94:0047 3A07        CMP     AL,[BX]                        DS:0162=65


AX=0A65  BX=0162  CX=0000  DX=015C  SP=0258  BP=0000  SI=0160  DI=0100
DS=0E9B  ES=0E9B  SS=0EB6  CS=0E94  IP=0049   NV UP EI PL ZR NA PE NC
0E94:0049 7509        JNZ     0054


AX=0A65  BX=0162  CX=0000  DX=015C  SP=0258  BP=0000  SI=0160  DI=0100
DS=0E9B  ES=0E9B  SS=0EB6  CS=0E94  IP=004B   NV UP EI PL ZR NA PE NC
0E94:004B 4B          DEC     BX


AX=0A65  BX=0161  CX=0000  DX=015C  SP=0258  BP=0000  SI=0160  DI=0100
DS=0E9B  ES=0E9B  SS=0EB6  CS=0E94  IP=004C   NV UP EI PL NZ NA PO NC
0E94:004C EBF4        JMP     0042


AX=0A65  BX=0161  CX=0000  DX=015C  SP=0258  BP=0000  SI=0160  DI=0100
DS=0E9B  ES=0E9B  SS=0EB6  CS=0E94  IP=0042   NV UP EI PL NZ NA PO NC
0E94:0042 3BF3        CMP     SI,BX


AX=0A65  BX=0161  CX=0000  DX=015C  SP=0258  BP=0000  SI=0160  DI=0100
DS=0E9B  ES=0E9B  SS=0EB6  CS=0E94  IP=0044   NV UP EI NG NZ AC PE CY
0E94:0044 7408        JZ      004E


AX=0A65  BX=0161  CX=0000  DX=015C  SP=0258  BP=0000  SI=0160  DI=0100
DS=0E9B  ES=0E9B  SS=0EB6  CS=0E94  IP=0046   NV UP EI NG NZ AC PE CY
0E94:0046 AC          LODSB


AX=0A64  BX=0161  CX=0000  DX=015C  SP=0258  BP=0000  SI=0161  DI=0100
DS=0E9B  ES=0E9B  SS=0EB6  CS=0E94  IP=0047   NV UP EI NG NZ AC PE CY
0E94:0047 3A07        CMP     AL,[BX]                        DS:0161=64


AX=0A64  BX=0161  CX=0000  DX=015C  SP=0258  BP=0000  SI=0161  DI=0100
DS=0E9B  ES=0E9B  SS=0EB6  CS=0E94  IP=0049   NV UP EI PL ZR NA PE NC
0E94:0049 7509        JNZ     0054


AX=0A64  BX=0161  CX=0000  DX=015C  SP=0258  BP=0000  SI=0161  DI=0100
DS=0E9B  ES=0E9B  SS=0EB6  CS=0E94  IP=004B   NV UP EI PL ZR NA PE NC
0E94:004B 4B          DEC     BX


AX=0A64  BX=0160  CX=0000  DX=015C  SP=0258  BP=0000  SI=0161  DI=0100
DS=0E9B  ES=0E9B  SS=0EB6  CS=0E94  IP=004C   NV UP EI PL NZ NA PE NC
0E94:004C EBF4        JMP     0042


AX=0A64  BX=0160  CX=0000  DX=015C  SP=0258  BP=0000  SI=0161  DI=0100
DS=0E9B  ES=0E9B  SS=0EB6  CS=0E94  IP=0042   NV UP EI PL NZ NA PE NC
0E94:0042 3BF3        CMP     SI,BX
```

**Figure 10.2 (cont.)**

```
AX=0A64  BX=0160  CX=0000  DX=015C  SP=0258  BP=0000  SI=0161  DI=0100
DS=0E9B  ES=0E9B  SS=0EB6  CS=0E94  IP=0044    NV UP EI PL NZ NA PO NC
0E94:0044 7408        JZ      004E

AX=0A64  BX=0160  CX=0000  DX=015C  SP=0258  BP=0000  SI=0161  DI=0100
DS=0E9B  ES=0E9B  SS=0EB6  CS=0E94  IP=0046    NV UP EI PL NZ NA PO NC
0E94:0046 AC          LODSB
```

{Note how DEBUG adds information at each compare instruction referring to memory locations to show the contents of the location in question (e.g. DS:0163=72, the ASCII code for 'r'). The error can now be spotted in the last but one instruction traced above. The centre of the phrase has been reached in the comparison process and the two pointers have crossed: an indication that the phrase is a palindrome. However, the je ispalindrome does not detect this and the loop is about to be obeyed for a fourth time. If the phrase had contained an odd number of characters the two pointers would by now be equal and all would be fine. We need to change the conditional jump instruction to jae for the even case to work properly.}

```
-a44
0E94:0044 jae 4e
0E94:0046
```

{The a (assemble) command is used above to change the conditional jump instruction and we may confirm this by displaying the relevant section of program using the u (unassemble) command. The printing of the equally acceptable jnb mnemonic by DEBUG cannot be helped – no record of the programmer's original choice is available to DEBUG.}

```
-u42

0E94:0042 3BF3        CMP     SI,BX
0E94:0044 7308        JNB     004E
0E94:0046 AC          LODSB
0E94:0047 3A07        CMP     AL,[BX]
0E94:0049 7509        JNZ     0054
0E94:004B 4B          DEC     BX
0E94:004C EBF4        JMP     0042
0E94:004E BA2301      MOV     DX,0123
0E94:0051 EB04        JMP     0057
0E94:0053 90          NOP
0E94:0054 BA3E01      MOV     DX,013E
0E94:0057 B409        MOV     AH,09
0E94:0059 E80A00      CALL    0066
0E94:005C EBC3        JMP     0021
0E94:005E A10000      MOV     AX,[0000]
0E94:0061 50          PUSH    AX
```

**Figure 10.2 (cont.)**

{The modified program can now be re-entered at the beginning with the g command. This time no breakpoints are set and the program runs to completion.}

```
-g=21

Type in a potential palindrome
redder

That was a palindrome!

Type in a potential palindrome
ridder

That was not a palindrome

Type in a potential palindrome
fredy

That was not a palindrome

Type in a potential palindrome


Program terminated normally
-q
```

{The debugger has now been left by the q (quit) command. We should not forget subsequently to edit the change into the assembly language source file for reassembly of the corrected program.}

**Figure 10.2**

# 11 | Input/Output

Traditionally, input/output is the area of greatest variation between different computer systems, both at the processor architecture level and at the programming language/operating system level. It is even the case that many programs written in high-level language still need to be modified substantially before they can be transported to a new computer. As far as smaller computer systems are concerned, the assembly language programmer's headaches have been relieved slightly in recent years by the adoption of a few 'standard' operating systems implemented on many different hardware systems. The earliest notable success in this direction was CP/M, developed by Digital Research for Intel 8080-based computers. This disk-based operating system was designed for relatively simple and rapid implementation on any 8080 (and, subsequently, Z80) computer. The substantial user base that grew up around this system ensured a wide range of applications software support, even on computers from the smallest manufacturer.

With the advent of popular 16-bit microprocessors such as the Intel 8086 came the CP/M-86 operating system. Such systems are often called 'industry standard' systems – they are standardized by market acceptance rather than by the deliberations of a national or international committee. The entry of the IBM Personal Computer into the market introduced a further system: the IBM Personal Computer Disk Operating System (referred to usually as simply DOS), written by Microsoft Inc. Many smaller manufacturers now produce computers with operating systems claimed to be more or less the same as that on the IBM, hence the 'IBM compatible' tag invariably attached to such systems.

To the assembly language programmer, DOS is compatible in many respects with CP/M-86. The important operating system function calls described later work in similar ways and have the same codes, for example. Some of the minor differences in assembly language format have already been considered in earlier chapters. Finally the position is further complicated by the periodic introduction of new versions of the operating systems in which new features are introduced and, less desirably, in which old features are omitted or changed. The most important of those considered later are the

224

more recent DOS versions 2 and 3, in which some important changes are made, particularly in respect of file handling. In general the designers of these systems try hard to maintain 'upwards compatibility' between their new and old versions. This is achieved if a program written for an earlier version of the operating system continues to work on newer versions.

With apologies for the need for a potted history, we now see that there are several operating systems in use on the IBM PC. In the introduction which follows, the overall emphasis is placed on the use of DOS (the versions covered are abbreviated to DOS 1, DOS 2 and DOS 3 except where a specific release is referred to), with accompanying comments regarding the use of CP/M-86 and the steps needed to maintain some degree of compatibility between both systems.

The instructions in the 8086 for input and output (IN and OUT) are not normally used directly by a programmer on the IBM PC. To do so would bypass the operating system, one of whose main reasons for existence is to monitor and control the use of the computer's resources, including I/O. It is usual to leave the low-level access of I/O devices (via ports, using IN and OUT) to the operating system and to make use of function calls provided for this purpose.

## 11.1   OPERATING SYSTEM FUNCTION CALLS

All of the operating systems DOS 1, DOS 2, DOS 3 and CP/M-86 provide function calls for device I/O and file handling. Each call has a function code by which it is identified and most require further information to be passed over in particular registers. Some calls refer to blocks of memory locations whose start addresses may also be passed over in registers.

The method of calling the functions varies in detail between the different systems. These differences were explained in Section 5.2.6 but they are effectively hidden in the skeleton program routines called dobdos in Appendix C. Thus, we may assume that a function may be invoked by setting its code in AH and making a call of dobdos, regardless of the operating system. We should note, however, that this code is transferred to the CL register by the dobdos routine for CP/M-86 and that calls in this latter system tend to affect values in the general-purpose registers, even those not used for parameters.

Within the dobdos routines, the actual call on the operating system is performed by a software interrupt instruction (INT 21h in DOS; INT 0E0h in CP/M-86). DOS provides other interrupts for activities such as program termination and error trapping (see Section 11.8). Note, however, that a label finished is provided in the skeleton program for program termination.

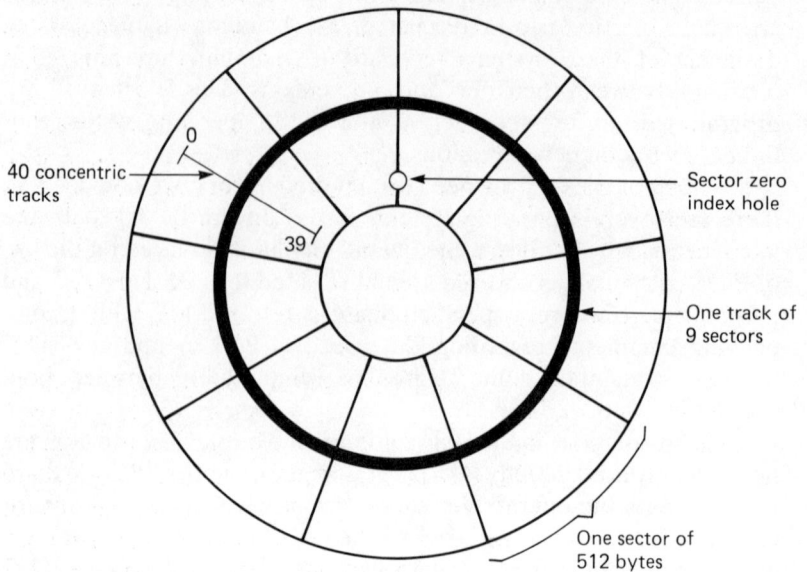

**Figure 11.1**   Diskette storage organization.

Not all of the operating system functions are described in detail in this introduction, though a fairly comprehensive index to the file handling functions is presented in tabular form.

## 11.2   DISK FILES

All of the operating systems provide file handling facilities for files held on diskettes and, where present, on larger capacity fixed disks. A 'file' in this context is a collection of data recorded on backing store and identified by a unique **filename**. Physically, the data are recorded on concentric **tracks** on the surface of the diskette, divided further into a number of **sectors** as shown in Figure 11.1.

The number of tracks and sectors varies for different disk drives. IBM single-sided diskettes under DOS 2 and 3 have 40 tracks, 9 sectors per track, with each sector containing 512 bytes of data, for example. The tracks are numbered in this case from 0 (outer) to 39 (inner), and the sectors on each track from 1 to 9. Each sector is identified by writing a unique address onto the disk at the beginning of the sector. Only the sector 1 position for all tracks is recognized by the hardware by sensing the position of an index hole. Simple arithmetic gives the total storage capacity of this diskette as $40 \times 9 \times 512 = 184\,320$ bytes or 180 Kbytes, not quite all of which will be available for user files. A single read/record head moves in and out across the tracks as the diskette rotates in order to access a given sector of data. Double-sided diskettes employ two read/record heads, one per side, and may record data using both heads at once to minimize the movement of the heads. Head movement accounts for a substantial proportion of the disk access time.

A higher storage capacity on a diskette can be produced by either increasing the number of tracks – making them narrower and placing them closer together – or by changing the recording technique to increase the number of bytes stored on each track. Fixed disks (sometimes called Winchester or hard disks) employ a much more refined and precise technology to permit far denser recording techniques at much higher access speeds, still based on the same logical division into tracks and sectors.

It is unattractive for the programmer to address a diskette directly in terms of physical movements across the diskette. In practice, special-purpose hardware (a disk controller) is used to provide a higher-level interface for accessing disks but even this is not a 'user friendly' interface. General housekeeping activities associated with the management of data on the disks are better provided by the operating system at large than by the individual user. File structure can be imposed: data can be grouped into single files and associated with a filename for user access. Access to the files for reading or writing can be controlled; filenames on a diskette can be listed, or files deleted and their space reused for subsequent files. These are routine activities which the normal user should have no desire to implement in order to make use of disk files.

One or more physical disk units may be connected to the system – diskettes or fixed disks – and these are separated by the operating system and referred to by different logical **drive names** (A, B etc.). Within a file on any particular drive, data are recorded in fixed-length **blocks** divided into fixed-length **records** numbered upwards from 0 within the block. Thus the sector and track structure is effectively hidden from the programmer in normal file accessing.

The operating system maintains a **directory** of the files on a drive and this directory is itself stored on the drive, normally in some of the sectors of track 0. The directory contains information about the names and locations of files on the disk with additional data which depends to some extent on the operating system being used. Typically this information includes attributes such as 'read-only' access permission or 'system file' status, whose meanings are explained in Section 11.6.5. Date and time of file creation or last update, and size in bytes may also be recorded in the directory entry for a file. The initialization of all sectors on a disk and the creation of a blank directory is the task of the disk formatting program.

Two comments may be made on the subject of directories. Firstly, the sectors used to store each file are mapped in an accompanying table (the file allocation table or FAT) such that any 'cluster'

– a unit of one or more sectors, depending on the disk type – on the disk can be allocated in any order to any file. This flexible management scheme means that the storage space on a disk is not fragmented into unusable chunks by frequent creation and deletion of files. Clusters released by deleting one file immediately become available for re-allocation to other files and the absolute number of each cluster used to store the data in a file is recorded in the FAT. A typical size of cluster on a diskette is one sector of 512 bytes and this is the minimum unit of allocation of storage on the disk. Larger capacity fixed disks may have cluster sizes of two, four or even more sectors and the minimum file allocation unit is correspondingly larger. This explains why the same file can be reported to be of a different size when stored on media of different types.

The second point to note is that the number of files permitted on one drive is governed by the number of sectors reserved for directory entries in DOS 1 and CP/M-86. This will vary from perhaps 64 for smaller capacity diskettes up to 512 or more for hard disks. The subdirectory structure of DOS 2 and 3 (see later) removes this restriction on the number of possible files on a drive, however.

In the description of file handling facilities which follows, mention is made of the **Program Segment Prefix** (PSP). This is a block of 100h bytes allocated by the operating system at the base of the memory available to the program. The operating system reserves some of these locations for its own use but some of the data fields in the PSP are useful to the programmer.

Unfortunately, the PSP (under DOS) occupies a region of memory that is outside the data segment defined by the skeleton program. To circumvent this problem the skeleton program places a copy of the PSP into the first 100h locations of the data segment before executing the user's program. Thus, a program can address data in the PSP and the skeleton program provides labels for some of the commonly required regions in the PSP.

The next few sections introduce the basic facilities for file processing in assembly language programs.


## 11.3   FILE CONTROL BLOCK (FCB)

File Control Blocks (FCBs) form an essential part of file access facilities for programmers using DOS 1 or CP/M-86. The approach is very similar to that used in the earlier CP/M operating system. For compatibility, the more recent DOS 2 and DOS 3 systems will allow the use of File Control Blocks but they provide in addition an improved and rather simpler interface for file handling. Programmers writing only for DOS 2 or later can ignore FCBs and move directly to Section 11.5.

A File Control Block is a data structure through which an assembly language programmer can establish access to a disk file. It consists of an array of 33 or more bytes divided into a number of fixed-length fields representing features of the disk access. Some of these fields can be addressed sensibly by the programmer; some – such as the filename fields will normally be initialized by a program prior to file access. Other fields are maintained partly or entirely by the operating system to record information such as the current read or write position within the file. Indeed, a block of bytes in the middle of an FCB is 'reserved for system use' entirely.

Appendix D defines the fields of FCBs in DOS and CP/M-86. These are similar except that CP/M-86 uses one less byte for the final field and interprets some of the fields slightly differently. Also, an FCB in DOS only may be extended by an optional 7-byte prefix but the operating systems are in principle compatible in most of the FCB usage. The FCB for DOS 2 and later is identical to that for DOS 1 except for enhancement of the attribute types in the prefix (FCB − 1).

At first glance, the meaning and use of FCBs and their many fields can look confusing. Below we identify the common sequence of events required to establish an FCB for reading and writing to an existing file.

### Allocate space for the FCB
If only one file is to be accessed in a program it is often convenient to use the block of 36 bytes reserved in the program segment prefix specifically for an FCB. The start of this area is at offset 5Ch in the segment and defined in the DOS skeleton program as:

```
                 org 5ch
default_fcb      db 36 dup (?)
```

Certain DOS and CP/M-86 commands also make use of this buffer area in a way which may or may not be convenient; they are considered below. Alternatively, FCBs may reside anywhere in data space defined, for example, by:

```
    fcb2             db 37 dup (?)        ;DOS
```
or:
```
    fcb2             rb 36                ;CP/M-86
```

Note that an FCB in DOS (only) may need an extra byte on the end in cases where a record size of less than 64 bytes is used. The standard FCB at segment offset 5Ch does not have room for this extra byte, though it may be possible to allow overwriting of the first byte of the following buffer area in some circumstances. Since the default record size is 128 bytes, it is normally adequate to define FCBs to be a maximum of 36 bytes long and, if no random access calls are to be made, to shorten this to 33 bytes in all operating systems (but see Section 11.6.5 if using extended FCBs).

### State the file to process

To access a given file the drive, filename and filename extension (file type) must be entered into the FCB (bytes 0–11):

1. The drive code is written as an integer between 0 and 16 in FCB byte 0. Drives A, B etc. are represented by integers 1, 2, etc. A zero entry in the drive field requests the system to use the current default drive.

2. The filename is written in upper case ASCII into FCB bytes 1–8 inclusive. Byte 1 must contain the first character of the filename, with trailing spaces inserted to fill out to eight characters.

3. The filename extension is written in similar fashion into bytes 9–11, and may be all spaces if no extension is required.

The colon and full-stop characters used as separators when writing filenames are *not* entered into the FCB. Note that the characters which may be used in filenames vary slightly between the operating systems and for this reason it is probably wise to use only alphabetic characters and digits in filenames. One or two special cases are considered later, where a search is made in a directory for the file specified in an FCB. In these circumstances only, an ambiguous file reference character (?) may be inserted in the filename or filename extension fields and will be matched in the search by any character in that position.

CP/M-86 also insists that the 'extent' field of an FCB be set by the user to identify the extent (a group of records) in the file to be accessed. The normal procedure is to write a zero into this byte (byte 12) of the FCB before the file is opened, in order to identify the first extent of the file.

### Open the file

An FCB in the above state is said to be 'unopened'. Before issuing any read or write requests, for example, a file must be 'opened' by means of the system function call 0Fh (all function codes are quoted in hex). The calling mechanism for this, and other basic calls is described shortly. Note, for the moment however, the following summary of the effect of an open:

1. In the FCB, a zero drive code is replaced by the actual (default) drive code (DOS only).

2. The file is located in the directory of the specified drive (an error condition is signalled if the file cannot be found).

3. The system fills in many of the FCB fields ready for subsequent file operations.

## Initialize the FCB

The 'open' FCB created by the above system call is not quite ready for file operations. The system needs to know the record position within the file at which processing is to commence. For sequential access to the file all that is needed is to write a zero into FCB byte 32, the current relative record number (the current relative block number – bytes 12 and 13 – is zeroed by the open call). To perform random access operations on a file the relative record number (bytes 33–35 or 36) must first be set to the required record number relative to the start of the file (see Section 11.6.3).

## 11.4  BASIC FILE HANDLING CALLS

As described in Section 11.1, file handling is carried out in all the operating systems by issuing function calls to the system. The calls summarized in this section are valid for DOS 1, CP/M-86 and DOS 2 or 3, though a simpler interface is available with the latter two if preferred (see Section 11.5). In each case, the function number is placed in AH before calling dobdos as described earlier. Furthermore, in the absence of the skeleton program (see Chapter 5), it is the programmer's responsibility to ensure that the DS register has been set to the current data segment base address. Other parameters are specified in most cases – see the relevant operating system manual for detailed definitions.

### Open file (fn 0Fh)

    on entry: DX = FCB offset
    on exit:  AL = return code

This is the function referred to in the previous section for 'opening' an FCB in cases where an existing file is to be accessed. The return code will be 0 (DOS) or 0–3 inc. (CP/M-86) for a successful open, and 0FFh for a failed open (the file cannot be found).

### Create file (fn 16h)

    on entry: DX = FCB offset
    on exit:  AL = return code

This is the call used in place of 'open file' when an unopened FCB refers to a new file to be created in the filestore. A return code of 0 (0–3 in CP/M-86) signifies successful creation and opening such that a subsequent open file call is not required. 0FFh is returned in AL if there is no room in the directory for a new file. In CP/M-86 only, an error is also returned if the file by the requested name already exists, hence a 'delete file' call is a sensible preamble to a 'create file' call in CP/M-86. DOS will automatically reuse a directory entry, deleting any contents that may be resident in the old file.

### Delete file (fn 13h)

on entry: DX = FCB offset
on exit:   AL = return code

Any directory entry matching the file specified in the unopened FCB is deleted. The file specification may contain ambiguous references (?s), resulting, potentially, in more than one file deletion. The return code is 0 for a successful delete and 0FFh for a failure due to the file not being found, or to a file protected from deletion.

### Set disk transfer address (fn 1Ah)

on entry: DX = new DTA

The disk transfer address (DMA address in CP/M-86) is the memory address of the buffer used to hold the actual data record involved in a disk access. Thus, a read operation of standard record length will read a block of 128 bytes from disk into memory, starting at the DTA. This address is set by default to the second half of the program segment prefix (offset 80h) which is labelled default_dta in the skeleton program. It can be altered as required by the Set DTA function call.

### Sequential read (fn 14h)

on entry: DX = FCB offset
on exit:   AL = return code

The FCB addressed must be open prior to this call. The record (default length 80h bytes) in the file identified by the combination of the current block and record fields in the FCB is read into memory at the current disk transfer address. This record address is then incremented so that the next read operation will access the following record. Return codes are:

0  Read successful
1  End of file (no data in this record)
2  Not enough space at the DTA
3  End of file (a partially full record has been read and filled out with 0s).

Only codes 0 and 1 are returned in CP/M-86.

### Sequential write (fn 15h)

on entry: DX = FCB offset
on exit:   AL = return code

A record is written from the DTA to the disk record identified by the current block and record fields in the open FCB. The FCB record address is then incremented. Return codes are:

0  Write successful

*DOS*

1  Disk full

2  Not enough space at DTA to hold the record to be written

*CP/M-86*

1  No available directory space (the directory space needed grows larger as files grow larger in this system)

2  Disk full

### Close file (fn 10h)

> on entry: DX = FCB offset
> on exit:   AL = return code

A call of `close file` forces the system to update the directory on the disk. Directory information and buffered file data are held in memory during file operations for efficiency reasons and may not be updated on disk correctly if an explicit close file is not performed. The return code is 0 (0, 1, 2 or 3 in CP/M-86) for a successful close and 0FFh for a failure due to the file not being found or, possibly, due to a diskette change since the file was opened.

It is not necessary to close an FCB if only read operations have taken place, except in DOS 3 and later where it is advisable to close all unwanted files, regardless of their mode of access.

### A simple file copy program

The next program is presented as an example of File Control Block definition and function calling. It is written in DOS (1, 2 or 3) assembly language and requires the skeleton program in Appendix C. See also the comments in Chapter 5 regarding the alterations needed to assemble this program under CP/M-86 and the earlier comments in this chapter on creating and opening files in this operating system. The program must be called with two filenames as parameters:

```
fcopy  <source>  <destination>
```

On entry, it is assumed that the command processor has decoded `<source>` and placed it in the default FCB at 5Ch in the program segment prefix (see Section 11.6.1 for command decoding details). `<destination>` is also decoded, this time into the buffer from 6Ch. The routine must move this file specification to a user defined FCB before opening the default FCB.

Records are copied one at a time from `<source>` to `<destination>`, using the default DTA (Disk Transfer Address) at 80h. In an efficient file copy program it is considerably faster to read as many records as possible into a large buffer in memory before writing them out to <destination> because of the physical characteristics of disks, notably head movements. This is particularly true if the two files are accessed by the same disk head or heads.

*In the DATA section*

```
            ;The default fcb at 5ch and default DTA are defined
            ;in the skeleton program.

fcbout          db  fcblength dup (?)  ;Destination FCB.

            ;Function call definitions.

openf           equ  0Fh               ;Open file.
creatf          equ  16h               ;Create file.
closef          equ  10h               ;Close file.
readf           equ  14h               ;Sequential read.
writef          equ  15h               ;Sequential write.
printf          equ  09h               ;Print string.

        ;Messages

source_error    db  'Source file not found$'
create_fail     db  'Unable to create destination file$'
disk_full       db  'Disk full$'
write_fail      db  'Unable to write to destination file$'
done_ok         db  'Copy complete$'
close_error     db  'Unable to close destination file$'
newline         db  cr,lf,'$'
```

*In the CODE section*

```
copy_file:

        ;Move the <destination> filename to a new FCB
        ;using a block copy.

        mov    si , 6Ch             ;The start of <destination>.
        mov    di , offset fcbout   ;The new FCB address.
        mov    cx , 12              ;Filename length.
        rep    movsb                ;Block move.

        ;Open the <source> FCB.
```

```
open_fcbin:
        mov     dx , offset default_fcb
        mov     ah , openf
        call    dobdos

        inc     al                      ;Error OFFh becomes zero.
        jnz     open_fcbout

        ;Open failed - file not found.

        mov     dx , offset source_error ;Display an error
        mov     ah , printf              ;message and then exit.
        call    dobdos

        jmp     exit

open_fcbout:
        ;Create the <destination> file.

        mov     dx , offset fcbout
        mov     ah , creatf
        call    dobdos

        inc     al                      ;Error OFFh becomes zero.
        jnz     fcb_init

        ;Failed to create (e.g. bad or missing filename
        ;or disk directory full).

        mov     dx , offset create_fail ;Display an error
        mov     ah , printf              ;message and then exit.
        call    dobdos

        jmp     exit

fcb_init:
        ;Zero the current record field in both FCBs.

        mov     default_fcb + 32 , 0
        mov     fcbout + 32 , 0

copy_loop:
        ;Read one record of default length (80h bytes) into
        ;the default DTA at 80h.

        mov     dx , offset default_fcb
```

```
        mov     ah , readf
        call    dobdos

        dec     al                      ;AL = 1 at end of file.
        jz      end_copy

;Write a record to the <destination> file.

        mov     dx , offset fcbout
        mov     ah , writef
        call    dobdos

        or      al , al                 ;AL = 0 if write was OK.
        jz      copy_loop               ;Copy the next record.

;Write error.

        dec     al                      ;AL = 1 for a full disk.
        jnz     write_error

        mov     dx , offset disk_full   ;Display an error
        jmp     werror_print            ;message and then exit.

write_error:
        mov     dx , offset write_fail

werror_print:
        mov     ah , printf
        call    dobdos

        jmp     close_exit              ;Close file before exit.

end_copy:
        ;Copy complete, display success.

        mov     dx , offset done_ok
        mov     ah , printf
        call    dobdos

close_exit:
        ;Close the <destination> file.

        mov     dx , offset fcbout
        mov     ah , closef
        call    dobdos

        or      al , al                 ;AL = 0 if closed OK.
```

```
          jz       exit

          ;Unable to close <destination> (e.g. diskette swop?).

          mov      dx , offset close_error ;Display an error
          mov      ah , printf             ;message and then exit.
          call     dobdos

exit:
          ;Common exit point: print newline at end of message.

          mov      dx , offset newline
          mov      ah , printf
          call     dobdos

          jmp      finished
```

## 11.5    TREE-STRUCTURED FILES

Particularly with the advent of large capacity fixed disks, the limitations of a single, 'flat' directory structure for files have been recognized in the design of DOS 2 and later versions. The tree-structured filestore of this operating system encourages the user to define a hierarchical directory structure in which files can be grouped sensibly in sub-directories. It provides a consistent and powerful filing mechanism owing much to the tradition of the well-respected UNIX operating system.

At the same time, the assembly language programmer's interface to the filing system has been raised to a higher level in DOS 2. Thus, for programs which do not need to run on earlier systems, DOS 2 and later versions are provided with more convenient facilities for file accessing. For consistency with earlier systems, however, the new facilities are provided in parallel to the old and upwards compatibility is maintained.

Filenames in tree-structured directories may be specified in one of two different ways: by giving the complete path from the top of the hierarchy (the **root directory**) or by expressing the path relative to the **current directory**. A typical example of a complete path is:

```
\usr\chris\source\othello.asm
```

which may be interpreted informally as meaning 'in the usr (user) sub-directory of root there is a further sub-directory for chris containing a further directory of his called source which in turn contains othello.asm, one of his source program files'. The path may be preceded by a drive code, as in:

```
B:\usr\chris\source\othello.asm
```

for cases where the current default drive is not appropriate. The current directory of a drive is the default directory which will be searched for files specified by only a partial path. If the current directory is \usr\chris, for example, then the above file can be specified as:

```
source\othello.asm
```

The initial current directory is root, but this may be changed by the CHDIR command or by a function call from within a program. Note that the leading backslash (\) will only be present when a full path is given. See the DOS manuals for more detailed description of tree-structured directories. In the description which follows, 'DOS manual' refers to the DOS version 2 or 3 manual containing the DOS function call descriptions.

The extended directory and file management calls of DOS 2 and later versions must be used to take full advantage of the facilities for manipulating tree-structured files. File Control Blocks are not used. Rather, on initiating a file access the programmer is given a 16-bit value called a **handle** with which to identify that file in subsequent operations. A file handle may refer also to a peripheral device such as the 'standard input device' (normally the keyboard) or 'standard output device' (normally the screen). The functions themselves are called in a similar way to those described earlier.

The following introduction to the new function calls presents the equivalent calls to those described earlier for the FCB approach.

### Open file (fn 3Dh)

on entry: DX = file specification address
AL = access code
(open code, DOS 3)
on exit:   AX = file handle

The file to be opened is specified as a character string in memory, the address of which is placed in DX before the call. The file may be described by either of the full or relative path approaches described earlier, with an optional drive code; the DOS manual calls this an 'ASCIIZ' string – it is a string of ASCII characters terminated by a zero. Unlike the DOS 1 calls, the programmer is obliged to specify an access (or open) code to open the file explicitly for reading (access code 0), writing (1) or both reading and writing (2). The file must exist and must not be protected against the requested mode of access (e.g. no attempt to open a read-only file for writing will be permitted).

DOS 3 uses a more complicated range of bit assignments in the open code field (AL). The increased complexity is due to the need to state criteria for shared access to files in the DOS 3 networking environment.

Note that the complete set of error codes returned from the new calls is grouped into a single error return table (see the DOS manual and Section 11.8.3). The carry flag is set on return from such a call if an error is detected; the error code is returned in AX.

If the open is successful, a 16-bit handle is returned in AX. This must be saved and used in subsequent calls which access the opened file. Note that, from DOS 3, there are predefined handles for some peripheral devices (e.g. the standard printer device) which do not need to be opened before use (see the DOS manual).

### Create file (fn 3Ch)

on entry: DX = file specification address
          CX = attribute mask
on exit:   AX = file handle

The file specification is in the same format as for 'open file'. This file may already exist: it is truncated to zero length if it does. In creating a new file, DOS places certain attributes in its directory entry which will stay with that file until deletion or until the attributes are changed by a 'change mode' function. Attributes are defined by a bit mask in CX and can be used to define a file as being read-only, or to hide it from normal directory searches, for example (see the DOS manual for further details). If successful, the file is opened in read/write mode and a file handle returned in AX. An error code is returned in AX with carry bit set after a failure.

### Delete file (fn 41h)

on entry: DX = file specification address
on exit:   AX = error return

The directory entry for the specified file is deleted, assuming the file can be found and is not protected by a read-only attribute.

### Read (fn 3Fh)

on entry: BX = file handle
          CX = no. of bytes to read
          DX = buffer address
on exit:   AX = no. of bytes read

The current position within a file at which read/write operations take place is maintained in the 'read/write pointer', initialized to the start of the file on opening. Unlike the fixed length record reading in the more primitive FCB-controlled calls, the programmer can request a read of any (16-bit) number of bytes and place them into store at any buffer address specified in the call. The number of bytes actually read may be less than that requested due to encountering the end of a file, for example. When input is directed from a device such as the keyboard, input will be at most one line of text. In the extreme case, AX is set to zero if the read/write pointer is at the end of the file on entry to the call. An invalid handle or insufficient access permission results in an error code returned in AX, with carry flag set. Both read and write calls manipulate the read/write pointer to achieve sequential file access.

### Write (fn 40h)

    on entry: BX = file handle
              CX = no. of bytes to write
              DX = buffer address
    on exit:  AX = no. of bytes written

As in the read call, the quantity and location of the bytes to output are stated flexibly in this call. The programmer should check that the actual number of bytes written is the same as the number requested as this is the only way to detect an event such as a full disk. Error codes as in the read call may also be returned.

### Close file (fn 3Eh)

    on entry: BX = file handle
    on exit:  AX = error return

The file identified by the handle in BX is closed. Note that, for efficiency reasons, an operating system will hold data output to a file in the internal memory until complete sectors are built up. Only on closing the file will any remnants of this output be 'flushed', that is written out to disk. An error code will be returned if the file handle is invalid, with the carry flag set.

Because of the possibility of shared access to a file by other network users in DOS 3, all files should be closed as soon as they are no longer needed (see the DOS manual for further details of shared access to files).

### Another simple file copy program
The following example is the file copy routine of Section 11.4 implemented in DOS 2 or later version using the advanced file handling calls introduced above.

Unlike the previous example, no FCB definitions are required to write this program using the DOS 2 extensions. It is assumed on entry that the program is called with the full or relative path names of the source and destination files, as in:

    fcopy  doc\chmemo.txt  doc\memo\ch

Note that the relative path names in this example refer to subdirectories of the current directory called doc and doc\memo which must already exist. In particular, the program will only create the destination file ch; it will not create the subdirectory doc\memo in which to place it.

The DOS command processor – that part of the operating system which processes the fcopy command – will automatically place the command tail (the two filenames) into memory from offset 81h in the Program Segment Prefix, with the length of this tail in offset 80h (see Section 11.6.1). We shall leave these filenames here, and determine the start address of each to use in the DOS calls.

As in the previous example, 80h bytes are read at a time into a buffer in memory. This unit of transfer can be increased easily by changing the data buffer size constant in the program.

*In the DATA section*

```
              ;Parameter buffer addresses in the Program Segment Prefix
              ;are defined in the skeleton program.

              ;Define a buffer area to hold a data record.

record_size      equ  80h                    ;Change as desired.
data_buffer      db   record_size dup (?)

              ;Variables to hold the source and destination file handles.

source_handle    dw   0
dest_handle      dw   0

              ;Function call definitions.

openf            equ  3Dh                    ;Open file.
creatf           equ  3Ch                    ;Create file.
closef           equ  3Eh                    ;Close file.
readf            equ  3Fh                    ;Read.
writef           equ  40h                    ;Write.
printf           equ  09h                    ;Print string.

         ;Messages.

param_error      db   'Two filenames expected$'
done_ok          db   'Copy complete$'
error_mess       db   'Error $'
newline          db   cr,lf,'$'
```

*In the CODE section*

```
copy_file:

        ;Find the start address of the source filename.
        ;param_length and param_buffer are defined in the
        ;skeleton program.

        mov     ch , 0
        mov     cl , param_length       ;Count of characters.
        mov     di , offset param_buffer ;Start of filenames.

        call    find_filename

        push    si                      ;Save the current position
        push    cx                      ;in the parameter string.

        ;Open the source file.

        mov     dx , di                 ;Start of source filename.
        mov     al , 0                  ;'Read' access code.
        mov     ah , openf
        call    dobdos                  ;Open file.

        jc      error

        ;Save the source file handle.

        mov     source_handle , ax

        ;Scan the command tail for start of the destination file.
        ;Restore the buffer count and pointer.

        pop     cx
        pop     di

        call    find_filename

        ;Create a new destination file or truncate an old one to
        ;zero length.

        mov     dx , di                 ;Start of dest. filename.
        xor     cx , cx                 ;Zero the attribute parameter.
        mov     ah , creatf
        call    dobdos
```

```
        jc     error

        ;The destination file is now open in read/write mode.
        ;Save the destination file handle.

        mov    dest_handle , ax

copy_loop:
        ;Read one data record into the buffer.

        mov    bx , source_handle
        mov    cx , record_size
        mov    dx , offset data_buffer
        mov    ah , readf
        call   dobdos

        jc     error

        or     ax , ax
        jz     end_copy                    ;AX = 0 at end of file.

        ;Write a data record out to the destination file.
        ;AX contains the size of data record actually read

        mov    bx , dest_handle
        mov    cx , ax
        mov    dx , offset data_buffer
        mov    ah , writef
        call   dobdos

        jc     error

        jmp    copy_loop                   ;Keep going.

end_copy:
        ;Copy complete, display success.

        mov    dx , offset done_ok
        mov    ah , printf
        call   dobdos

        ;Close the destination file.

        mov    bx , dest_handle
        mov    ah , closef
        call   dobdos
```

```
          jc      error

          jmp     exit

error:
          ;Error routine.
          ;Print the error return table entry number.
          ;This number is in AX on entry.
          ;
          ;Uses the +ve integer print routine 'print_num'
          ;given in 6.2.2.

          push    ax                      ;Save the error code.
          mov     dx , offset error_mess
          mov     ah , printf
          call    dobdos                  ;Print error message.

          pop     ax
          call    print_num               ;Print error number.

exit:
          ;Common exit point - print a newline at end of
          ;the message and exit.

          mov     dx , offset newline
          mov     ah , printf
          call    dobdos

          jmp     finished


find_filename:
          ;Scans a parameter string for a valid (tree-structured)
          ;filename.
          ;On entry,
          ;   CX = remaining length of string.
          ;   DI = pointer to filename string.
          ;On exit,
          ;   DI = address of start of filename.
          ;   SI = address of end of filename + 2.
          ;   CX is updated.
          ;   the filename is terminated by a zero, i.e. it is a
          ;      valid ASCIIZ string.
          ;

          or      cx , cx
```

```
            jle      p_error              ;No characters there at all.

            mov      al , ' '
            repe     scasb                ;Skip leading spaces.
            je       p_error              ;Nothing but spaces there.

            dec      di                   ;DI = start of filename.
            inc      cx

            mov      si , di

scan_loop:
            dec      cx
            lodsb                         ;Scan to end of filename.
            cmp      al , ' '
            ja       scan_loop

            mov      byte ptr [si-1] , 0  ;Add ASCIIZ terminator.

            ret

p_error:
            mov      dx , offset param_error ;Display an error
            mov      ah , printf             ;message and then exit.
            call     dobdos

            pop      cx                   ;Remove the return address
            jmp      exit                 ;before exit.
```

The error handling in this program is not very friendly: an improved program would store the error return table and print out an error message in place of the number (but see also Section 11.8.3 on error handling).

Note that FCB function calls can be used in a tree-structured file environment but only files in the current directory can be addressed by an FCB call.

## 11.6   FILE HANDLING UTILITIES

In addition to the basic calls described in the previous sections, an operating system provides a range of further functions for file handling. A summary of all file handling functions and their availability in the various operating systems is given in Table 11.1, with the tree-structured file utilities shown separately in Table 11.2.

**Table 11.1**   FCB file handling utilities.

| Operating system | | | Fn. | Function | Group |
|---|---|---|---|---|---|
| DOS 1 | DOS 2/3 | CP/M -86 | no. (HEX) | | |
| Y | Y | Y | 0F | Open file | File status |
| Y | Y | Y | 10 | Close file | |
| Y | Y | Y | 16 | Create file | |
| | | | | Sequential: | |
| Y | Y | Y | 14 | Sequential read | |
| Y | Y | Y | 15 | Sequential write | |
| | | | | Random: | |
| Y | Y | Y | 21 | Random read | |
| Y | Y | Y | 22 | Random write | |
| Y | Y | Y | 24 | Set random record | |
| Y | Y | N | 27 | Random block read | |
| Y | Y | N | 28 | Random block write | |
| N | N | Y | 28 | Write random (fill) | Read/write |
| Y | Y | Y | 1A | Set disk transfer address | |
| Y | Y | N | 2E | Verify switch | |
| N | Y | N | 2F | Get disk transfer address | |
| N | N | Y | 33 | Set dta base | |
| N | N | Y | 34 | Get dta base | |
| Y | Y | Y | 11 | Search for first | |
| Y | Y | Y | 12 | Search for next | Filename and |
| Y | Y | Y | 13 | Delete file | directory |
| Y | Y | Y | 17 | Rename file | operations |
| Y | Y | N | 29 | Parse filename | |
| N | N | Y | 1E | Set file attribute | |
| Y | Y | Y | 23 | File size | |
| N | Y | N | 36 | Free space | |
| Y | N | N | 1B | FAT address | |
| N | Y | N | 1B | FAT info (default drive) | Directory |
| N | N | Y | 1B | Get ADDR (ALLOC) | enquiries |
| N | Y | N | 1C | FAT info (specific drive) | |
| N | N | Y | 31 | Sysdat address | |
| N | N | Y | 1F | Get ADDR (Disk Parameters) | |
| Y | Y | Y | 0D | Disk reset | |
| Y | Y | Y | 0E | Select disk | |
| Y | Y | Y | 19 | Current disk | |
| N | N | Y | 18 | Login vector | |
| N | N | Y | 1C | Write protect | System/drive |
| N | N | Y | 1D | Get R/O vector | status |
| N | N | Y | 20 | Set/get user code | |
| N | N | Y | 25 | Reset drive | |

**Table 11.2**    Tree-structured file handling utilities (DOS 2/3)

| Function number (HEX) | Function | Group |
|---|---|---|
| 3C | Create file | |
| 3D | Open file | |
| 3E | Close file | File status |
| 5A | Create unique file (3.00) | |
| 5B | Create new file (3.00) | |
| 5C | Lock/unlock file access (3.00) | |
| 3F | Read | |
| 40 | Write | |
| 42 | Move read/write pointer | Read/write |
| 44 | I/O Control | |
| 2E | Verify switch | |
| 54 | Get verify state | |
| 39 | Create sub-directory | |
| 3A | Remove directory | |
| 3B | Change directory | |
| 41 | Delete file | |
| 43 | Change mode | Filename/directory operations |
| 47 | Get current directory | |
| 4E | Find first | |
| 4F | Find next | |
| 56 | Rename file | |
| 45 | Duplicate file handle | Concurrent file access |
| 46 | Force duplicate | |
| 59 | Get extended error (3.00) | New DOS 3 general calls |
| 62 | Get program segment prefix address (3.00) | |
| 5E00 | Get machine name (3.10) | |
| 5E02 | Set printer setup (3.10) | |
| 5E03 | Get printer setup (3.10) | Device control |
| 5F02 | Get redirection list entry (3.10) | |
| 5F03 | Redirect device (3.10) | |
| 5F04 | Cancel redirection (3.10) | |

(functions available from DOS 2.00 onwards unless otherwise indicated)

Clearly, it is in the interest of those implementers writing software to run on all operating systems to stick as far as possible to those functions present in all DOS versions and in CP/M-86.

The detailed operation of the above function calls is documented in the relevant operating system manuals. Below, we consider some of the more useful programming techniques involving the FCB-oriented functions described in Table 11.1.

### 11.6.1  Command and filename parsing

A common way of specifying a file on which a program is to operate is to append the filename after the command. In general, one or more filename parameters could follow a command, as illustrated by the typical command structure:

```
compare thisfile.txt thatfile.txt
```

Assistance is available for the programmer who wishes to accept filenames in this format and translate them into FCB format. In the simplest case where just one filename follows the command, this filename is automatically decoded by the command processor of DOS and inserted in the default FCB at offset 5Ch in the Program Segment Prefix. The format is that expected in an FCB, making it possible to open the FCB without further manipulation of the filename fields (other than to zero the extent field in CP/M-86).

If two filenames are present the second is also decoded, this time into an FCB beginning at offset 6Ch in the Program Segment Prefix. This is not a convenient place to open an FCB because it overlaps with the FCB of the first file parameter at 5Ch. It should be considered to be a holding area for the FCB filename details which should then be copied to an FCB area defined in the program. The copying must take place before the first file FCB is opened in order to avoid corrupting the second filename.

In addition to the above, the entire command line after the command name is placed in an unformatted parameter area from offset 81h in the Program Segment Prefix, with the total number of characters placed in 80h. This allows parsing of the filename or other parameters under control of the programmer. The buffered keyboard input routine (function 0Ah) provides an alternative for reading filenames from within a program.

The skeleton program (Appendix C) defines labels for many of the above addresses in the Program Segment Prefix.

Note finally that DOS provides a useful 'parse filename' function (29h) for flexible decoding of filenames presented in this latter way. This function correctly decodes ambiguous filenames containing ? or * characters – the * is expanded into ?s in the FCB filename or extension fields. Default options are provided for special cases of decoding, such as default drive specification.

### 11.6.2  Directory searching

The two functions 'search for first' (11h) and 'search for next' (12h) are normally used to scan a disk directory for filenames which match an ambiguous file specification (i.e. one containing the global filename character '?'). Typically, a programmer wishes to perform some processing on all files which match a particular ambiguous specification – all *.TXT files, for example.

The filename is placed in an unopened FCB, with ?s in all positions where any character will be acceptable (*.TXT expanded to ????????.TXT, for example). 'Search for first' attempts to locate a matching filename in the directory and, if found, returns the unambiguous filename. 'Search for next' continues the directory search and returns a subsequent match in the same manner. The programmer can continue to issue 'search for next' calls to locate the entire set of matching directory entries.

There are two important points to note when using these functions. Firstly, the system keeps track of the current search position in the directory by inserting information into the unopened FCB area. Thus, it is generally unsafe to perform any file operations between search for first/next calls, even though this is precisely what we most often wish to do! The secure, if inconvenient approach is to retrieve and store a complete list of unambiguous matching filenames in an array (in FCB filename format) prior to processing them. Beware of using shortcuts such as a 'search for first' on the unambiguous filenames in turn, followed by a 'search for next' on the ambiguous one – this will not work on all systems. If speed is not of the essence, however, one could start the search from the beginning each time, keeping a count of how many matches to skip over to the next unprocessed file.

The second point refers to the difference in operation between DOS and CP/M-86. In the former, a successful search returns a valid, unopened FCB at the disk transfer address containing the matching filename. CP/M-86, however, returns a complete directory record at the DTA containing a block of four 32-byte FCB formatted entries, with the particular entry identified by a 0–3 code in AL. To write programs which will work in either system it is sufficient to program the CP/M-86 variant, since DOS returns 0 in AL for both search calls, correctly mimicking the equivalent CP/M-86 structure.

### 11.6.3 Random access

In sequential reading and writing the operating system maintains pointers to the next record in the file to be accessed. This record is in fact identified by the current record position in the current block ('extent' in CP/M-86); both of these values are contained in the FCB at bytes 32 and 12 (12/13 in DOS) respectively. The programmer is only obliged to set the current record field of the FCB once, to zero, after opening the FCB.

To enable a random access to be made to any record in the file, each record is identified absolutely by a single integer from zero upwards. Bytes 33–36 (DOS) or bytes 33–35 (CP/M-86) of the FCB are used to hold this integer identifier and, hence, space for these must be allocated in the FCB declaration when using random access calls. In practice, we can unify the procedure required to work in all operating systems by assuming that only default length records (128 bytes) will be accessed. In this simplified case, byte 36 (DOS) is not used and byte 35 (all operating systems) should be set to zero. Thus, the two remaining bytes represent a 16-bit unsigned integer (byte 33 is the least significant byte) identifying file records in the range 0–65 535 decimal. Note, incidentally, that there is no space for byte 36 (DOS) in the default FCB at 5Ch without overlapping into the unformatted parameter area at 80h but it is not necessary to allocate byte 36 at all if the above simplification is adopted.

The system does not set this random record number field automatically during file accessing. The programmer should set byte 35 to zero and bytes 33 and 34 to the number of the required record, relative to the start of the file. Once this field is set, a random read or write call (functions 21h and 22h) can be issued to access the specified record.

Sequential accesses may be mixed with random accesses, but note that a random access call does not automatically advance the current record position held in the FCB to the next record, as does a sequential operation. Thus, a sequential read (write) following a random read (write) will access the same record twice. A 'dummy' sequential read call is sufficient to skip to the next record.

Regardless of the mode of access, an FCB must be *open* before performing accesses.

Typically, a programmer may wish to determine the current random record number of a record just read or written, in order to save it, in a table perhaps, for later random access of that record. The 'set random record' function (24h) translates the internal block (or extent) and record information in the FCB, and sets the random record field to the correct value for the current record. The 2-byte integer at FCB bytes 33 and 34 is the value which should then be saved for future random accessing.

When writing random records it is quite possible to leave 'gaps' in a file by not writing to all random record numbers in the range used for that file. This feature should be used with care since the unwritten records will not contain sensible data and may not even have space allocated on the disk if the gaps are large. In many applications it may be better to avoid gaps developing by ensuring that all records are initialized. The 'random block write' (DOS) or 'write random with zero fill' (CP/M-86) functions (both 28h) may be useful in this respect, though they are not compatible with each other.

Finally, note that a convenient way to append records to an existing file is to use the 'compute file size' function (23h). It returns the number of records in the file in the random record number field of the FCB. As a bonus, this is precisely the number of the record following the last one in the file, requiring no further action before performing a random write of a record to be appended.

### 11.6.4  Resetting and changing diskettes

Care must be taken when a program requires a change of diskette since the operating system cannot always adjust automatically to such a dramatic upheaval in its filestore. It is possible, for example, that updated directory information and buffered file output may not have been written out prior to removing a diskette, with unfortunate consequences.

The main function involved in diskette changing is the 'disk reset' function (0Dh). It may be called *before* a diskette change in order to guarantee that any buffered data in open files will be written to diskette (an activity called buffer **flushing**) and the directory on diskette updated. However, this is not needed if all files written are closed before the change takes place. The reset disk function should certainly be called *after* the diskette change to restore the system to a stable, reset state.

The 'reset disk' call may have other effects. In CP/M-86, the default drive is reset to drive A. Thus, to perform a reset in CP/M-86 while retaining the previous settings of these values, the following sequence is recommended:

1. Determine the current default drive using the 'current drive' function (19h) and save this code.
2. Reset the diskette (function 0Dh) – this can be omitted if all files written have been properly closed.
3. Make the diskette change.
4. Reset the diskette (function 0Dh).
5. Reset the default drive using function 0Eh.

The procedure is more complicated if accesses to a file on a different drive are to continue unaffected by a disk system reset. The current random record position should be determined, saved, and restored when the file is reopened after the reset.

The cautious programmer may choose to issue a similar sequence of calls (omitting steps 2 and 3) prior to the first access to any diskette drive, even when diskette changes are not normally expected.

### 11.6.5  File attributes

A file **attribute** is a marker attached to a directory entry in order to define a particular characteristic of a file's behaviour. A typical example is the 'read-only' attribute which may be set to prohibit write or delete access to a file. Two of the other attributes available in some, but not necessarily all of the operating systems are given in this chapter.

#### *'System file attribute'*

This makes the filename 'invisible' to normal directory searches. It is often used in conjunction with the read-only attribute to protect system command and data files and to reduce the background clutter in directory listings and searches.

### 'Archive bit attribute'

This is set by the operating system whenever the file has been written to and closed. An 'archiver' is a program that makes copies of files on a back-up disk for recovery in cases of accidental data loss. It is often run regularly, e.g. once per day, to limit the damage that can be caused by disk failure or inadvertent file destruction. An archiver may inspect the 'archive bit' attribute and update its copy of the file only if changes have been made to the file since it was last archived. The archive bit can then be reset by the archiver.

Attributes have been implemented differently in the various operating systems and the relevant manual should be consulted to determine the range of attributes supported and the required procedures.

Note that an *extended* FCB is a feature used by DOS only to hold the attributes of a file. It consists of a standard FCB with a 7-byte prefix, the first byte of which contains 0FFh so that DOS can recognize it as an extended FCB. Any of the DOS function calls referring to an FCB will also accept the address of the start of this 7-byte prefix.

### 11.6.6   File access table

A number of the directory enquiry type of function calls refer to the File Access Table (FAT) in DOS, or to ADDR/ALLOC in CP/M-86. This information relates to the way in which logical disk records are mapped onto the physical locations (tracks/sectors etc.) on the disk. In practice, the method of access to this information is complicated and it is rarely required by a programmer. In the absence of a suitable function call, however, it may be necessary to access this information. One example of this is to calculate the amount of free space left on a disk, though a function call is now available in DOS (only) to do this. The relevant documentation should be studied carefully before using the access table information.

### 11.7   ENVIRONMENT CALLS

Many additional operating system function calls are provided to support various non-file and non-I/O operations. These include access to the date and time settings, and to the operating system version number, for example. One set of calls is concerned with controlling the dynamic allocation of memory to a user program. Interrupt activity can be monitored and directed by other calls. Control over the execution of programs, such as to run a second program from within a program, may also be provided.

There is virtually no compatibility between DOS and CP/M-86 in these environment calls, the majority of which have been tagged onto versions of the operating systems. It seems likely that the range of calls will be extended significantly at each new release, and the programmer must study the relevant documentation carefully to choose the correct function for a particular purpose.

## 11.8   DOS SOFTWARE INTERRUPTS

DOS reserves a block of interrupts (from INT 20h to INT 3Fh) for its own use. These transfer control to routines whose addresses are stored in an area of memory reserved by DOS. This mechanism is designed to provide efficient implementation of certain fundamental activities, a few of which are introduced next. See the DOS manuals for further information.

### 11.8.1   Program termination
A software interrupt call INT 20h is one way to exit from a program. Certain DOS parameters which may have been modified temporarily by the program are reset and all file buffers are flushed (though files must be closed properly in order to update directory information correctly). It is important to ensure when using this interrupt that, on entry, the CS register refers to the Program Segment Prefix.

DOS 2 and later versions remove this restriction on CS provided INT 21h is used instead of INT 20h, with AH containing 4Ch on exit.

The skeleton program (Appendix C) label finished provides a convenient program termination technique.

### 11.8.2   Function calling
INT 21h has already been described as the mechanism for invoking all DOS function calls.

### 11.8.3   Error handling
When a 'critical error' occurs, DOS will transfer control with an INT 24h instruction. A critical error is a serious failure typified by an abortive attempt to write to a disk due to write protection or a disk controller error. It may be possible for a user program to take sensible recovery actions in such cases or to 'degrade gracefully', i.e. to finish the program execution in orderly fashion, with a sensible error message. Detailed information on the exact nature of the error can be deciphered from the register and user stack values established in an INT 24h call, as explained in the DOS manual.

From DOS version 3.00 a function call (59h) has been introduced in an attempt to unify error handling. This function may be called by the user after an error is detected by an INT 24h, for example, but it may also be called after any INT 21h function call, including the FCB calls. An error code is returned, together with information on the class of the error (hardware, internal, system etc.) and its location (serial device, memory etc.). An action code is also specified: this offers a recommended action (retry, abort, etc.) mainly for use in handling errors whose precise cause and treatment is not anticipated in a particular application.

# 12| Segments

## 12.1 INTRODUCTION

Throughout this book there have been casual references to segments. Data items have appeared in the data segment and instructions have appeared in the code segment. A segment is simply a designated section of the 1 Mbyte of memory available to the 8086 processor. All references to memory provide two items of information in order to locate the required object. Firstly the segment within which the required data object resides must be named. Secondly the offset of that data object within the segment is given. It is for this reason that the word 'offset' has usually been used rather than the more common term of an 'address'. The address is more correctly the combination of the segment name and the offset. As we shall discover in the next section, the naming of the segment can be made quite invisible to the programmer. Segments can be nominated as 'current segments' and future access requires only the specification of an offset. This initialization of current segments is one of the functions of the skeleton program.

## 12.2 USING SEGMENTS

The available memory in an 8086 system may be as large as 1 Mbyte. Each byte has an address within the range 0 to FFFFF in hexadecimal notation. The 8086 calculates the address from the segment name and the offset.

A segment name is a number specifying the start of that segment. The starting address of a segment is within the range 0 to FFFFF with the restriction that the last four bits – the last hexadecimal digit – must be zero. This restriction means that only the first four digits of the 5-digit address need to be given as the last digit is known to be zero. This first 4-digit address is the segment name. It is exactly accommodated within 16 bits, which conforms with the 8086 16-bit architecture. For example suppose we had defined a segment which starts at address 12340h. This segment would be situated within the one megabyte memory as shown in Figure 12.1.

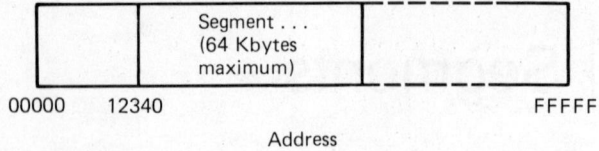

**Figure 12.1**   Example of segment memory layout.

The segment's name is 1234. We may now access data within this segment by presenting the segment name and the offset of the data. The fourth byte in the segment has an offset of three. The byte is identified as:

```
Segment name 1234    Offset  0003
```

The byte's address is calculated by adding the offset to the starting address of the segment. The starting address of the segment is simply the segment name with a zero digit appended:

```
12340
 0003 +
─────
12343   Final address
```

This process occurs for every access to memory. There are two restrictions placed on segments. Firstly, because the last digit of the starting address must be zero, segments may only start on 16-byte intervals. Secondly, because the offset is a 4-digit (16-bit) value, the maximum size of a segment is 64 Kbytes. Segments may then be of any size which is a multiple of 16 bytes up to a maximum of 64 Kbytes. The size of a segment is, however, conceptual and no attempt is made by the 8086 processor to stop a program accessing data which follows a segment which is not of the maximum size. If our segment 1234 were preceded by a small segment 1230 then the memory layout would appear as in Figure 12.2.

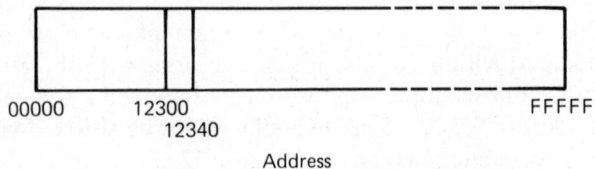

**Figure 12.2**   Adjacent memory segments.

The bytes within segment 1230 have offsets in the range 0000 to 003F. If an offset larger than this were given then an object in segment 1234 would be found. The byte with offset 0003 in segment 1234 could equally be accessed as the byte with offset 0043 in segment 1230! In practice such overlapping impingements are dangerous to use and should be avoided.

This arrangement of segments is made much more convenient to use than the above description might imply. The allocation of space to segments is performed by the operating system which passes the segment names to the program. The 8086 also simplifies matters somewhat by having a concept of 'current segments'. There are always four segments which are nominated as being current. The current segments are called:

- data segment;
- code segment;
- stack segment;
- extra segment.

The name of the segment currently known as the data segment is in the data segment register DS. The name of the segment currently known as the code segment is in the code segment register CS. Similarly the names of the segments currently known as the stack and the extra segments are in the registers SS and ES. The four segment registers DS, CS, SS and ES were introduced in Chapter 4. There are very few instructions which can be used to manipulate them. The MOV, PUSH and POP instructions may be used on the segment registers DS, SS and ES. There are special jump and call instructions which are the only way to alter the CS register.

Only segments which are current can be accessed. Programs written in this book have only used three distinct segments. These are the code, date and stack segments and have always been current. The skeleton program has ensured that the segment registers are correctly initialized. An extra segment is declared by the skeleton program as exactly overlapping the data segment. Memory access is normally made by providing an offset. The segment which is used with this offset is determined by context under the following rules:

1. All instructions are in the code segment and so jumps and calls refer to an offset in the code segment.
2. Stack instructions access the stack pointer SP which always contains an offset within the stack segment.
3. All other memory references are to data within the data segment.

There are two exceptions to rule 3 and there are also mechanisms for overriding these rules. These matters are explained in later sections.

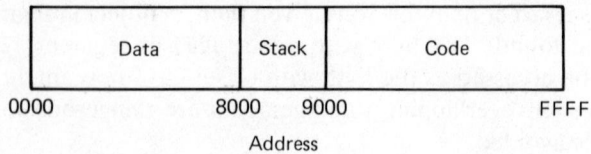

**Figure 12.3**   A typical large program layout.

It appears that no use is made of the extra segment. In our programs we have ensured that the data and extra segments are the same segments. Access to the extra segment is also explained later.

There are two main advantages of a segmented memory scheme. Firstly there is a vast increase of memory size available. Secondly there are several conceptual benefits permitting many features hitherto found only in large computer systems. These two advantages are discussed in turn.

### 12.2.1   Increased memory capacity

The 8086 processor has a 16-bit architecture and this limits its normal number range to FFFF in hexadecimal. Such a range would only allow an accessible address space of 64 Kbytes. This is the upper limit on most early microprocessors which similarly employ 16-bit addressing. A typical large program layout on such a machine might be as shown in Figure 12.3.

The program's data exists within the memory range 0000h to 7FFFh followed by an area for the stack in the range 8000h to 8FFFh which is followed by the code in the range 9000h to FFFFh.

These three divisions of data, stack and code are conceptual as well as physical. Normally we would neither normally wish to jump into the stack nor would we store values into the code. Each instruction would sensibly use an address which is known to relate to either data, stack or code. One way to take advantage of this fact would be to provide three separate memories, as shown in Figure 12.4.

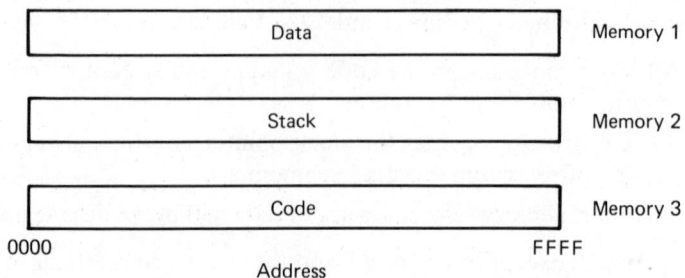

**Figure 12.4**   Separated memories.

In this situation an instruction such as:

    jmp 89ADh

could be interpreted by the processor as:

Jump to offset 89AD hex in memory 3

The instruction:

    mov  ax , 89ADh

could be interpreted by the processor as:

Move into register AX the data with offset 89AD hex in memory 1

The instruction:

    push ax

could be interpreted by the processor as:

Decrement the stack pointer and then store register AX at the offset into memory 2 given by the stack pointer.

By giving each individual instruction a default memory to which it applies we have effectively tripled our available memory while still using the same 16-bit addresses. There would be occasions when we wish to alter these defaults – for example when initially writing the program's instructions into memory 3. Many such memories could be provided and special instructions could be incorporated such as:

Memory 4 is now the data memory

By providing many memories the program's size is unlimited. Subroutines could each access 64 Kbytes of personal data by starting with an instruction such as that above. Upon return from the subroutine the data memory number would then be reset. Subroutines' instructions could exist in different memories. The subroutine call-and-return mechanism need only remember and restore such changes to the 'current code memory'.

This hypothetical system has provided a much larger memory capacity and parallels between it and the 8086's segmented approach should be becoming obvious. By recognizing that each instruction applies to a unique application of memory the physical size of programs is not restricted to the simple address range.

In practice a fourth kind of memory would be required. For example, a program which reads the user's program into memory would have to have access to at least one more currently accessible memory into which it places, in turn, the user's program's data, stack and code. This extra memory completes the parallel with the 8086's concept of an 'extra segment'.

Finally the programmer could be given the flexibility to change from a rigid structure with, say, sixteen 64 Kbyte memories to suit differing requirements. The total available memory could alternatively be divided into:

1 × 64-Kbyte code memory
10 × 32-Kbyte data memories
32 ×  4-Kbyte code memories (for small subroutines)

This would still leave half of the total memory available which could be used by another program. This final alteration is permitted by the 8086 and, while not advancing the overall memory available, permits some of the benefits described in the next section.

### 12.2.2  Conceptual benefits
The ability to split a program into several segments of the kind described earlier has many important benefits. The logical distinction between code and data gives a degree of protection in that some of the erroneous actions otherwise allowable – such as altering instructions or jumping into data – are not allowed directly. By suitable means these actions can be achieved but the instructions to do so are different and the intention is clear.

Program development is made easier and less error prone. A program can be developed as several small programs, each performing some designated task. These small programs can be written and tested separately. This greatly assists the programmer. Each program can be restricted to its own segment and is then unlikely to interfere erroneously with another program. A newly written component may then be added to a set of already tried and tested programs in the knowledge that it will not corrupt the existing working programs. Any errors found in subsequent testing can reasonably be assumed to lie in the new program. This confinement of errors makes them much easier to locate.

### *Relocation*
Perhaps the major benefit of a segmented memory is the ability to relocate segments during a program's execution. It is desirable that a program can be placed anywhere within memory when it is first loaded. In this way several independent programs can coexist running concurrently. Some systems allow the processor's time to be shared between several programs. The user may set a particularly lengthy program running which requires no interaction and then carry on with a second program. In such a dynamic environment programs must be relocatable. This means that when a program is loaded it can be placed at a different absolute position each time.

In a non-segmented machine this is achieved by the assembler translating the program as though it were to be loaded at address zero. Each instruction and data word containing a memory address is marked. When the program is loaded the actual address where loading commences is added to each marked word. The problem with this system is that, once running, a program cannot be safely relocated. If the program were to be moved and the marked words altered accordingly this would not suffice. By then, return addresses of subroutines and addresses of data objects may have been stored in locations unknown to the operating system.

With a segmented machine dynamic relocation is simple. The segment would be copied to its new location and the segment name – the starting address of the segment – altered accordingly. As all accesses to this segment are relative to this name the relocation is complete. The ability to relocate programs dynamically has two important consequences. Firstly in an environment where different programs start and finish the memory can become fragmented. That occurs because when a program finishes, its memory space can be reclaimed. Several free 'holes' of differing sizes appear. A situation can then arise where there is sufficient memory available to load a new program but it is not in a usable form, as shown in Figure 12.5.

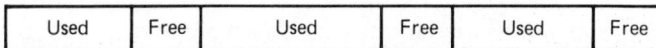

| Used | Free | Used | Free | Used | Free |
|------|------|------|------|------|------|

**Figure 12.5**    Fragmented memory.

In this case the segments in use can be relocated downwards to fill in the intervening holes, creating one large free space at the top of memory, as shown in Figure 12.6.

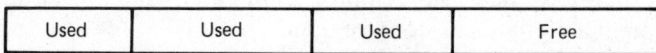

| Used | Used | Used | Free |
|------|------|------|------|

**Figure 12.6**    Memory layout after relocation.

The second advantage to dynamic relocation is that individual segments can vary their sizes. If a segment needs to expand as a program's data requirements temporarily become larger then this would otherwise be impossible unless there happened to be sufficient free space following the segment. However with this system the segment is simply relocated to an area which has sufficient free space.

## 12.3   SEGMENT DEFAULTS

When an instruction accesses memory an offset is produced which is applied within one of the four current segments. Section 12.2 gave three rules governing which segment is used and noted that there are two exceptions to those rules. The rules are:

1. A jump or call produces an offset into the code segment.
2. The stack pointer contains an offset into the stack segment.
3. Other memory accesses are within the data segment.

The two exceptions are exceptions to the third rule. They are:

1. Any memory access using the BP register produces an offset into the stack segment.
2. With the string instructions STOS, MOVS, CMPS and SCAS the DI register contains an offset into the extra segment.

The first exception means, for instance, that the following instructions will fetch the word at the top of the stack into the AX register and without altering the state of the stack:

```
mov     bp , sp            ;Offset of top of stack.
mov     ax , word ptr [bp]  ;Fetch word into AX.
```

The BP register can be used to access any part of the stack in this way. It is because of this exception that the cryptic comment in Chapter 4 warns against using the BP register as a pointer.

The main reason for this exception is in recognition of the common stack usage of block-structured high-level programming languages. In such languages local data space is allocated on procedure entry and released on procedure exit. This means that it is not necessary to reserve space for every procedure all the time. It also permits procedures to call themselves without the subsequent alteration of their local data, as each procedure entry would result in the allocation of a new area of store for data.

This system is achieved by allocating space in the stack for local data. On procedure entry the stack pointer is moved over the required space and the BP register used to access this space. A typical sequence of events on procedure entry might be:

```
BP := SP - 2                first free position
SP := SP - space required   skip over local data
```

The local data is referred to as, for example:

```
word ptr [bp - 6]
```

or:

```
byte ptr [bp - 10]
```

Procedure exit would then reset the stack pointer to the value in the BP register plus two.

The second exception appears at first sight peculiar. It is, however, the only sensible means of allowing string instructions to apply to two strings in different segments. When the operations are on strings which are both in the data segment all that is required is to ensure that the data and extra segments are the same. This simply means that the ES register should contain the same value as the DS register. The skeleton program ensures that this is the case when a program starts.

Data can be copied from the data segment into any other segment by placing that destination segment's name into the ES register. When the current data segment is not the source of a string instruction then the DS register must be altered temporarily. Great care must be taken not to access any data segment objects while the DS register holds this temporary value. If a data object is declared in the data segment as:

```
data_obj        dw        10
```

Then the instruction:

```
mov     data_obj , ax
```

simply moves the value in the AX register into the word with the same offset as data_obj in the segment currently named in the DS register. The general procedure for performing a string operation is as follows:

1. Set up registers SI, DI and CX as appropriate.
2. If DS is not the source segment then save DS.
3. If ES is not the destination instruction then save ES.
4. Alter DS and ES as necessary.
5. Perform the string operation.
6. Restore DS and ES as necessary.

For example, suppose we wish to copy the top 10 words currently on the stack into the data segment. The words are copied into an array called stack_ten_words. The following instructions will achieve this:

```
mov     si , sp                          ;Top of stack offset.
add     si , 18                          ;Move a further 9 words
                                         ;into the stack.
mov     di , offset stack_ten_words  ;Destination.
mov     cx , 10                          ;10 words.

push    ds
push    es                ;Save DS and ES.

mov     ax , ds           ;Destination segment is current DS.
```

```
mov     es , ax         ;Copy this into ES.

mov     ax , ss         ;Source segment is current SS.
mov     ds , ax         ;Copy this into DS.

rep     movsw           ;Copy ten words.

pop     es
pop     ds              ;Restore the ES and DS registers.
```

## 12.4  SEGMENT OVERRIDES

The rules and exceptions for segment access were discussed in the previous section. There are occasions when the required segment is not the one that would be used by default. This situation can be overcome by temporarily altering the relevant current segment as was done in the example which copied information from the stack.

Such saving and restoring of segment names is clumsy when only a few instructions are required. The segment used for the memory access of an instruction can be explicitly named as one of the other three current segments. This is achieved by prefixing the instruction with a segment override instruction. The assembler syntax for this prefix is to prefix the memory operand with one of:

```
DS:  CS:  SS:  ES:
```

This actually causes one of the four segment override instructions to appear immediately before the affected instruction. As an example the following instruction moves a word from the code segment into the AX register:

```
mov     ax , cs:word ptr [bx]
```

The word moved is in the code segment and its offset is the value in the BX register. This instruction was in fact encountered in Chapter 7 in connection with the case construct.

The string instructions may also be prefixed in this way. Some string instructions have two memory operands. Only the source operand as given by the SI register is affected. The DI register *always* contains an offset into the extra segment and, presumably for consistency, this is the case with the instructions STOS and SCAS which only have one memory operand. Any segment prefix to these two instructions is ignored. Problems can arise when a segment prefix is applied in addition to a repeat prefix:

```
rep cs: movsb
```

This sort of construct should not be used, as any external interrupt will result in one of the prefixes being 'forgotten' by the processor. For these reasons it is safest never to use a segment override on any string instruction.

## 12.5  SUMMARY

The segmented architecture of the 8086 has been described and can be seen to be one of the major reasons for this processor's vast superiority over most previous microprocessors. Most of the advantages described will be taken automatically by the operating system and the average user need not be concerned with the complications that arise. It is sufficient for most programs simply to use the skeleton program and effectively ignore the existence of segments. The sophisticated programmer should take more advantage of the facilities available. While the details of such use of segments is beyond the scope of this book the manufacturer's documentation provides full details and should be consulted.

# Appendix A

# Summary of the instruction set

**KEY:**

### Operand(s)
Operands are shown as:

r  Any of the registers AH, AL, BH, BL, CH, CL, DH, DL, AX, BX, CX, DX, SP, BP, SI, DI

r8  Any of the 8-bit registers AH, AL, BH, BL, CH, CL, DH, DL

r16  Any of the 16-bit registers AX, BX, CX, DX, SP, BP, SI, DI

sr  Any of the segment registers CS, DS, ES, SS

m  Any memory operand (byte or word)

m8  Any byte memory operand

m16  Any word memory operand

d  A constant number (literal operand)

d8  A constant number less than 256 (8 bits)

d6  A constant number less than 64 (6 bits)

L  Any label name

l  Any label name within 128 bytes of the instruction

DX, CL, AX, AL  The named register

Alternatives are shown separated by /. For example:

r/m

means either a register or memory operand.

Where two operands are shown the destination operand is given first separated from the source operand by a comma. For example:

r/m, r/m/d

means that the destination operand is either a register or memory object and the source operand is either a register, memory or constant number object. Note that when two operands are given as either r, m or d then both operands must be the same size – both bytes or both words – and both cannot be memory operands.

## Flags

The flags are:

| | |
|---|---|
| O | Overflow |
| D | Direction |
| I | Interrupt |
| T | Trap |
| S | Sign |
| Z | Zero |
| A | Auxiliary carry |
| P | Parity |
| C | Carry |

The effect of each instruction on the flags is shown next to the instruction mnemonic. If the column is blank then that flag is not affected by the instruction, otherwise the effect is:

| | |
|---|---|
| 0 | The flag is set to zero |
| 1 | The flag is set to one |
| x | The flag is set according to the instruction result |
| ? | The flag is affected in an indeterminate manner. |

| Mnemonic | Operand(s) | O | D | I | T | S | Z | A | P | C | *Flags* |
|---|---|---|---|---|---|---|---|---|---|---|---|
| AAA | | ? | | | | ? | ? | x | ? | x | *ASCII adjust for addition* Correct the result in AL after adding two ASCII operands. |
| AAD | | ? | | | | x | x | ? | x | ? | *ASCII adjust for division* Adjust the dividend in AL prior to an instruction to divide two ASCII operands. |
| AAM | | ? | | | | x | x | ? | x | ? | *ASCII adjust for multiply* Correct the result in AX after multiplying two ASCII operands. |
| AAS | | ? | | | | ? | ? | x | ? | x | *ASCII adjust for subtraction* Correct the result in AL after subtraction between two ASCII operands. |
| ADC | r/m, r/m/d | x | | | | x | x | x | x | x | *Add with carry* Add the source and the carry flag to the destination. |
| ADD | r/m, r/m/d | x | | | | x | x | x | x | x | *Addition* Add the source to the destination. |

| Mnemonic | Operand(s) | O | D | I | T | S | Z | A | P | C | |
|---|---|---|---|---|---|---|---|---|---|---|---|
| AND | r/m, r/m/d | 0 | | | | x | x | ? | x | 0 | *Logical AND* Form the logical bitwise AND of the two operands returning the result to the destination. |
| CALL | L/m16/r16 | | | | | | | | | | *Call a procedure* Push IP onto the stack and then jump to the offset given. (Return with the RET instruction). |
| CBW | | | | | | | | | | | *Convert byte to word* Perform a sign extension of AL into AH: i.e. replicate bit 7 of AL throughout AH. |
| CLC | | | | | | | | | | 0 | *Clear the carry flag* The C flag is set to 0. |
| CLD | | | 0 | | | | | | | | *Clear the direction flag* The D flag is set to 0 so that future string instructions will increment the SI and/or DI register(s). |
| CLI | | | | 0 | | | | | | | *Clear the interrupt flag* The I flag is set to 0 thereby disabling interrupts. |
| CMC | | | | | | | | | | x | *Complement the carry flag* Switch the value of the C flag between 0 and 1. |
| CMP | r/m, r/m/d | x | | | | x | x | x | x | x | *Compare* Compare the operands by performing a subtraction of the source from the destination and setting the flags accordingly: the operands are unaffected. |

| Mnemonic | Operand(s) | O | D | I | T | S | Z | A | P | C | |
|----------|-----------|---|---|---|---|---|---|---|---|---|---|
| | | | | | | Flags | | | | | |
| CMPSB | | x | | | | x | x | x | x | x | *Compare string byte* Compare the bytes addressed by SI and DI by performing a subtraction of the SI byte from the DI byte and setting the flags accordingly: the operands are unaffected: SI and DI are altered by 1. |
| CMPSW | | x | | | | x | x | x | x | x | *Compare string word* Compare the words addressed by SI and DI by performing a subtraction of the SI word from the DI word and setting the flags accordingly: the operands are unaffected: SI and DI are altered by 2. |
| CWD | | | | | | | | | | | *Convert word to doubleword* Perform a sign extension of AX into DX: i.e. replicate bit 15 of AX throughout DX. (See the DIV instruction). |
| DAA | | ? | | | | x | x | x | x | x | *Decimal adjust for addition* Correct the result in AL after an addition of two decimal operands. |
| DAS | | ? | | | | x | x | x | x | x | *Decimal adjust for subtraction* Correct the result in AL after a subtraction of two decimal operands. |
| DEC | r/m | x | | | | x | x | x | x | | *Decrement by one* Subtract one from the operand. |
| DIV | r/m | x | | | | x | x | x | x | x | *Division (unsigned)* Divide AX (for a byte operand) or the pair DX:AX (for a word operand) by the operand. For a byte operand, the result is in AL and the remainder in AH. For a word operand the result is in AX and the remainder in DX. |

| Mnemonic | Operand(s) | O | D | I | T | S | Z | A | P | C | Flags |
|----------|-----------|---|---|---|---|---|---|---|---|---|-------|
| ESC | d6, m/r | | | | | | | | | | *Escape to other processor* The ESC instruction causes an attached external processor to be sent the instruction d6 and the given register or memory operand. |
| HLT | | | | | | | | | | | *Halt the processor* The processor is halted: it can be restarted by an external interrupt or a reset. |
| IDIV | r/m | x | | | | x | x | x | x | x | *Division (signed)* This instruction performs a division in the same way as DIV except that both operands are taken as signed two's complement. |
| IMUL | r/m | x | | | | ? | ? | ? | ? | x | *Multiplication (signed)* This instruction performs a multiplication in the same way as MUL except that both operands are taken as signed two's complement numbers. |
| IN | AL/AX, d8/DX | | | | | | | | | | *Input byte or word* A byte or word is input from a port depending upon whether the destination is AL or AX: the port is specified by a constant 8 bit number or as DX where the contents of DX give the port number. |
| INC | r/m | x | | | | x | x | x | x | | *Increment by one* Add one to the operand. |
| INT | d8 | | | 0 | 0 | | | | | | *Interrupt* Push the flags onto the stack; clear the I and T flags; push the CS and IP registers onto the stack and replace them with the words at (d8*4)+2 and d8*4: This effects a far call. |

| Mnemonic | Operand(s) | O | D | I | T | S | Z | A | P | C | Flags / Description |
|---|---|---|---|---|---|---|---|---|---|---|---|
| INTO | | | | x | x | | | | | | *Interrupt if overflow* <br> Obey an INT 4 instruction if the overflow flag is set. |
| IRET | | x | x | x | x | x | x | x | x | x | *Return from interrupt* <br> A return is made from an interrupt whether external or generated by the INT instruction. The IP, CS and flags registers are popped off the stack. |
| JA | l | | | | | | | | | | *Jump if above* <br> Jump to the label if both the C and Z flags are 0. (Same as JNBE). |
| JAE | l | | | | | | | | | | *Jump if above or equal* <br> Jump to the label if the C flag is 0. (Same as JNB and JNC). |
| JB | l | | | | | | | | | | *Jump if below* <br> Jump to the label if the C flag is 1. (Same as JNAE and JC). |
| JBE | l | | | | | | | | | | *Jump if below or equal* <br> Jump to the label if either the C flag or the Z flag is 1. (Same as JNA). |
| JC | l | | | | | | | | | | *Jump if carry* <br> Jump to the label if the C flag is 1. (Same as JNAE and JB). |
| JCXZ | l | | | | | | | | | | *Jump if CX is zero* <br> Jump to the label if the CX register is 0. |
| JE | l | | | | | | | | | | *Jump if equal* <br> Jump to the label if the Z flag is 1. (Same as JZ). |
| JG | l | | | | | | | | | | *Jump if greater* <br> Jump to the label if the Z flag is 0 and the S flag has the same value as the O flag. (Same as JNLE). |

| Mnemonic | Operand(s) | Flags O D I T S Z A P C | |
|---|---|---|---|
| JGE | l | | *Jump if greater or equal* Jump to the label if the S flag has the same value as the O flag. (Same as JNL). |
| JL | l | | *Jump if less* Jump to the label if the S flag has a different value to the O flag. (Same as JNGE). |
| JLE | l | | *Jump if less or equal* Jump to the label if *either* the Z flag is 1 *or* if the S flag has a different value to the O flag. (Same as JNG). |
| JMP | L/m16/r16 | | *Jump* Jump to the label or the offset given by the memory or register operand. |
| JNA | l | | *Jump if not above* Jump to the label if either the C flag or the Z flag is 1. (Same as JBE). |
| JNAE | l | | *Jump if not above or equal* Jump to the label if the C flag is 1. (Same as JB and JC). |
| JNB | l | | *Jump if not below* Jump to the label if the C flag is 0. (Same as JAE and JNC). |
| JNBE | l | | *Jump if not below or equal* Jump to the label if both the C and Z flags are 0. (Same as JA). |
| JNC | l | | *Jump if no carry* Jump to the label if the C flag is 0. (Same as JNB and JAE). |

| Mnemonic | Operand(s) | O | D | I | T | S | Z | A | P | C | |
|----------|------------|---|---|---|---|---|---|---|---|---|--|
| JNE | l | | | | | | | | | | *Jump if not equal*<br>Jump to the label if the Z flag is 0. (Same as JNZ). |
| JNG | l | | | | | | | | | | *Jump if not greater*<br>Jump to the label if *either* the Z flag is 1 *or* if the S flag has a different value to the O flag. (Same as JLE). |
| JNGE | l | | | | | | | | | | *Jump if not greater or equal*<br>Jump to label if the S flag has a different value to the O flag. (Same as JL). |
| JNL | l | | | | | | | | | | *Jump if not less*<br>Jump to the label if the S flag has the same value as the O flag. (Same as JGE). |
| JNLE | l | | | | | | | | | | *Jump if not less or equal*<br>Jump to the label if the Z flag is 0 and the S flag has the same value as the O flag. (Same as JG) |
| JNO | l | | | | | | | | | | *Jump if no overflow*<br>Jump to the label if the O flag is 0. |
| JNP | l | | | | | | | | | | *Jump if no parity*<br>Jump to the label if the P flag is 0. (Same as JPO) |
| JNS | l | | | | | | | | | | *Jump if no sign*<br>Jump to the label if the S flag is 0. |
| JNZ | l | | | | | | | | | | *Jump if not zero*<br>Jump to the label if the Z flag is 0. (Same as JNE) |

| Mnemonic | Operand(s) | Flags | | | | | | | | | |
|----------|------------|-------|---|---|---|---|---|---|---|---|----|
| | | O | D | I | T | S | Z | A | P | C | |
| JO | l | | | | | | | | | | *Jump if overflow* Jump to the label if the O flag is 1. |
| JP | l | | | | | | | | | | *Jump if parity* Jump to the label if the P flag is 1. (Same as JPE) |
| JPE | l | | | | | | | | | | *Jump if parity even* Jump to the label if the P flag is 1. (Same as JP) |
| JPO | l | | | | | | | | | | *Jump if parity odd* Jump to the label if the P flag is 0. (Same as JNP) |
| JS | l | | | | | | | | | | *Jump if sign* Jump to the label if the S flag is 1. |
| LAHF | | | | | | | | | | | *Load AH from the flags* Bits 7, 6, 4, 2 and 0 of AH are loaded with flags S, Z, A, P and C respectively. The remaining bits of AH are indeterminate – they may be loaded with either 1 or 0. AH \|S\|Z\|?\|A\|?\|P\|?\|C\|  7 6 5 4 3 2 1 0 |
| LDS | r16, m16 | | | | | | | | | | *Load DS register* The destination register is loaded from the source word: the DS register is loaded from the word following the source word. |
| LEA | r16, m | | | | | | | | | | *Load effective address* The destination register is loaded with the offset of the source memory operand. |

| Mnemonic | Operand(s) | Flags | | | | | | | | | |
|----------|------------|---|---|---|---|---|---|---|---|---|---|
| | | O | D | I | T | S | Z | A | P | C | |

| Mnemonic | Operand(s) | Description |
|----------|------------|-------------|
| LES | r16, m16 | *Load ES register*<br>The destination register is loaded from the source word: the ES register is loaded from the word following the source word. |
| LOCK | | *Lock the bus*<br>Set the special bus-lock signal for the duration of the *next* instruction. In this way, a system of several processors can mutually exclude each other when necessary: each processor is held up while the bus-lock signal is present. |
| LODSB | | *Load string byte*<br>Load the byte addressed by the SI register into AL: alter SI by one. |
| LODSW | | *Load string word*<br>Load the word addressed by the SI register into AX: alter SI by two. |
| LOOP | l | *Loop until (CX is zero)*<br>Decrement CX by one: if the result is not 0 then jump to the label. |
| LOOPE | l | *Loop while equal*<br>Decrement CX by one: if the result is not 0 and if the Z flag is 1 then jump to the label. (Same as LOOPZ). |
| LOOPNE | l | *Loop while not equal*<br>Decrement CX by one: if the result is not 0 and if the Z flag is 0 then jump to the label. (Same as LOOPNZ). |
| LOOPNE | l | *Loop while not zero*<br>Same as LOOPNE. |

| Mnemonic | Operand(s) | O | D | I | T | S | Z | A | P | C | |
|---|---|---|---|---|---|---|---|---|---|---|---|
| LOOPZ | l | | | | | | | | | | *Loop while zero* <br> Same as LOOPE. |
| MOV | r/m, r/m/d <br> or <br> sr, <br>  r16/m16 <br> or <br> r16/m16, <br>  sr | | | | | | | | | | *Move* <br> Copy the value of the source operand into the destination operand. |
| MOVSB | | | | | | | | | | | *Move string byte* <br> Move the byte addressed by SI into the byte addressed by DI: alter SI and DI by one. |
| MOVSW | | | | | | | | | | | *Move string word* <br> Move the word addressed by SI into the word addressed by DI: alter SI and DI by two. |
| MUL | r/m | x | | | | ? | ? | ? | ? | x | *Multiply (unsigned)* <br> Multiply the operand by AL (for a byte operand) or AX (for a word operand) returning a double-length result in AX (byte operand) or the pair DX:AX (word operand): the carry and overflow flags are set if the high order half of the result is not zero – otherwise they are both unset. |
| NEG | r/m | x | | | | x | x | x | x | x | *Negate – two's complement* <br> Subtract the operand from 0 and return it forming the two's complement negative of the original value. |
| NOP | | | | | | | | | | | *No operation* <br> Continue to the next instruction: (often used to 'pad' out sections of a program). |

| Mnemonic | Operand(s) | O | D | I | T | S | Z | A | P | C | |
|---|---|---|---|---|---|---|---|---|---|---|---|
| | | | | | *Flags* | | | | | | |
| NOT | r/m | | | | | | | | | | *Logical NOT* <br> Form the logical NOT of the operand by inverting all 0s and 1s and return the result to the operand: (note that this is the only arithmetic/logical instruction which does not affect the flags). |
| OR | r/m, <br> r/m/d | 0 | | | | x | x | ? | x | 0 | *Logical OR* <br> Form the logical bitwise inclusive OR of the operands returning the result to the destination. |
| OUT | d8/DX, <br> AL/AX | | | | | | | | | | *Output byte or word* <br> A byte or word is output to a port depending upon whether the source operand is AL or AX: the port is specified by a constant 8-bit number or as DX where the contents of DX give the port number. |
| POP | r16/m/sr | | | | | | | | | | *Pop a word from the stack* <br> The word addressed by SP in the stack segment is transferred to the operand: SP is then incremented by 2. |
| POPF | | x | x | x | x | x | x | x | x | x | *Pop the flags from the stack* <br> The word addressed by SP in the stack segment is transferred to the flags register: SP is then incremented by 2. |
| PUSH | r16/m/sr | | | | | | | | | | *Push a word onto the stack* <br> SP is decremented by 2: the word operand is then transferred to the word addressed by SP in the stack segment. |
| PUSHF | | | | | | | | | | | *Push the flags onto the stack* <br> SP is decremented by 2: the flags register is then transferred to the word addressed by SP in the stack segment. |

| Mnemonic | Operand(s) | O | D | I | T | S | Z | A | P | C | |
|---|---|---|---|---|---|---|---|---|---|---|---|
| | | | | | | | | | | *Flags* | |
| RCL | r/m, 1/CL | x | | | | | | | | x | *Rotate left through the carry* The destination operand is rotated left bit-wise through the carry flag: the C flag moves into the right of the destination and the high order bit moves into the C flag This operation is carried out once or the number of times given by CL: the O flag is undefined if CL is specified. For a count of 1, the O flag is set to 0 if the final high order bit is equal to the C flag; otherwise it is set to 1. |
| RCR | r/m, 1/CL | x | | | | | | | | x | *Rotate right through the carry* The destination operand is rotated right bit-wise through the carry flag: the C flag moves into the left of the destination and the low order bit of the destination moves into the C flag. This operation is carried out once or the number of times given by CL: the O flag is undefined if the source is CL. For a count of 1 the O flag is set to 0 if the final two high order bits of the destination are equal otherwise it is set to 1. |
| REP | | | | | | | | | | | | *Repeat string instruction* The following string instruction is repeated while the CX register is non-zero: after each repetition CX is decremented by 1. In the case of a repeated CMPS or SCAS instruction, repetition will also cease if the Z flag becomes 0: (REP is an alternative mnemonic to REPE). |

| Mnemonic | Operand(s) | Flags | | | | | | | | | |
|----------|-----------|---|---|---|---|---|---|---|---|---|---|
| | | O | D | I | T | S | Z | A | P | C | |

| | | | |
|---|---|---|---|
| REPE | | | *Repeat while equal* The following string instruction is repeated while the CX register is non-zero: after each repetition CX is decremented by 1. In the case of a repeated CMPS or SCAS instruction, repetition will also cease if the Z flag becomes 0: (Same as REPZ and REP). |
| REPNE | | | *Repeat while not equal* The following string instruction is repeated while the CX register is non-zero: after each repetition CX is decremented by 1. In the case of a repeated CMPS or SCAS instruction, repetition will also cease if the Z flag becomes 1: (Same as REPNZ). |
| REPNZ | | | *Repeat while not zero* Same as REPNE. |
| REPZ | | | *Repeat while zero* Same as REPE. |
| RET | <none>/d | | *Return from procedure* The return offset, as placed on the stack by a previous CALL, is popped off the stack and jumped to: SP is incremented by 2. If an operand is given then it must be a constant and this is additionally added onto SP. |
| ROL | r/m, 1/CL | O:x C:x | *Rotate left* The destination operand is rotated left bit-wise: the high order bit moving into the low order bit position: the high order bit is also moved into the C flag This operation is either carried out once or the |

| Mnemonic | Operand(s) | O | D | I | T | S | Z | A | P | C | Flags |
|----------|------------|---|---|---|---|---|---|---|---|---|-------|
| | | | | | | | | | | | number of times given by CL: if the count was CL, then the O flag undefined; otherwise the O flag is set to 0 if the C flag equals the new high order bit and to 1 if they are unequal. |
| ROR | r/m, 1/CL | x | | | | | | | | x | *Rotate right* The destination operand is rotated right bit-wise: the low order bit moves into the old high order bit position and also into the C flag. This operation is carried out once or the number of times given by CL: if the count is CL the O flag is undefined otherwise, the O flag is set to 0 if the new two high order bits are equal and it is set to 1 if they are not equal. |
| SAHF | | | | | | x | x | x | x | x | *Store AH into the flags* Bits 7, 6, 4, 2 and 0 of AH are stored into the S, Z, A, P and C flags respectively.<br>AH     \|S\|Z\|?\|A\|?\|P\|?\|C\|<br>       7 6 5 4 3 2 1 0 |
| SAL | r/m, 1/CL | x | | | | x | x | ? | x | x | *Shift arithmetic left* The destination operand is shifted left bit-wise: the high order bit moves into the C flag and 0 moves into the old low order bit position: this operation is carried out once or the number of times given by CL: if the count was not 1 then the O flag is undefined: otherwise the O flag is set to 0 if the new high order bit equals the C flag (the old high order bit) and it is set to 1 if they are not equal. (Same as SHL) |

| Mnemonic | Operand(s) | O | D | I | T | S | Z | A | P | C | Flags / Description |
|---|---|---|---|---|---|---|---|---|---|---|---|
| SAR | r/m,<br>1/CL | x | | | | x | x | ? | x | x | *Shift arithmetic right* The destination operand is shifted right bit-wise: the low order bit moves into the C flag and the high order bit *retains* its original value. This operation is carried out once or the number of times given by CL: if the count is 1 then the O flag is set to 0 if the new two high order bits are equal and to 1 if they are not equal: if the count is CL then the O flag is set to 0. |
| SBB | r/m,<br>r/m/d | x | | | | x | x | x | x | x | *Subtract with borrow* Subtract the source operand and the C flag from the destination operand. |
| SCASB | | x | | | | x | x | x | x | x | *Scan string byte* Compare the byte addressed by DI with AL by subtracting the DI byte from AL and setting the flags accordingly: neither operand is affected. Then alter DI by 1. |
| SCASW | | x | | | | x | x | x | x | x | *Scan string word* Compare the word addressed by DI with AX by subtracting the DI word from AX and setting the flags accordingly: neither operand is affected. Then alter DI by 2. |
| SHL | r/m,<br>1/CL | | | | | | | | | | *Shift left* Same as SAL. |
| SHR | r/m,<br>1/CL | | | | | | | | | | *Shift right* The destination operand is shifted right bit-wise: the low order bit moves into the C flag and 0 moves into the old high order bit position. This operation is carried out once or the number of times given by CL: |

| Mnemonic | Operand(s) | O | D | I | T | S | Z | A | P | C | Flags |
|---|---|---|---|---|---|---|---|---|---|---|---|
| | | | | | | | | | | | if the count is 1 then the O flag is set to 0 if the new two high order bits are equal and it is set to 1 if they are not equal: if the count is CL then the O flag is undefined. |
| STC | | | | | | | | | | 1 | *Set the carry flag* <br> The C flag is set to 1. |
| STD | | | 1 | | | | | | | | *Set the direction flag* <br> The D flag is set to 1 so that future string instructions will decrement the SI and/or DI register(s). |
| STI | | | | 1 | | | | | | | *Set the interrupt flag* <br> The I flag is set to 1 thereby enabling interrupts. |
| STOSB | | | | | | | | | | | *Store string byte* <br> Store AL into the byte addressed by the DI register: DI is then altered by 1. |
| STOSW | | | | | | | | | | | *Store string word* <br> Store AX into the word addressed by the DI register: DI is then altered by 2. |
| SUB | r/m, <br> r/m/d | x | | | | x | x | x | x | x | *Subtract* <br> Subtract the source from the destination. |
| TEST | r/m, <br> r/m/d | x | | | | x | x | ? | x | x | *Test (logical compare)* <br> Perform a bit-wise logical AND between the two operands and set the flags accordingly: neither operand is affected. |

| Mnemonic | Operand(s) | Flags | | | | | | | | | |
|----------|-----------|-------|---|---|---|---|---|---|---|---|----|
| | | O | D | I | T | S | Z | A | P | C | |
| WAIT | | | | | | | | | | | *Wait* <br> The processor waits for an external interrupt thus allowing it to synchronize with external hardware. |
| XCHG | r/m, <br> r/m | | | | | | | | | | *Exchange* <br> Exchange the values of the two operands. |
| XLAT | | | | | | | | | | | *Translate* <br> Move the byte addressed by BX+AL into AL. |
| XOR | r/m, <br> r/m/d | 0 | | | | x | x | ? | x | 0 | *Logical exclusive OR* <br> Form the logical exclusive OR bit-wise between the operands, returning the result to the destination operand. |

# The ASCII Character Set

To determine the code for a given character, read first the number at the side of the *row* (in hex or binary) and then the number at the head of the *column*.

| | 0<br>000 | 1<br>001 | 2<br>010 | 3<br>011 | 4<br>100 | 5<br>101 | 6<br>110 | 7<br>111 |
|---|---|---|---|---|---|---|---|---|
| F<br>1111 | SI | VS | / | ? | O | _ | o | DEL |
| E<br>1110 | SO | RS | . | > | N | ^ | n | ~ |
| D<br>1101 | CR | GS | - | = | M | ] | m | } |
| C<br>1100 | FF | FS | , | < | L | \ | l | \| |
| B<br>1011 | VT | ESC | + | ; | K | [ | k | { |
| A<br>1010 | LF | SUB | * | : | J | Z | j | z |
| 9<br>1001 | HT | EM | ) | 9 | I | Y | i | y |
| 8<br>1000 | BS | CAN | ( | 8 | H | X | h | x |
| 7<br>0111 | BEL | ETB | ' | 7 | G | W | g | w |
| 6<br>0110 | ACK | SYN | & | 6 | F | V | f | v |
| 5<br>0101 | ENQ | NAK | % | 5 | E | U | e | u |
| 4<br>0100 | EOT | DC4 | $ | 4 | D | T | d | t |
| 3<br>0011 | ETX | DC3 | # | 3 | C | S | c | s |
| 2<br>0010 | STX | DC2 | " | 2 | B | R | b | r |
| 1<br>0001 | SOH | DC1 | ! | 1 | A | Q | a | q |
| 0<br>0000 | NUL | DLE | SPACE | 0 | @ | P | ` | p |

# Appendix C
# The Skeleton Programs

## C.1   The DOS skeleton program

```
stack      segment   para stack 'stack'
           db    100 dup ('STACK')
stack      ends

data       segment   para public    'data'
saveprefix     dw    0

    ;Constants.

cr         equ       0dh
lf         equ       0ah

    ;Program Segment Prefix data.

fcblength equ        33

    org 5ch
defaultfcb     db    fcblength dup (?)

    org 80h
param_length db     0
param_buffer db     7fh dup (?)

    org 80h
diskbuffer    db     80h dup (?)

    org  100h


    ;INSERT DATA HERE .............
    ;****************


data       ends
```

```
code segment    para public    'code'
assume    cs:code, ds:data, es:data, ss:stack

mainentry:
    push ax
    mov  bx , ds                 ;Save segment start in bx.
    mov  ax , data               ;Fetch data segment start.
    mov  es , ax                 ;Copy PSP to new data segment.
    xor  si , si
    mov  di , si
    mov  cx , 80h
    rep  movsw
    mov  ds , ax                 ;Data segment start into ds.
    mov  saveprefix , bx         ;Save original segment start.
    mov  dx , 80h                ;Set new dta
    mov  ah , 1ah
    call dobdos
    cld                          ;Clear the direction flag.
    pop  ax


    ;INSERT CODE HERE ............
    ;****************


finished:
    mov  ax , saveprefix
    push ax
    xor  ax , ax
    push ax
finito    proc far
    ret
finito    endp

dobdos:
    int  21h
    ret

code ends

end  mainentry
```

## C.2  Explanation of the DOS skeleton program

The DOS skeleton program starts with a declaration of a segment which will be used to hold the stack. The segment has therefore been called stack. This segment is defined to contain 100 occurrences of the sequence of characters STACK. This is done in order that, in a debug session, that portion of the stack which has been used is readily seen where the sequence of the word STACK has been overwritten.

The declaration of the data segment follows. It is named data. When the program starts, a special segment is created called the Program Prefix. This segment is explained in Chapter 11. The location of this segment is required in order to finish the program gracefully and the word saveprefix is declared for this purpose. The program prefix contains much useful information, most of which is transferred to the data segment for easier access. The first 100 hexadecimal bytes are reserved for this purpose. The most useful two sections of the prefix are given the names defaultfcb and disk_ buffer when they are copied into the data segment. The same memory area as disk_buffer is also labelled by param_length and param_ buffer for use in accessing the parameter string placed here by the command processor as described in Section 11.6.1.

Finally the program's own data may be declared immediately after the comment stating where data is to be inserted. The data segment end is signalled to the assembler by the line:

```
data ends
```

The code segment follows and is also appropriately named code. It begins with 15 instructions which are concerned with setting up the current data and extra segments to be the segment named as data above, and with saving the program prefix. The default transfer address for disk transfers is set up at location 80 hexadecimal. After the program prefix has been moved to the start of the data segment, the first word, saveprefix, is overwritten. This first word is, however, of no interest as it is only normally used in the original program prefix segment.

The user program's instructions follow after the indicating comment.

Next the instructions which terminate the program appear labelled as finished. These instructions cause a jump to the first word of the (original) program prefix where the necessary book-keeping and general tidying up is performed before the processor hands control back to DOS.

The short subroutine dobdos appears next. This subroutine simply issues the interrupt instruction which causes a DOS function call to be performed and then returns.

Finally the code segment is terminated and the last line:

```
end   mainentry
```

informs the assembler that the program as a whole is complete and that the first instruction to be obeyed is labelled mainentry.

## C.3   The CP/M-86 skeleton program

```
      dseg

      ;Constants.
cr          equ   0dh
lf          equ   0ah

      ;Data segment prefix locations.

fcblength         equ   33
      org   5ch
default_fcb   rb    fcblength

      org   80h
param_length  db    0
param_buffer  rb    7fh

      org   80h
disk_buffer   rb    80h


      org   100h

      ;INSERT DATA HERE ............
      ;****************


      cseg
      org   0

mainentry:
      mov   ax , ds
      mov   es , ax
      cld                     ;Clear the direction flag.


      ;INSERT CODE HERE ............
      ;****************


finished:
      mov   cl , 0
      mov   dl , cl
      int   0e0h
```

```
dobdos:
     push es
     mov  cl , ah
     int  0e0h
     pop  es
     ret

end
```

## C.4   Explanation of the CP/M-86 skeleton program

The CP/M-86 skeleton is simpler than the DOS version. CP/M-86 provides a stack for the program and so there is no need to declare one unless the standard stack as provided is too small. There is no separate segment for the program prefix which always occupies the first 100 hexadecimal bytes of the user program's data segment. For these reasons, the skeleton merely declares the names of the most used sections of the prefix in the data segment. The same memory area as disk_buffer is also labelled by param_length and param_buffer for use in accessing the parameter string placed here by the command processor as described in Section 11.6.1.

The code segment is next introduced by the word cseg. Two instructions follow which ensure that the extra segment is equivalent to the data segment. Following those is the comment showing where the user program's instructions may be placed.

Next are the instructions which terminate the program and they are labelled finished. These simply call bdos function zero.

Finally is the subroutine dobdos. This firstly saves the extra segment register, as some (most) versions of CP/M-86 overwrite this register. The function number is transferred from the AH register to the CL register. CP/M-86 uses the CL register for passing over the function call number whereas DOS uses the AH register. In order to eliminate as many as possible of the differences between the two systems we have always used the AH register to hold the bdos function value. This is because, while some of the advanced DOS functions not available under CP/M-86 use the CL register as a parameter, none of the CP/M-86 functions uses the AH register. The bdos is entered by an interrupt instruction. Finally the dobdos subroutine returns.

The end mnemonic signals the end of the program to the assembler.

# Appendix D
# File Control Block Layouts

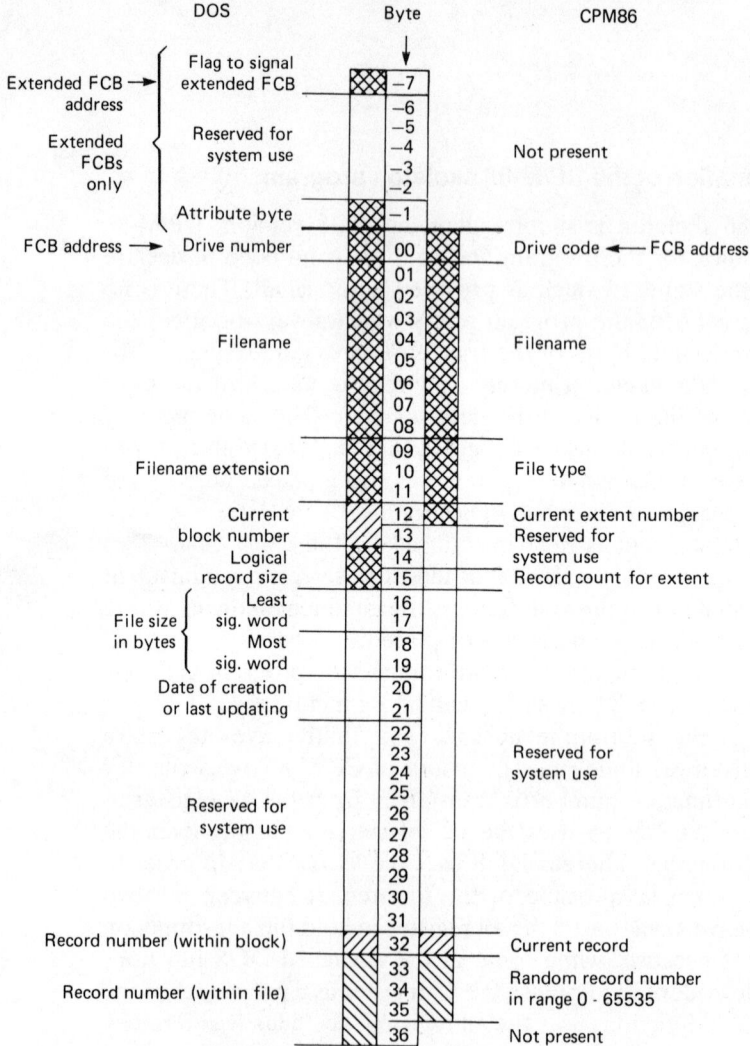

| DOS | Byte | CPM86 |
|---|---|---|
| Flag to signal |  |  |

Extended FCB → Flag to signal extended FCB   −7

address

Extended FCBs only { Reserved for system use   −6 −5 −4 −3 −2    Not present

Attribute byte   −1

FCB address → Drive number   00   Drive code ← FCB address

Filename   01 02 03 04 05 06 07 08   Filename

Filename extension   09 10 11   File type

Current block number   12 13   Current extent number / Reserved for

Logical record size   14 15   system use / Record count for extent

File size in bytes { Least sig. word   16 17 / Most sig. word   18 19

Date of creation or last updating   20 21

Reserved for system use   22 23 24 25 26 27 28 29 30 31   Reserved for system use

Record number (within block)   32   Current record

Record number (within file)   33 34 35   Random record number in range 0 - 65535

36   Not present

Shaded fields may be set by the user in:

sequential file accessing;

random file accessing;

both sequential and random file accessing.

Unshaded fields are maintained by the system and should not be altered.

# Index